Dynamic Media

Music, Video, Animation, and the Web in Adobe PDF

QA 76.76 .I59

Connolly, Bob, 1954-

Dynamic media

INCLUDES CD

DATE DUE

Bob Connolly

New England Institute
of Technology
Library

Win/Mac CD-ROM offers fully interactive PDF version of book, complete

#78212722

Dynamic Media: Music, Video, Animation, and the Web in Adobe PDF

Bob Connolly

Peachpit Press
1249 Eighth Street
Berkeley, CA 94710
(510) 524-2178
(800) 283-9444
(510) 524-2221 (fax)

Find us on the Web at: www.peachpit.com
To report errors, please send a note to errata@peachpit.com
Peachpit Press is a division of Pearson Education.

Copyright © 2007 Connolly Media LTD.

Editor: Becky Morgan
Production Editor: Connie Jeung-Mills
Indexer: James Minkin
Cover Design: Mimi Heft
Interior Design: Mimi Heft
Layout Artists: Peter Dudar and Jason Lee
Art Direction: Bob Connolly
Rich-Media Programming: Jason Lee
Interactive Index Programming: Sonar Bookends Activate™

This book, eBook, and CD-ROM were produced by Connolly Media LTD, operating as pdfPictures.

For technical support and more information about this pdfPicture Book, visit our companion Web site: www.DynamicMediaBook.com

Colophon
This book was set using Berthold Akzidenz Grotesk (Adobe, Inc.) and Chalet (House Industries). It was written and composed in Adobe InDesign CS2. Final output was PDF to plate at Courier, Kendallville, Indiana.

Notice of Rights
All rights reserved. No part of this book may be reproduced or transmitted in any form or by any means, electronic, mechanical, photocopying, recording, or otherwise, without the prior written permission of the publisher. For information, contact permissions@peachpit.com.

Notice of Liability
The information in this book is distributed on an "as is" basis, without warranty. While every precaution has been taken in the preparation of this book, neither the authors nor Peachpit Press shall have any liability to any person or entity with respect to any liability, loss, or damage caused or alleged to be caused directly or indirectly by the instructions contained in this book or by the computer software and hardware products described herein.

Notice of Trademark
QuickTime and the QuickTime logo are trademarks or registered trademarks of Apple Computer, Inc., used under license therefrom. Many of the designations used by manufacturers and sellers to distinguish their products are claimed as trademarks. Where those designations appear in this book, and Peachpit was aware of a trademark claim, the designations appear as requested by the owner of the trademark. All other product names and services identified throughout this book are used in editorial fashion only and for the benefit of such companies with no intention of infringement of the trademark. No such use, or the use of any trade name, is intended to convey endorsement or other affiliation with this book.

ISBN 0-321-43083-2

0 9 8 7 6 5 4 3 2 1
Printed and bound in the United States of America.

The Making of Dynamic Media

If you take into consideration the mountain of "content" that was involved in making this book and companion eBook, you'll understand why it took almost five years to produce.

I use the word "produce" instead of "write" because the writing is only one part of the product that you now hold in your hands or view on your computer. The companion eBook and CD-ROM, which contain numerous rich-media PDF examples and case studies, were produced by my company for clients during the past five years. I am forever grateful for their permission to provide you with a behind-the-scenes look of their productions. I also want to thank the many freelance Flash artists and award winning "content" contributors who have submitted the additional digital media that helps bring the companion eBook to life.

A special place in my heart goes out to Andra Sheffer from the BellFund who provided the initial rich-media PDF research funding, and to Noha Edell for bringing the results of the grant to the attention of her associates at Adobe Systems. I truly appreciate the staff at Peachpit for seeing the rich-media PDF vision and allowing me to present it here to you as I intended.

But my greatest gratitude goes out to my friends and associates Jay, Peter, Martin, Tony, Len, and Thom who all played a vital role in the development of the book and the dynamic media workflow that we use to produce interactive rich-media PDF.

Bob Connolly
President, pdfPictures.com

Contents

Contents

Chapter 18: Flash SWF 242

Chapter 19: Flash Story eBooks 248

Chapter 20: Digital Magazines and Rich Media 264

Chapter 21: Server-Side PDF Custom Publications 280

In a culture like ours, long accustomed to splitting and dividing all things as a means of control, it is sometimes a bit of a shock to be reminded that, in operational and practical fact, the medium is the message. This is merely to say that the personal and social consequences of any medium—that is, of any extension of ourselves—result from the new scale that is introduced into our affairs by each extension of ourselves or by any new technology.

Marshall McLuhan

Understanding Media

Welcome to PDF, the Portable Document Format

PDF is like a digital briefcase. You can put television programs, videos, music, books, brochures, magazines, training manuals, flyers, catalogs, corporate reports, newsletters, bios, and many other forms of media inside it, and lock it up for safe keeping.

It's portable. Instead of carrying it to a meeting, you can transmit it via the Internet, anywhere in the world. If they have the password, recipients of the digital PDF briefcase can open it up using the free Adobe Reader application and then view or remove all of the media to convert it back to its original form. The media might be a printed document or an attached digital video file for use in an iPod or on a DVD.

This digital briefcase is much different when compared to a Web page. You can download it, email it, and print it with one click of a button. You can customize this PDF briefcase too. Instead of endlessly surfing web sites to find the information you require, you can build it "on the fly," download it, turn off your Internet connection, and view the "full screen" content offline at your leisure anywhere, anytime. Dynamic Digital Media on demand.

We are at the threshold of a brand new form of communication and if you intend to pursue this direction as a business, you need to realize that there are many obstacles that lie in the road ahead. Computer operating systems are constantly evolving.

New file formats for digital content are being invented. Traditional media workflows and methods must be updated, and with that comes retraining or replacing staff who might be too set in their ways to accept change.

Dynamic Media PDF creation requires producers who can see the big picture and lead their team toward the final goal. Desktop print designers, Flash programmers, audio and video editors, and Web site producers will need to work as a team and create workflows that suit their corporate structure.

Printed documents like this book can live online. In this fast-paced world of constantly evolving computer technology, a PDF can be quickly updated and can contain links to companion Web sites. For example, our Dynamic Media eBook has a companion Web site, www.DynamicMediaBook.com, where you can obtain the latest updates and news about rich-media PDF workflows, PDF tools, and tips that will make your rich-media PDF creation easier.

We invite you to explore the next generation of the Internet where HTML has evolved into rich-media PDF.

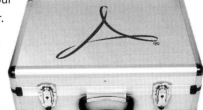

Introducing Dynamic Media

1

Welcome to the new world of convergence. In case you don't recognize that term, perhaps I should use the more fashionable term *dynamic media* that is now in vogue. Whatever your thoughts on dynamic media may be, in this book you'll learn about a new process through which you will be able to combine several types of digital media such as video, audio, and animation into one self-contained, easy-to-use rich-media PDF (Portable Document Format) document.

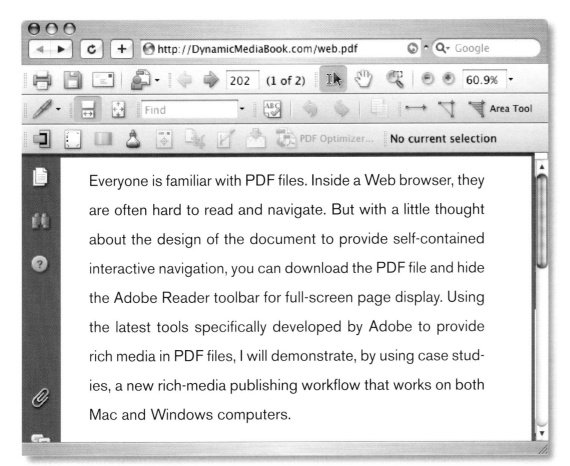

http://DynamicMediaBook.com/web.pdf

Google

202 (1 of 2) 60.9%

Find Area Tool

PDF Optimizer... **No current selection**

Everyone is familiar with PDF files. Inside a Web browser, they are often hard to read and navigate. But with a little thought about the design of the document to provide self-contained interactive navigation, you can download the PDF file and hide the Adobe Reader toolbar for full-screen page display. Using the latest tools specifically developed by Adobe to provide rich media in PDF files, I will demonstrate, by using case studies, a new rich-media publishing workflow that works on both Mac and Windows computers.

2004 Jaguar XJ
BORN TO PERFORM

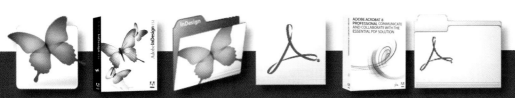

Who Should Read This Book?

If you publish books, magazines, flyers, catalogs, brochures, training manuals, or virtually any printed material, this book will show you how to make your publications interactive and easy to read on a computer. Writers will benefit from understanding how the various forms of digital media are integrated into a PDF so they can also become "content" providers of photography and digital audio for interviews and testimonials.

Producers of music, video, and Flash animation will learn how to format their productions to best view them inside electronic editions of traditional print publications. Web developers will learn how to create dynamic Web sites based entirely on PDF where users can create their own personalized custom PDF publication on demand.

This book is not meant to replace the manuals that come with the computer applications you'll use to produce the projects I will showcase. Consider this to be the documentation that will guide you through the endless possibilities with numerous limitations of the rich-media PDF format so you can make an informed decision about whether it will be useful to you.

Even if you are not involved with actually producing or marketing media, you can still enjoy this book. Any person who is interested in the past, present, and future of media—especially the impact that rich-media PDF will have on traditional institutions of education—will soon realize that learning about rich-media PDF creations can be fun.

What's in the Book?

The first part of the book introduces you to the history of interactive media production and how it has evolved to include PDF. You'll then learn about the many types of digital media file formats that can be used with PDF and how best to implement them into your production. The rich media you'll study includes QuickTime VR (virtual reality), interactive U3D (the new universal 3D format), interactive video, interactive audio, and many forms of Flash animation, known as SWF.

The last part of the book features a number of case studies where you will see how rich media is being used in eBooks, eBrochures, digital music booklets, electronic model and photography portfolios, comic books, technical publications, games, and much more.

What's on the CD-ROM?

At the back of the book, you will find a companion hybrid CD-ROM that includes a rich-media eBook to allow you to experience for yourself rich-media video tutorials and the interactive rich-media case studies via your computer. The CD also includes complete versions of the rich-media publications I profile throughout the book. Here you will find eBooks with audio, automotive eBrochures with virtual tours of the car, digital music booklets that include music video, travel eBrochures, interactive Flash comic books, and many more samples of rich-media PDF.

What's on the Companion eBook?

What makes this print book so different from other print books is that it has a companion rich-media eBook. The print book and the eBook are identical. Read the chapter in the book and then watch it come to life with embedded audio, video, virtual reality, and Flash animation inside the eBook. It's a rich-media eBook about creating rich-media publications!

Here you will find video testimonials from the artists and producers who are documented in the case studies. QuickTime video tutorials bring the "how-to" text alive by showing the functions of the various application tool menus and windows that are used to create the rich media and the interactive PDF.

What's on the Companion Web site?

www.DynamicMediaBook.com

Here you will my Web blog that provides the latest news concerning rich-media PDF technology. If you are experiencing technical difficulties with the companion eBook, I have a category dedicated to the bugs and limitations you will find with the various versions of Adobe Acrobat and Reader for Mac and Windows.

Case Studies and Rich-Media Creations

In Chapter 9, learn the production techniques to convert a printed travel brochure into an interactive eBrochure that can be downloaded from a Web site.

In Chapter 10, you'll examine the workflow for producing an interactive short-story eBook called *The Evil Governor*, which contains an audio narration that automatically turns the pages of the book to keep the audio and text in sync. Hyperlinks in the pages of the book allow you to jump to additional reference material for an in-depth explanation of the subjects addressed in the story. At the end of the eBook, you'll find an interactive quiz that can be used for testing students.

In the case study of Flash comic animation production companies in Chapter 19, you'll learn how traditional cell animators have now embraced Flash to produce characters that come to life in full-motion video when you click the pictures in the eBook. Learn how a popular cartoon series called 6Teen that was made for broadcast television can be reformatted for delivery inside a rich-media PDF file.

Digital music can also be downloaded as an attachment inside a PDF file. In Chapter 12, learn how one musician has created

his own promotional digital music booklet that contains pictures, a virtual reality tour of the music studio where his music was recorded, a music video, and an attached music file that can be removed from the PDF and placed on an iPod.

In Chapter 13, you'll take an in-depth look at how Jook Leung, an award-winning Virtual Reality photographer, promotes his work via an interactive PDF portfolio. Here you'll see the equipment and methods that he uses to take 360-degree pictures of world-famous locations such as Times Square on New Year's Eve.

Each year, automotive companies produce millions of expensive, glossy, high-quality print brochures to promote their cars. In Chapter 16, learn how Volvo creates electronic brochures that contain more than 70 videos demonstrating the various accessories available for its line of automobiles.

The customization of electronic brochures is now possible via server-side PDF. In Chapter 21, you'll learn how to create electronic rich-media documents that are built on the fly, open full screen, and contain video selected by the user from a list of search results on a Web page. Think Google meets rich-media PDF.

The Evolution of Rich Media

Many prospective clients ask me, "What is different about PDF? Why should I care? I already have a Web site." To them I reply, "Can you download your Web site? Can you email your entire Web site—the text, the videos, and the animation—to someone as an attached file?" Their response is usually, "Why would someone want to do that?" Well, there are many reasons, but it's best explained by looking at the history of rich media via the Internet to show you why PDF is now ready to become a major competitor of the Web browser.

Web Content: The Beginning

The Internet has become one of the most powerful forms of media in a relatively short period of time, when compared to radio and TV. It started as text over telephone lines and was extremely slow, but it was a great communication tool for universities and government organizations.

Soon, the private sector became involved through companies such as CompuServe and America Online (AOL) offering easy access to the Internet via tools that permitted email and Web browsers that were customized for their content.

These Web browsers became the main interface to the Internet, but they were built on a primitive computer language called HTML. Although the Web pages of today can do some pretty spiffy things, they are not backward compatible with early versions of Web browsers, and therefore you cannot ensure that they'll work everywhere. The Web browser was not created to display video and required clunky plug-ins to allow video to appear inside the browser. Even today, these plug-ins are subjects of patent disputes which have caused Microsoft to alter its browser to not automatically play Flash and QuickTime.

Adobe's Vision

For many years, Adobe's vision of the Internet has been a world that operates in PDF, outside a Web browser, and outside the limitations of HTML. Browser wars are meaningless. In a PDF document, text is razor sharp at any font size. The file's resolution is not fixed at 72 dpi, which allows for higher-quality printing. It's also a world where high-speed broadband connections allow for the delivery of any digital content inside one self-contained PDF file. PDF, not HTML, efficiently controls the flow of the rich media that the world now craves. But before PDF can become the publication of choice, content providers must agree on the vision.

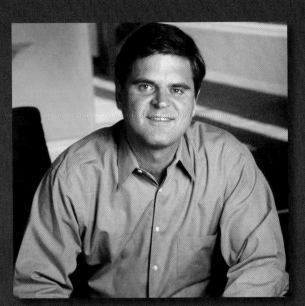

Steve Case, founder of AOL Photo courtesy of AOL

The Birthing Pains of Rich Media

During the dotcom boom, AOL was singing the praises of convergence to its subscribers to raise investment capital to purchase "content" that could be digitized and delivered to homes via AOL's Internet service. The public bought into this vision, causing the value of AOL to grow to record heights nearing 163 billion dollars.

On January 10, 2000, AOL made good on its promise by acquiring Time Warner and its associated companies with the hopes that television from CNN, music and movies from Warner, and publishing interests from Time could be formatted for digital delivery into the homes of its subscribers.

Computer companies such as Apple and Adobe shared the convergence vision and began the process of creating tools that could create this type of "new media." Unfortunately, the Internet gold rush fever hurt many prospectors who bought into worthless Internet ventures that were doomed to fail.

When intelligent or unscrupulous investors in the high-tech industry saw that the dotcom game had reached a point of no financial return, they cashed out, the dotcom bomb went off, and the term convergence took on a distasteful meaning throughout the world. Millions of people lost money, and many brilliant minds that had accurately predicted the benefits of convergence were ridiculed and escorted out the door. Other companies such as Apple and Adobe secretly carried on with their dynamic media aspirations.

The Birth of Broadband

AOL had the right idea; the crash just came too early in its business plan. Plus, the corporate executives at the new AOL Time Warner had a great unwillingness to work together. Several other market forces would first have to align themselves to produce an environment where the flow of digital information could pass swiftly, securely, and in a manner that could be appreciated. Since this converged content would be quite large in file size, too big for AOL's dial-up connections, the majority of home users would first have to upgrade to a high-speed Internet connection known as broadband.

AOL was not a telephone company. To get a high-speed connection for their subscribers, AOL had to partner with telephone companies or with cable TV companies, and these players had their own visions and business plans, which did not include AOL. The broadband wars began when companies such as Verizon and even DIRECTV began offering high-speed Internet access to places that were out of the range of Asymmetric Digital Subscriber Line (ADSL) services.

Five years later, in 2005, high-speed Internet connections in the US broke the magic 50-percent barrier, partially because of a young audience that preferred to download or "rip and burn" music instead of buying CDs. Broadband also provided additional benefits, such as free Voice over IP services such as Skype, which allows anyone to make free voice and video calls anywhere in the world via their Internet connection **(FIGURE 1-1)**.

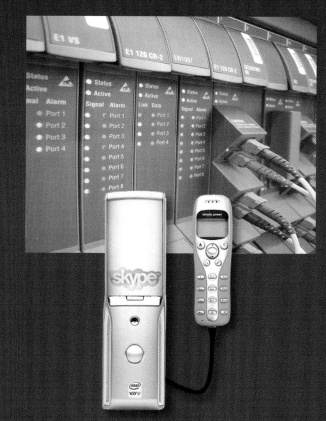

FIGURE 1-1 Simply Power Skype compatible phones connect to the USB port on a laptop or PC, and the integrated keypad manages both the Skype application and all your calls.

The Digital "Download" Revolution

The next convergence alignment came from copyright holders. During the early days of the AOL Time Warner merger, its music divisions chose to ignore digital delivery opportunities for its content because file-sharing services such as Napster were starting to seriously erode their sales of music CDs. Although AOL and Warner Brothers Records had a perfect opportunity to create their own online digital music stores, the music industry decided to focus their attention on suing the public that downloaded songs illegally. Apple Computer was even running campaigns promoting the CD-recordable "Rip. Mix. Burn." capability of their computers, which added fuel to the fire.

But the public was hooked. Downloading huge music files via high-speed connections took only a few minutes. Independent artists with no radio airplay were suddenly becoming popular via file-sharing services. The major labels that were paying attention began to sign those groups. The music industry was in a panic, and they knew there was really no way to turn back the clock. The timing was perfect for Steve Jobs to present his vision of convergence, so Apple offered a viable alternative: iTunes and the iPod.

Music artists were also becoming dismayed by the trend of fans downloading only their hit songs, and thus hastening the death of the CD album format that included artwork and lyrics. But Steve Jobs thought if you provide the music in a manner conducive to the on-demand needs of the modern consumer who prefers to download content, they will pay for it—especially if you offer them an incentive, such as pictures of the band. To inspire the sale of the complete album, Apple started providing the capability to download a "bonus" interactive PDF "digital booklet" of bands that shows up inside iTunes along with the music. (I will show you in Chapter 12 how to make one.)

The business model provided by iTunes and the iPod was initially perceived as a risk, but Jobs assured the copyright holders that they had a secure digital rights management system in place. Well, that's all history now. After witnessing many billion downloads of songs from iTunes, the entertainment industry agreed to include music videos, popular television series and movies for Apple's Video iPod.

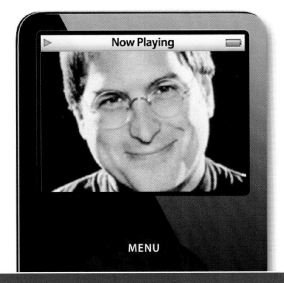

Printed Pages to Web Pages

The final convergence alignment came from print publishers. Millions of printed books, newspapers, and magazines tried to follow a route similar to the one embraced by the music industry by going digital. However, one of the greatest digital hurdles that print publishers faced was the original contract that authors signed for their written stories. Few legal departments anticipated that magazine articles could one day appear on a computer screen via the Internet. So when the newspaper and magazine publishers attempted to repurpose their stories for the Web, writer's guilds cried, "You don't own the electronic rights! You have to pay an additional fee for that!" Meanwhile, Apple's iTunes Music Store was able to add audio eBooks as an alternative to audiocassettes and CDs because the rights to that content had been negotiated up front with the author.

After many years of unsuccessful lawsuits and negotiations between the writers and publishers, the US Supreme Court supported the right of the publisher to display the publication on the Internet electronically in its original form without paying additional fee. But all the advertising, the page layout, and the written words had to remain intact, which made the publication practically impossible to read on a computer monitor. If you download some magazines in the Zinio format, you will know what I mean. Repurposing the publication for the Web under these conditions was just not financially feasible.

These legal issues led to a situation where almost all new contracts between an author and a publisher include "all forms of media," even those not yet invented! Many writers who had initially upheld their copyright decided to release their previous works to remain employed in the new digital evolution of the Internet.

Internet Television, Apple, and Intel

Today, broadband has started to move into the living room, supplying content for "Internet appliances" such as Intel's Viiv entertainment center **(FIGURE 1-2)** and Apple's wireless media receiver. These are computers with remote control that can hook up to a wide-screen high-definition TV. You can download your movie or your full-screen rich-media PDF and watch it back in full screen on your TV—outside the Web browser.

South Korea is the most broadband-connected country in the world with more than 80 percent of the households enjoying an always-on high-speed connection. The high-tech TV industry is led by Samsung, who champions Digital Light Processing (DLP) chips for viewing video and is making several Internet set-top appliances that allow the Internet to interface to their sets using Intel's Viiv technology.

If you look at countries that invent and currently enjoy these broadband home entertainment devices on a wide scale, you'll see that nearly all Japanese customers have access to "high-speed" 20 Mb broadband, with an average connection speed 16 times faster than in the United States, for $22 a month. Even faster "ultra-high-speed" fiber-optic cable is available with speeds up to 100 Mb per second. In Japan, your family could use a broadband connection to download music from iTunes and watch several high-definition movies on demand while talking long distance on Voice over IP telephones—all at the same time!

FIGURE 1-2 Broadband has started to move into the living room, supplying content for "Internet appliances" such as Intel's Viiv entertainment center and Apple's wireless media receiver.

According to the Computer Industry Almanac, in June of 2005, there were more than 217 million worldwide subscribers to high-speed Internet connections, and one quarter, or 47 million, were in the US. As we become more dependent on the Internet for our business and entertainment, the need for bandwidth like the Japanese enjoy will inspire the data service providers to offer even faster, lower-cost Internet connections than we experience today. And with that big pipe, out will come the content that the publishers have locked safely away in their vaults, waiting for the day when they could sell it online and on demand to allow the viewer to experience the content in the best way—full screen outside a Web browser.

Merging PDF with Traditional Media

Today, the majority of media industry professionals think the Web page is the place where convergence is most relevant. It might consist of text from a back-issue magazine article or book, video footage from historical TV programs, and a bit of Flash animation to liven up the page. The media all resides on a Web server and plays inside a Web browser. But there is an alternative to this type of media access: Adobe PDF.

The latest versions of Adobe Reader PDF files can provide a similar experience to that which is currently found on highly sophisticated Web sites. Video, audio, and animation can stream into a PDF page; interactive 3D models from computer-assisted design (CAD) applications can be manipulated to obtain 360-degree views; and database-driven message boards, Weblogs, news engines, and e-commerce are now all possible via Flash in a PDF.

As with Apple's iTunes/iPod, rich-media PDF offers a dramatic advantage over a Web page because you can download a PDF and own it just like music files, email it to your friends, and disconnect from your Internet connection and take it on the road. All the rich media will play back because it's embedded inside the PDF document. You can remove any attached files such as video to burn a DVD or MP3 music to transfer to your iPod. You can watch the PDF in full screen on your computer or TV. You can print one page of reference materials for school reports, or you can print the whole document in high resolution at an instant-print shop such as FedEx Kinko's. And if you are making a special presentation at a large corporate function, quality counts, and PDF can provide that quality.

Rich Media Book

It's convergence that works.

Defining
Rich-Media Terms

Naming technology is something of an art form. Who would have thought the iPod would become a household word? In this book, I define many new terms that are also used for Web site production. In this chapter, I'll try to differentiate the terms for their specific use in PDF in a layman's way with the hope that you will be able grasp their meanings as I refer to them throughout this book.

Digital Video
RealPlayer
Web Sites
Cross-Media
Digital Audio
Adobe
Banner Ads
Flash
Interactive PDF
Animation
Macromedia
DVD
Web Server
QuickTime
Animated Gif
Windows Media
Linked Rich Media
Convergence
CD-ROM
Broadband
Adobe Acrobat
MPEG
Virtual Reality
Codec Internet
RealPlayer
Cross-Media
Adobe
Flash
Interactive PDF
Animation
Macromedia
DVD
Web Server
QuickTime
Animated Gif
Windows Media
Linked Rich Media
Convergence
CD-ROM
Broadband
Embedded Media

Advertising agencies originally adopted the term *rich media* to describe animated banner advertisements for use on Web sites. Rich-media banner ads are more appealing than a flashing graphic known as an *animated* GIF. The "media" is "richer" looking with dissolves, animated text, panning graphics, and in some cases video. Typically this form of rich media is created using an application known as Flash, and the file format is .SWF (pronounced "swiff"). Many applications can create .SWF files, and in most cases I will refer to .SWF files as just Flash files.

For this book, rich media describes any form of media beyond text and still pictures, so it includes digital audio, digital video, slide shows, or Flash animation; in our case, this rich media is targeted for playback inside PDF documents, not Web sites.

The rich media that plays inside a PDF may reside on an Internet Web server, but instead of being viewed on a Web page, our rich media will be attached, streamed, or "embedded" in a PDF page that resides on a computer hard drive or some other form of physical media such as CD, DVD, or CompactFlash.

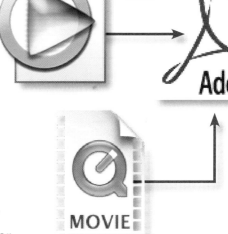

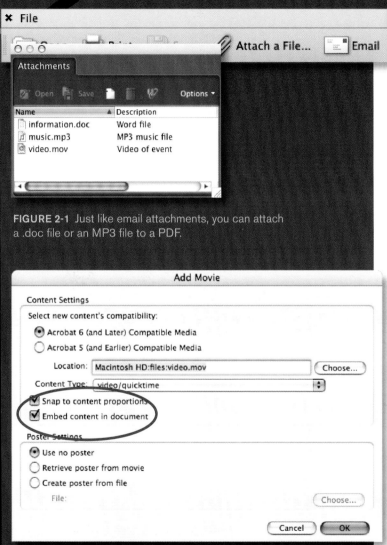

FIGURE 2-1 Just like email attachments, you can attach a .doc file or an MP3 file to a PDF.

FIGURE 2-2 Acrobat allows audio or video to be embedded into a PDF file, but unlike attached files, the user cannot remove them.

Attached Rich Media

A file *attachment* is often a file such as a .pdf or .doc that you can add to your email message; once received via email, recipients can extract the attachment to open it in their word processor or Adobe Reader.

You can also attach rich-media files to PDF files **(FIGURE 2-1)**. Just like email attachments, you can attach a .doc file or an MP3 file to a PDF and then send the PDF file as an attachment with the email message. When I talk about file attachments with PDF, don't get confused with the two ways you can attach files: in an email or inside a PDF file. You cannot view attached files inside a PDF; you must remove them and open them in a compatible application.

In Chapter 12, you will learn about attaching music MP3 files to a PDF that can be removed later for playback on an iPod.

Embedded Rich Media

Embedded rich media are files inserted into a PDF file, but unlike attached files, the user cannot remove them. You embed media such as audio or video into the PDF document **(FIGURE 2-2)**, and all the rich media is presented to the user as one self-contained file. After you email or download the PDF file to your computer, you don't need an Internet connection to view the rich media inside the PDF. You will learn more about that process in Chapter 13.

Linked Rich Media

Linked rich-media files are files that are not self-contained inside the PDF file **(FIGURE 2-3)**.

In most cases, the linked rich-media files remain on a Web server. Once you have downloaded the PDF document, you will need an Internet connection to play any linked rich-media files inside the document.

You will learn more about this process in Chapter 7.

Convergence

Convergence occurs when you combine several types of digital media such as video, audio, and animation in one document, and convergence that works is the theme for this book. I will cover digital publications such as rich-media eBooks in Chapter 10, rich-media eBrochures in Chapter 13, and rich-media magazines in Chapter 20, such as electronic PDF documents that have been converged or enhanced with digital content from production companies that specialize in radio, television, feature film, and animation production.

Your *convergence strategy* is the workflow that is best used to capture the various types of media, convert them to digital formats, insert them into a PDF file, make the file interactive, and then make it available for distribution.

Add Movie

Content Settings

Select new content's compatibility:

○ Acrobat 6 (and Later) Compatible Media

◉ Acrobat 5 (and Earlier) Compatible Media

Location: http://www.aruba.tv/videos/qtlarge/diving.mov

☑ Snap to content proportions

Poster Settings

◉ Use no poster

○ Retrieve poster from movie

Cancel

FIGURE 2-3 A video that is too large to embed inside a PDF file can be streamed from a Web server.

Convergence:

Combining several types of digital media such as video, audio, and animation into one interactive document.

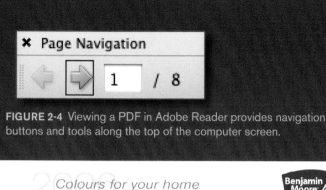

FIGURE 2-4 Viewing a PDF in Adobe Reader provides navigation buttons and tools along the top of the computer screen.

FIGURE 2-5 Viewing a PDF in full-screen mode hides the Adobe Reader navigation buttons, so you need to create interactive navigation buttons in the PDF.

Cross-Media Applications

The term *cross-media* is often used in place of the word *convergence*, which seems to have taken on a negative meaning since the dotcom bomb era.

Computer programs that can produce more than one form of digital media are often called *cross-media applications*. For example, Adobe InDesign can produce printed media and interactive media, whereas QuarkXPress, by itself, can produce only a file for printing.

Adobe Illustrator is a cross-media application because it can create a print file and a rich-media Flash file. Many applications that produce Flash files can also produce a file capable of high-resolution printing.

Some cross-media applications are capable of converging various forms of media such as audio and video into an entirely new form of media such as rich-media PDF files.

Interactive PDF

I will often refer to the capabilities of *interactive* PDF files. An interactive PDF document features some form of user interaction beyond what is provided by the standard Adobe Reader and Adobe Acrobat navigation tools **(FIGURE 2-4)**. For example, when you view a PDF in full-screen viewing mode, the Adobe Reader toolbar is hidden from view, so buttons, fields, and drop-down menus are added to the PDF page to allow the user to navigate through the document, to turn the page, or to jump to a particular place in the middle of the document **(FIGURE 2-5)**.

Interactive Rich Media

Interactive rich media is digital content that has interactive hot spots within the rich media, such as a Flash movie that will animate when you click it. A digital video might jump to a particular part of the movie when you click a hot spot. Interactive rich media usually has some form of user interface that allows you to interact with that media.

An audio file might trigger a page to turn when it reaches the end of a page. In this case, the rich-media audio is interactive because you can control the playback of the audio, which in turn controls the interactive PDF page.

Rich Media Players

Rich media players are applications installed on a computer to play back some form of digital media such as video, audio, and animation. Examples of rich media players are Apple QuickTime Player, Microsoft Windows Media Player, RealNetworks RealOne (formerly RealPlayer), and Adobe Flash Player. It is extremely important to understand the capabilities of these players if you want to make a rich-media PDF that works on all computers.

Rich Media Players can be downloaded for free online.

Apple QuickTime Player
www.QuickTime.com

Windows Media Player
www.WindowsMedia.com

RealNetworks RealPlayer
www.Real.com

Adobe Flash Player
www.Flash.com

FIGURE 2-6 Consumer DV (digital video) cameras capture video and then compress the data to the DV format.

FIGURE 2-7 QuickTime VR allows the user to look around virtual environments that were photographed or computer generated.

Codec

A *codec* is a short-form term for two words: *compressor* and *decompressor*. Codecs are the names for the various types of digital video and digital audio formats. For example, a consumer DV (digital video) camera will capture the video and then compress the data to the DV format; therefore, DV cameras use the DV codec to compress the data. To view the compressed digital video on a computer, the DV media player must have the DV codec installed to decompress the video **(FIGURE 2-6)**.

The world of digital video codecs is confusing and keeps evolving as new codecs are invented and become available, almost on a daily basis. If you will be producing video content for rich-media PDF, this is the most important part of the workflow. You will learn more about codecs in Chapter 5.

Virtual Reality

Virtual reality (VR) is a broad term. It usually refers to a computer simulation of a place or 3D model. You can experience the best examples of VR simulations at museum exhibitions by wearing a headset that contains a viewing apparatus hooked up to a computer. As you move your head in all directions, the computer renders the corresponding angle of view of a virtual world. For our purposes with rich-media PDF, virtual reality provides a similar interactive experience by using a mouse **(FIGURE 2-7)**.

Another form of the VR experience is manipulating a 3D object with a glove. The user picks up the virtual object with the glove and then rotates the 3D object to view it from all sides and angles. When you use VR in a rich-media PDF, you can create a similar experience by using a mouse. The user can click and drag the object to rotate it in a 360-degree view. You will learn more about VR in Chapters 14 through 16.

Broadband

Rich-media PDF file sizes are usually big, and a true broadband connection is preferable for downloading them from a Web site.

When signing up to receive a "high-speed" Internet connection from a service provider, most people believe they are getting a broadband connection to the Internet, which in many cases is not true. A *broadband* connection should deliver at least 1 megabit per second (1 Mbps) of data as a download stream.

Terms such as *high-speed lite* signify an Internet connection that is twice as fast as the dial-up speeds of 56 Kbps, or just more than 100 Kbps, which is a far cry from true broadband.

If you are thinking of upgrading to broadband, make sure you understand the various options of available high-speed connections.

The Phazer USB cable modem is capable of transfer rates of up to 42 Mbps.

Broadband Connection

A broadband connection should deliver 1 megabit per second (1 Mbps) of data or higher as a download stream.

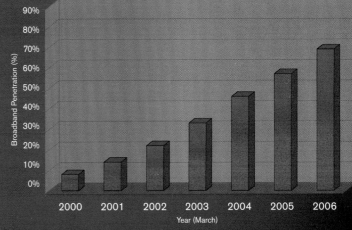

Broadband Internet Access Penetration in USA

Year (March)

Source: Ipsos-Reid and Nielsen/NetRating

21

Adobe's Trials and Tribulations Toward Rich-Media PDF

3

If you are planning to produce an interactive PDF that will contain some form of audio, video, or animation, it's important to understand the limitations of the PDF specifications. Not everyone has Adobe Reader 5 or later installed, which is required to play the basic rich-media file formats available inside a PDF. If you "overbuild" your production, assuming it will work everywhere, you will become frustrated by the complaints you'll soon receive from people who can't view your work as you intended.

File format and version incompatibilities, not to mention the "bugs" that slip by Adobe's quality control department, are found in the PDF format. Many multimedia developers to this day have simply abandoned the PDF multimedia format after unsuccessful attempts to produce a working product.

I'll warn you right now: You must move carefully through a minefield to reach your final destination. Use this chapter as a map to learn Adobe's vision for Acrobat and how it gradually grew to become a multimedia application that allows PDF to replace the Web browser. You'll soon understand the reason why many Web page developers and others creating traditional forms of media have classified PDF as a disruptive technology.

macromedia®
SHOCKWAVE®
ENABLED

Through the years of the development of Acrobat, many companies have tried to hinder (and still do) the progress of rich-media PDF. One of Adobe's visions of the Internet is where all the current media that you can view on a Web page—such as text, pictures, video, animation, ecommerce, message boards, RSS news feeds, and so on—is delivered to your desktop and viewed inside a PDF file. Yes, this would eliminate the Web browser, and with Adobe's purchase of Macromedia Flash, this is now possible. Let's take a look at the trials and tribulations of Adobe's journey.

macromedia®
FLASH™
ENABLED

The Race to Rich-Media Domination

In the mid-1990s, the most well-known rich-media application was Macromind Director, which became successful after being purchased by Macromedia, a company that could supply substantial marketing support. Most multimedia developers at that time were using Director to make rich-media applications that could play on interactive touchscreen displays, floppy disks, and (later) commercial CDs. Director gave birth to thousands of commercial creations such as interactive games, animated storybooks for children, and edutainment–a whole new category for learning.

Director was a challenging application to learn because the engineers at Macromedia had developed their own code language called Lingo to make production interactive. Except for the tools that were needed to produce digital video, Director had everything needed to create the document, make it interactive, and provide playback on a user's computer. The program created a "projector" file that could be distributed freely to anyone, and it was compatible on both Mac and Windows computers– a real nice multimedia package **(FIGURE 3-1)**.

FIGURE 3-1 Director created a "projector" file that could be distributed freely to anyone, and it was compatible on both Mac and Windows computers.

Adobe Steps into the Interactive Arena

Over the years, Adobe slowly enhanced the PDF specifications to include audio and video, and with each new version of the free Acrobat Reader (now known as Adobe Reader), Adobe increased the rich-media playback functionality (although Adobe never promoted this functionality until just recently).

In 1996, when Adobe released the specifications of PDF 1.2 (Acrobat 3.1), the capability to make the PDF document interactive became a reality. Instead of writing its own scripting language like Macromedia did, Adobe based its engine on ECMAScript (more commonly known as JavaScript). Today JavaScript is a popular, well-adopted scripting language for the Web, but in the early days of PDF, it was just in its infancy.

PDF 1.2 allowed interactive buttons and menus such as you see on Web pages to be placed into PDF documents and perform the same functions as the Acrobat toolbar, such as turning the page, printing the page, quitting the program, and so on. Quick-Time video could also now stream into the document. Adobe thought these additional interactive features would mean that PDF in full-screen mode could replace Microsoft PowerPoint for creating presentations. When Reader was in full-screen mode, the navigation toolbars were no longer visible, but with the use of JavaScripted menus in the PDF, the presenter could control the presentation by jumping to a page or playing video.

The strength that PDF had over a Director presentation was that it could launch full screen and fill the window using Adobe Post-Script graphics. Director presentations were fixed to the user's computer display size, and users were often presented with black frames if they did not reset their monitors manually.

Unfortunately, the multimedia community concluded that PDF was for printing only, and admin assistants were happy to stick with the simple-to-use features of PowerPoint.

Adobe's Mission: One Application for Print and Interactivity

Looking far ahead into a future where digital information would flow over telephone lines and wireless airwaves, Adobe wanted to evolve from being the leader in the print industry to being a leader in the interactive multimedia market. Instead of purchasing a contender to Director from a third-party company as Macromedia did, Adobe decided to continually enhance the interactive capabilities of PDF via Acrobat using the JavaScript language so it would have both print and multimedia in one application, which Adobe thought was a more logical solution. The Acrobat workflow would entail creating the document in a page layout program such as Adobe PageMaker or QuarkXPress and then having Acrobat convert (*distill*) it to PDF. Then, once the PDF document was opened in Acrobat, interactive functions and video could be added to the document and saved for playback via Reader. The only drawback to early editions of this presentation system was that a user needed the full version of Acrobat to view the video. Viewing rich media in a PDF would require a considerable cost from the user. Adobe thought this would be a good place to find revenue.

For Adobe it was a real gamble to assume that multimedia developers would go to these lengths to make an interactive publication when Director had such a strong user base. Macromedia Director created a "projector" that was a play-only version of the Director authoring application; it contained everything needed to view the presentation. But Adobe had to rely on the public to buy a copy of Acrobat to view the rich-media video.

Knowing that the general public would never pay for a copy of Acrobat, the multimedia industry declared interactive PDF a lost cause and thought it was much better suited to the print industry. Adobe took that cue and put its energy into refining the print portions of the PDF specification; as a result, PDF is the *de facto* standard for the print publishing industry today. Still, Adobe didn't give up on the interactive rich-media PDF; the company just went underground and regrouped its multimedia troops.

Tip: Developers have to pay attention to backward-compatibility. Remember, not everyone has the latest version of Reader installed.

Adobe Redefines the Office Workflow

Although rich-media developers turned away from the PDF format, Adobe kept refining its own version of JavaScript just for PDF to make it much more robust for multimedia and, specifically, for the interactive forms widely used by the business community. Many types of PDF forms could be downloaded, filled out offline, and submitted to a database.

Promoting PDF as a paperless office solution was paying off handsomely for Adobe, its third-party PDF application developers and the JavaScript developer community. Adobe was making millions of dollars creating enterprise systems for the financial community, and it was working frantically to stay ahead of the competition by refining its interactive forms using JavaScript, XML, and updated PDF libraries.

Adobe continuously improved the functionality and security of the PDF specification. Unfortunately, in some of the versions that were released, Adobe altered the JavaScript calls to provide improved security, and sometimes the new versions of the documents were not compatible with previous versions of Reader. So unless the home user upgraded to the latest free version of Reader, some interactivity in certain PDF documents would not work. Adobe is very concerned about the security of its PDF file format and goes to great lengths to ensure that viruses do not plague PDF files.

Page-Based vs. Timeline Formats

One big complaint about PDF that multimedia developers had (and still do to this day) was that Adobe uses a page-based interactive format, where Director (and its later incarnation called Flash) uses a timeline "cell-based" format **(FIGURE 3-2)**.

The majority of digital video editing and multimedia authoring applications are based on timelines where you move the playback head to a cell or frame to program interactivity for a particular scene. When these timeline-based developers opened Acrobat to see how the interactive part worked, they were quite perplexed because of the nontraditional programming methods for each PDF page.

Although it is fairly easy to work with once you get used to the pull-down menus and pop-up windows with check boxes, the page-based model was radically different from what developers were used to doing in Director.

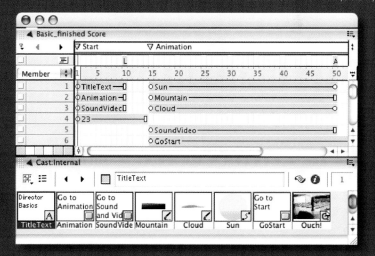

FIGURE 3-2 Adobe PDF uses a page-based interactive format (above). Macromedia Director and Flash use a timeline "cell-based" format (below)

The Cost of Playback

Another reason for the slow adoption of rich-media PDF was the financial decision to charge for the enhanced rich-media playback capabilities that were possible only from Acrobat. Even though you could link audio and video to a PDF file since version 1.1 (Acrobat 2), the home user needed to own the full version of Acrobat 2 to play the rich media! If you put an interactive PDF with a linked video on a CD and sent it to a customer, the user would need Acrobat installed to play it; Reader would not play the video! The additional fee for video playback was becoming a major complaint from developers.

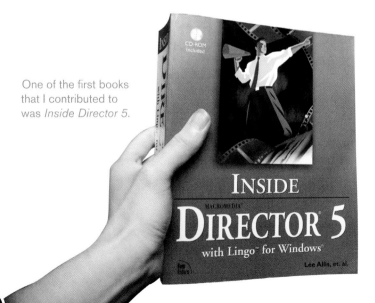

One of the first books that I contributed to was *Inside Director 5*.

Adobe Introduces Reader 5.1

Apparently, Adobe heeded the outcry of the multimedia industry and decided to bite the bullet when it introduced PDF 1.4 (Reader 5.1). For the majority of the Acrobat developer community, Reader 5.1 became the turning point for the rich-media PDF. The JavaScript code was robust and solid, and the free version of Reader 5.1 allowed QuickTime video to be streamed into the PDF from a CD, from a corporate network, or even from the Internet via a Web server.

Now the multimedia industry returned to PDF for a second look to see whether there was a viable solution to Macromedia Director, and decided that there was. The Adobe–Macromedia multimedia battle had begun.

At the turn of the millennium, the Internet was just starting to become a powerful force for delivering multimedia. The majority of North America was still using a dial-up connection, so streaming video into a PDF was not reasonable. Corporations and schools were experimenting with PDF and QuickTime video on internal networks and CDs, but few commercial titles were being released using that format.

Director had become the preferred application for authoring interactive CDs, and every multimedia company had at least one experienced staff member to create Director-based presentations. Macromedia altered Director to produce small interactive "Shockwave" animations with the hope that they would find a place on the Internet–this was the first incarnation of the SWF Flash format that is so popular today.

Multimedia Moves to the Web Page

As the Internet continued to grow, the sales of Director—once one of Macromedia's largest revenue generators—began to plummet when easy-to-use Web page–authoring tools such as Microsoft FrontPage became available. The multimedia world was moving to the Web, and Adobe was having tremendous success with Acrobat because its PDF files could be downloaded from Web sites and printed in perfect detail. Acrobat's strength was bandwidth-efficient PostScript text and vector graphics, but it was not capable of playing animation.

Macromedia wanted its Internet tools to provide a rich, highly interactive, Director-like experience and entered the ring with a vector-based application known as Flash for Web animation. But to make Flash work in a dial-up environment, Macromedia had to be conscious about the size of the plug-in that was required to play Flash SWF files in the Web browser.

Adobe, on the other hand, knew that high-speed Internet connections would soon become the norm, and it was at this time it envisioned a future where all forms of rich media could converge inside a PDF file instead of a Web page. Its vision to turn PDF into a downloadable browser that could provide everything a Web page could do without an Internet connection was gradually approaching. All Adobe had to do was just be patient, refine the PDF specifications, and wait for the arrival of broadband.

3

Acrobat's Best Friend— Adobe InDesign

Although Acrobat had finally become an alternative to Director for multimedia authoring, it was difficult to create pages that could be easily modified in Acrobat. The rich-media PDF workflow at that time consisted of creating pages in QuarkXPress, creating a PDF document in Acrobat Distiller, and then adding interactivity via Acrobat. The drawback to this workflow was that if you needed to make changes to text or graphics, you would have to return to QuarkXPress and start the process all over again!

Adobe saw the frustrations that the multimedia community was having with QuarkXPress and upgraded InDesign, its newly introduced page layout application, so that it could create print publications and author rich-media PDF—something QuarkXPress could not accomplish.

InDesign Gets Interactive

InDesign CS was a remarkable achievement for Adobe. The desktop print publishers could now become involved with multimedia using the traditional tool sets they had grown up using. You could "place" QuickTime and Flash files just like you place Adobe Photoshop files, export the PDF, click the Play Video button, and—presto!—the video or Flash file played right there inside the PDF. It was really simple.

With the release of PDF 1.5 (Acrobat/Reader 6), the rich-media PDF had matured into a full-featured multimedia format with the potential to replace the HTML Web page. You could now use Real Media, QuickTime, Windows Media, and Flash files inside a PDF. In addition to linking to videos that would stream into the PDF, you could also embed the video right inside the document. This allowed you to download the PDF, turn off your Internet connection, and still be able to play the video because it was embedded inside the PDF!

Well, after the folks at Macromedia saw Flash running inside a PDF, out came new versions of SWF that would not work in PDF. Then Macromedia provided the print functionality that was lacking inside Flash with a version of Flash called FlashPaper. Adobe was not at all happy about the new print feature of Flash. Then, out came the lawsuits over tool menus!

A Polarized New-Media Industry

A real war started taking shape among the multimedia developers, too. Even though the generally good-natured Mac community was still mainly print publishing–centric, "Mac-head" camps were divided between Web site developers using Flash and print developers using InDesign and PDF.

Because the world of the interactive CD was dying a slow death, the Director developers decided to port their skills to Flash and spent an enormous amount of time and money doing so. Instead of large bitmapped pictures, Flash requires vector graphics, and it was a real grind for them to relearn their craft to make highly interactive presentations that were bandwidth efficient for the Web.

The Flash camp saw the possibility of interactive QuickTime video inside full-screen interactive PDF as a threat that could make their talents obsolete. Flash had grown to be more than just flashing banner advertising and was now capable of providing cool navigation for Web pages. In some cases, entire Web sites that included video were being created in Flash. Rich-media PDF was clearly disrupting their plans to have SWF files replace HTML Web pages.

PDF 1.7 (Acrobat/Reader 8) has the potential to replace the HTML Web page.

Click here to download our PDF eBrochure

Rich-Media PDF and Disruptive Technologies

When a new technology causes another technology to become less valuable or even obsolete, it is often described as a *disruptive* technology. Many corporate Internet developers who created Web pages and cool Flash movies realized they might now be relegated to making a single button on a home page that says *Click Here to Download Our PDF eBrochure*. Since that eBrochure was probably created by the print designers, the Web designers would be left out of the creative process. In addition, if the PDF was successful, the budgets for "Internet media" might move to the print divisions, and because eBrochures do not have to be printed, the budget

for printing would be cut back too. As a result, the Web developers and the printers would be paid less, and the print developers would be paid more. Thus, the introduction of rich-media PDF into the workflow would cause a lot of disruption to the very employees who originally created the media for a company.

So, it was in the printers' and the Web developers' best interests to make sure rich-media PDF eBrochures would never replace their jobs—this is probably the reason you see so many bad PDFs on the Web today. The Flash developers and the print department weren't focused on making a pleasurable experience for the end user. They were not thinking "convergence."

It's a broadband experience targeted to people who have high-speed Internet connections.

Building a Team That Includes Everyone

In my many meetings with marketing managers of large corporations, the consensus has been that they love the benefits of interactive rich-media PDF eBrochures. "Astounding," they say. "All this inside a PDF file. Why have I not seen this before?" Now, because of my past experience in this situation, my reply will vary depending on who is in the room at the time. For example, I know the Web developers do not want to lose control of the Web site. And print publishers will be worried that their printing budgets will be cut.

The way I approach the situation is by introducing the rich-media PDF as a totally new form of media—a sort of Internet 2.0. I say it's a broadband experience targeted to people who have high-speed Internet connections. I say it's an opportunity to "converge" all their talents and reuse the content. "Don't stop making printed brochures," I say to the desktop publishers. "Just give us the files that you use to produce your brochures, and we will optimize them for Internet delivery. It will all be based on your design. Think of us as your service bureau." That sometimes works.

Webmasters are usually the toughest cookies to convince because they have the most to lose. To them I reply, "Those Flash animations on your site are wonderful. Did you know that all your forms, message boards, and booking engines that you create in Flash can be included right inside the PDF with a little bit of reconfiguration?" That statement usually causes their jaws to drop a bit as they ponder their futures. Will they be open to embracing the future, or will they attempt to kill it? Unfortunately, 99 percent of the time the Flash developers will attempt to kill the proposal. They will look for the weakness of the format and reply, "Not enough people have upgraded to Reader 8 or newer, which is what you need to view Flash rich media." And in many cases that is true, so it has become a waiting game for Flash inside PDF.

Underbuild or Version Your PDF and Win!

Until that day arrives when everyone has installed Reader 5 or newer, which is required to play QuickTime, I always advise the client to take baby steps and create two versions of PDF files: Standard, which runs in Reader 4, and Full, which runs in Reader 6 or newer. They both are interactive, will play full screen, and are easy to read, but the Full version has the rich media. I have found that 75 percent of users, when given the choice, will choose the Full version that includes the rich media. If visitors have a high-speed or broadband Internet connection, they usually will upgrade to the latest version of Reader just to watch the video in the Full version. They pay good money for the broadband connection and want to get value for their dollar.

Reader 8 (PDF 1.7)

The resistance to rich-media PDF, up until this point, was widespread and felt by many print designers who now want to embrace the Internet. They are constantly told that Flash eBrochures are the way to go. Even the Acrobat sales reps inform me that the Flash Player plug-in is widely installed in most Web browsers, so advertising agencies and media companies favor a rich-media Web experience using Flash because they know the majority of Internet users will be able to have a flawless rich-media experience.

Adobe knows the challenges that lie ahead. But to upgrade to the newer versions of Reader that can play rich media, the user needs some incentive. It's sort of like the chicken and the egg. If there are no rich-media PDFs on the Internet, why would people upgrade? The installed base of Reader 6 or newer is rapidly growing, but incentives are needed to speed up the adoption. Other than creating a killer rich-media PDF title and giving it away, what can you do to get people to upgrade? The reps have now returned to the roots of Acrobat, stressing the benefits of a paperless office and providing other valid reasons to upgrade to Reader.

If there are no rich-media PDFs on the Internet, why would people upgrade?

Commenting and Forms

Adobe Reader 8 features commenting tools and the ability to save information that you fill out in a PDF form. If you own Acrobat 8 Professional, you know you can add Reader commenting and form-saving privileges to a PDF document. This feature has long provided Acrobat Professional users the capability to insert feedback in the document. But now the commenting tool, including its other useful features—such as notes, highlighting, striking out, underlining of words, plus the capability of saving the information that was filled out in a form—are all available in the free version of Reader 8 as well **(FIGURE 3-3)**. Reader 8 has the capability to fill in a form, save it to your computer, and send it to someone as an attachment to an email.

Attached Files

Another reason to upgrade to Reader 8 is the ability to extract attached files. Once again, using Acrobat 8 Professional, you can enable the document for commenting and then attach files to it. Think of PDF as a briefcase where you can hold images, audio, Microsoft Word documents, and so on, and then email one self-contained package to your clients. They can then open the attachments with Reader 7 or later, make their comments, add some different photos, save the document, and send it all back inside one PDF. It's like ZipIt or StuffIt for PDF but without the compression features. It's also a great way to get files through a firewall because rarely does an IT department block a PDF file.

FIGURE 3-3 Adobe Reader's basic tools (above) can be modified to allow users to add comments to PDF documents with the Comment & Markup tools (below). Adobe Acrobat 8 Professional is required to enable commenting with the free Adobe Reader.

7 / 11   125%   Find

Review & Comment   7 / 11

Enable Usage Rights in Adobe Reader

The following features will become available for this document when opened in the free Adobe Reader.

- Save form data (for a fillable PDF form only)
- Commenting and drawing mark–up tools
- Sign an existing signature field
- Digitally sign the document anywhere on the page (only supported in Adobe Reader 8.0)

Note: Once Reader Enabled, certain functions, such as editing document content or inserting and deleting pages, will be restricted.

Cancel   Save Now

Adobe Acrobat 8 Professional can enable the free Reader 8 with the capability to fill in a form, save it to your computer and send it to someone as an attachment to an email.

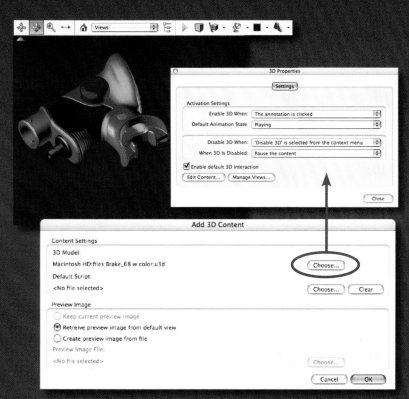

FIGURE 3-4 The CAD industry now has a way to share files with others who do not have the same application that created the model. U3D provides the capability to animate a 3D model—breaking it apart to show how the parts fit together.

Viewing Interactive 3D Rich Media

Reader 7 also provided a new rich-media PDF feature called U3D. The CAD industry now has a way to share files with others who do not have the same application that created the model. Acrobat initially had a Print to PDF option so anyone could read any document that could be printed in Reader. Well, once again Adobe has followed that business model; it has allowed 3D models and animations to be displayed inside PDF files so clients can view the model in 360 degrees. U3D also provides the capability to animate the model—breaking it apart to show how the parts fit together **(FIGURE 3-4)**.

JavaScript Is the Key

To bring this all back to the point at the beginning of this chapter, all of this interactivity inside PDF from Reader is provided by JavaScript, the original language that Adobe adopted in PDF version 1.2 (Acrobat 3.1). The latest version of Adobe JavaScript controls the interactivity of the PDF pages, the 3D models, the audio, the video, and now the Flash animation. To learn more about Adobe JavaScript visit Adobe.com and sign up to receive the Adobe Acrobat JavaScript Scripting Guide.

Adobe and Macromedia

The InDesign/Acrobat PDF platform has now matured into a robust authoring system that is capable of providing a much more compelling experience than a Web site. Even the folks at Macromedia saw that the future of the Internet could be one where Flash lives in harmony inside downloadable PDF magazines—magazines that are interactive and contain Flash advertising and e-commerce. Plus, these magazines can be printed in high quality.

In 2005, Adobe bought Macromedia and, using the Adobe brand name, began bundling its print products with Flash as part of the Adobe Creative Suite Premium, which allows you to create rich-media PDF documents with embedded Flash files that work! Imagine, InDesign and Flash in the same family of products. Armies of Adobe and former Macromedia salespeople are now singing the praises of Flash inside rich-media PDF.

The merger has had a dramatic effect on the multimedia industry. The Flash developers who despised PDF and Acrobat have been forced to take another look at rich-media PDF possibilities, because they know Adobe now controls both the PDF and SWF specifications. Press releases promote that the two formats now work together in harmony to provide the best experience possible—inside and outside a Web browser.

The former Macromedia engineers have even rewritten Adobe Acrobat 8 with a new look and have enhanced the capabilities of Flash playback inside PDF.

Adobe sees the browser as limiting because it was designed for text documents; the browser "chrome" (the tools at the top of the browser) is always in the way, and you have to be online. The Web document is not something portable enough to read at your summer cottage by the lake, for example. Adobe has created Digital Editions, an application (based on Flash, XHTML, and PDF) that will operate outside of the browser to read eBooks and more.

Try to think outside the box and outside the browser; the implications and possibilities are immense. Is this an effort to provide users with the best possible experience or an attempt to retire the browser to which we've grown addicted? It's probably somewhere in the middle. As a producer of interactive media, I welcome any technology that frees us from the constraints of a browser and the embedded media object patents that make the HTML Web-viewing experience unpleasant. The main purpose of this book is to introduce you to these new possiblities and workflows.

Adobe sees the browser as limiting because it was designed for text documents; the browser "chrome" is always in the way, and you have to be online.

Why Use PDF for Rich-Media Publishing?

In 1993, John Warnock invented PDF and Adobe Acrobat (originally called Camelot). As a cofounder of Adobe Systems, Warnock recognized the need to eliminate the difficulties impeding "our ability to communicate visual material between different computer applications and systems. Today's paper-based information is hampered by the physical media. Acrobat technology liberates information and the flow of ideas and allows it to enter the electronic age."

Acrobat and PDF have gone through a lot of growing pains since their inception. In fact, it took five years for the products just to gain momentum. Currently, PDF has a few competitors in the electronic document world, and they offer similar capabilities. In this chapter, you will learn about PDF, why it has become a world standard, and the reasons you should consider using it for rich-media publications.

"The products associated with the Internet are where I spend a lot of my time right now. It is a revolution that is bigger than the invention of printing. It is a revolution that's bigger than the invention of the telephone, radio, or any of the major revolutions that we've had in the past."

John Warnock
Chairman of the Board
Adobe Systems Incorporated
Inventor of PDF

4

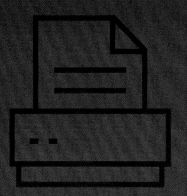

In the Beginning

PDF was initially used for in-house corporate communications to replace paper. Instead of printing a document to paper, you could use the Acrobat print driver to print to PDF, save the file on a floppy disk or CD, or send it to someone who didn't have the application that created the document. For example, if it was a Microsoft Excel document, the end user did not need Excel to view the file; they could view the layout using Acrobat Reader.

Companies that wanted to send an electronic document instead of printing and faxing it embraced Acrobat. Adobe then enhanced the PDF specification to include form fields, which allow the user to fill out a form online and submit the data electronically or save the completed form to the desktop as a PDF.

Adobe Acrobat (called Exchange in versions before 4.0) was used initially to create and view the PDF and cost $195; Adobe Acrobat Reader originally cost $50!

In 1996, the U.S. Internal Revenue Service (IRS) purchased the right to freely distribute Acrobat Reader 1.0 so U.S. taxpayers could fill out electronic versions of their tax returns. Instead of submitting returns with illegible handwriting, users could type their information into the appropriate form fields, print the documents, and send them to the IRS. This effectively made Acrobat Reader free to those who obtained it that way. Not long after, Adobe dropped the Acrobat Reader fee for version 2.

Adobe Acrobat Reader originally cost $50!

What's in a Name?

Adobe caused great confusion at the outset by naming the application that could create and alter PDF files Acrobat and then naming the application to read PDF Acrobat Reader. To the general public, the terms Acrobat and PDF were interchangeable. "Send me an Acrobat file" was the same as saying "send me a PDF." But PDF, Acrobat, and Acrobat Reader are very different creatures.

When the public visited the Adobe Web site to learn about downloading an upgrade of Acrobat to view a PDF document, many people thought you still had to buy a version of Acrobat just to view a PDF file. So many versions were available that most visitors couldn't figure out the difference between Acrobat and the free version of Acrobat Reader. It took Adobe ten years to finally drop Acrobat from Acrobat Reader. So thankfully, since version 6, it is now just called Adobe Reader. The name change has really cleared up a lot of confusion.

Reader Preinstalled

Acrobat is not free. But Reader is, and since it is also such a cool tool to have on your computer, almost every computer manufacturer preinstalls it on the operating system when you purchase a new computer. Another reason for this preinstall is that computer manuals often come as PDF files. So, Reader is currently installed on almost every computer except for the Mac—I'll get to that in just a bit.

PDF's Installed User Base

PDF has firmly entrenched itself in industries where the security and archiving of documents are vital, such as financial institutions for providing offline banking forms and legal documents. In addition, PDF has now become the *de facto* format for high-end printing of books, catalogs, and magazines—not to mention electronic publishing. If you visit Amazon or Google and search for eBooks, almost everything returned is exclusively in PDF. Google even returns links to PDF documents in its search results. It's the universal familiarity with PDF that provides an advantage over competing electronic publishing formats.

Although Reader is installed on almost a billion computers, you can't assume everyone has at least Reader 5, the version required to play Apple QuickTime video files. Many stragglers are happy with version 4 because their day-to-day business with PDF consists merely of viewing and printing pages of text. Others believe Reader still costs money.

Knowing this, if you make a PDF that contains rich media, it's extremely important to inform users that they need a compatible version of Reader to view the rich media. Provide a link from your Web page to Adobe.com/acrobat so they can get the latest version, and remind them Reader is free. When they see the special features in your PDF—rich media, video, or Flash—they will feel comfortable upgrading. Most users trust PDF since they are so familiar with it, and they also know it will be virus free.

PDF: A Universal Standard

PDF is a well-established file format. Adobe creates the portions of the PDF code called libraries and then licenses those libraries to other developers to create applications that utilize PDF. It's not open source code where everyone contributes to the development, but it's pretty close. Instead of locking down the file format so only Adobe developers can use it, Adobe wisely promotes PDF so it remains a global standard like JPEG and MPEG.

Third-Party Developers

Because of this open format, third-party vendors have embraced the PDF specification and have created hundreds of applications that can manipulate a PDF document. Some of these programs allow you to combine PDF pages from various sources on the desktop or "on the fly" via a Web server. Instead of downloading several individual PDF files from a Web page, you can select a checklist of PDF files to be combined and downloaded as a single file.

Developers who want to provide results as printable PDFs can incorporate HTML-to-PDF translators into their Web sites. For example, automotive Web sites often allow visitors to pick custom options for their cars and then provide the results as a downloadable PDF eBrochure with pricing specific to their choices.

Other companies have licensed the PDF specification to create proprietary versions of Reader such as the Zinio Reader. Many magazine publishers offer online versions of their magazines in the Zinio format. This makes it fairly simple for developers to take the high-resolution PDF print version and compress it to a low-resolution PDF that has been customized for the Zinio Reader, which uses a proprietary digital rights management (DRM) system (a way of protecting a document from being shared or pirated).

Even Apple has built into the release of OS X the ability to view a PDF file without Acrobat or Reader, in an application called Preview (which is why Reader is absent on new Mac computers). Since Preview is the default method for new Macs to view PDF files, you might have to supply a little technical support to any of your customers who might not have configured their Mac to use Reader to play the rich-media in the PDF.

Adobe's Advantage

Adobe often purchases companies that create cool PDF software and then brings their developers in-house to continue development under the Adobe brand. When Adobe purchased Macromedia, they brought in the interface designers and programmers from Macromedia to rewrite Adobe Acrobat 8, hence the new look and feel. The PDF specification has transformed itself from a low-resolution proofing format into a final high-resolution output file that is now the preferred printing format. In addition, Adobe's page layout application, InDesign, now allows users to embed rich media such as video and Flash; this is functionality that became available in PDF 1.5.

PDF Versions and Features

You can think of PDF as a container file, something like a briefcase that holds many types of media. The newer the briefcase, the newer the media it can hold. It has pockets (or layers) for text and graphics, it has locks for security, and it comes in several subset versions such as PDF-X1A for high-end printing. The version numbers of PDF and Acrobat/Reader are different, but you can figure out which PDF specification the document adheres to by adding the two numbers together. PDF 1.4 is compatible with Acrobat and Reader 5, for example.

If a PDF reader does not meet the PDF 1.5 specification, for example, you will not see embedded multimedia in the PDF file. If you have a Mac and view a PDF in Preview, you will not be able to see any multimedia because Apple has not licensed the libraries for the right specification of the document. The document will still be viewable; it just won't display any JavaScript menus or rich media. That data remains hidden inside the file.

Table 4.1 PDF Specifications and Features

Version	Year	Acrobat	Additional Features
PDF 1.0	1993	1.0, 2.0	Included PDFWriter printer driver and Acrobat Exchange application
PDF 1.1	1994	2.1	Document encryption (40 bit), external links, article threads, named destinations, link actions, notes, device-independent color resources, and multimedia support for audio and video
PDF 1.2	1996	3.x	Form fields, JavaScript, support for CMYK color space, spot colors, halftone screens and other advanced color features, and support for Chinese, Japanese, and Korean text
PDF 1.3	1999	4.x	Digital signatures, logical structure, embedded files, masked images, smooth shading, and support for additional color spaces and CID fonts
PDF 1.4	2001	5.0	Document encryption (128 bit), tagged PDF, accessibility support, transparency, improved JavaScript support, Tagged PDFs, metadata streams, and streaming QuickTime media
PDF 1.5	2003	6.0	Document encryption (Public Key), JPEG 2000 compression, optional content groups, support for layers, additional annotation types, and embedded rich-media content
PDF 1.6	2005	7.0	Document encryption (AES), increased maximum page size, support for U3D format, additional annotation types, and enabled commenting in free Adobe Reader
PDF 1.7	2006	8.0	Enabling form fields to be saved in free Adobe Reader

PDF Is Adobe PostScript

Although many of the other competing file formats such as DNL and readers such as Microsoft Reader can do a decent job displaying text and pictures, the quality of the document is nowhere near that of PDF. When PDF was first released, many thought it meant PostScript Document File because that is really what PDF is based on. PostScript is a programming language that describes the attributes of a page. PDF is a file format that reads the text and graphic elements of a PostScript file to display it on a computer monitor.

PostScript fonts and graphics are crystal clear at any size. The difference is most noticeable on a Web page viewed on a PC. If the text is plain text generated by the computer, the text will be very jagged at large font sizes because the Web page cannot display the text in PostScript. On a Mac, the OS X operating system's PostScript rendering engine displays everything as PostScript, so the difference between viewing Web page text on a PC and a Mac is like night and day. That is why the Mac is often chosen for graphic design—everything on the monitor is rendered in fine, crisp detail.

The text and PostScript graphics in a PDF document look perfect when enlarged to full screen on any platform because the fonts are embedded inside the PDF file, and the computer, with the aid of Reader, is rendering the PostScript fonts to the screen. If you use a graphic image that consists of vector art such as an EPS (Encapsulated PostScript) file that was created in Adobe Illustrator, the artwork will also display perfectly at any size. The curves of the graphics are clean and crisp. The print quality is also perfect. The reason why the Zinio Reader is based on PDF is because publishers want their magazine text and advertising to look just like the printed product that was printed from a PostScript file.

Security and Digital Rights Management

Adobe PDFs have been widely accepted as being safe and secure. Hence, most IT departments allow them through the corporate firewall. Adobe wants to preserve that track record. Consequently, in Adobe Reader 8 the user is repeatedly confronted with pop-up warnings when trying to view a file in full screen mode, accessing rich media, or clicking links to Web pages. Though well meaning, these intrusions can be annoying. Fortunately, there are options to minimize them.

If you program a PDF file to launch full screen, Reader 8 will pop up a Full Screen warning (**FIGURE 4-1**) when the PDF first appears on the viewer's screen. It cautions that full screen mode can be made to look like a different type of application, possibly for soliciting personal information from you. The message concludes with "Would you like to allow this document to enter full screen mode automatically?" Before clicking "Yes," the viewer can select "Remember my choice for this document" so this prompt need not repeat on subsequent viewings of the file.

To minimize the chances of viruses infecting the user's computer via embedded rich media, Adobe Reader 8 pops up a Manage Trust for Multimedia Content prompt, enabling the viewer to accept or deny the playback of rich media inside the PDF file (**FIGURE 4-2**). You have the opportunity to play the multimedia once or add all of the rich media in the PDF file to your list of trusted PDF documents and the warning will no longer appear for that PDF.

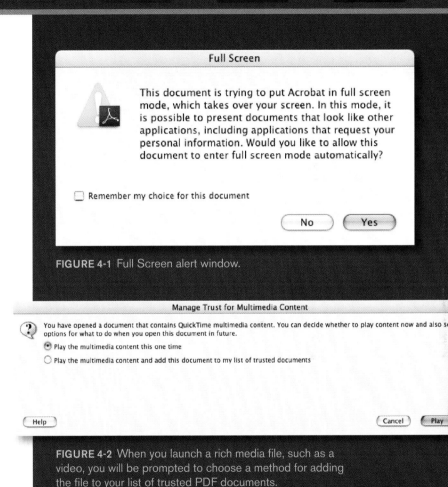

FIGURE 4-1 Full Screen alert window.

FIGURE 4-2 When you launch a rich media file, such as a video, you will be prompted to choose a method for adding the file to your list of trusted PDF documents.

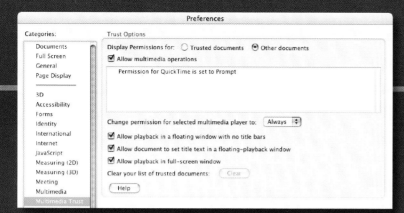

FIGURE 4-3 The Multimedia Trust category in Adobe Reader 8's Preferences dialog lets the viewer customize Reader 8's multimedia permissions.

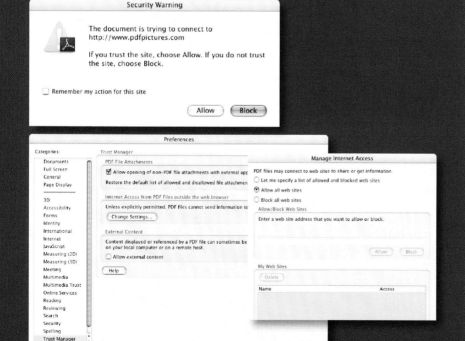

FIGURE 4-4 The Trust Manager category of Adobe Reader 8's Preferences lets the end user turn off Web site link warnings.

Multimedia Trust Preferences

The Multimedia Trust category in Adobe Reader 8's Preferences dialog lets the viewer customize Reader 8's multimedia permissions (**FIGURE 4-3**). Leaving "Allow multimedia operations" enabled (the default setting) enables all sorts of options, including "Allow playback in full-screen window" for any document type. Reader 8 recognizes two document types: the aforementioned "Trusted" as well as "Other." You can set differing options for each type. For each document type, the permission for a listed mutimedia player can be set to Always, Never, or Prompt. The Always option stops the repetition of warning pop-ups for the selected player for all PDF documents.

Trust Manager Category

The end user can turn off Web site link warnings by accessing the Trust Manager category of Adobe Reader 8's Preferences (**FIGURE 4-4**). Select the Change Settings button to call up the Manage Internet Access window. Then select the "Allow all Web sites" radio button to turn off all warnings when linking to Web pages.

To make this procedure easy for your end user, keep in mind that you can include a button in your PDF document using the Execute Menu Item Action command to launch the Reader 8 Preferences window.

Applying Passwords to a PDF

You can apply a password to view a PDF and to stop others from opening the PDF file to view the programming within the document. You can also stop people from copying and printing the document. Prohibiting the document from being copied requires special server software from Adobe, but it's quite simple to prohibit others from printing your PDF using the password security settings (**FIGURE 4-5**).

How Acrobat Uses Encryption

Print publishers also see huge companies such as Google beginning to digitize whole libraries and offer eBooks for free. Those who have cautiously decided to move to digital downloading know it is simple to duplicate a PDF and share it, so they are looking at the various digital rights management systems to safeguard their electronic documents from illegal copying.

Acrobat does not encrypt the entire PDF file; only streams and strings within the PDF file are encrypted. PDF 1.5 allows embedded rich-media files to be encrypted without encrypting other document contents. You can put two types of encryption on the document: 40 bit (Classic) and 128 bit (Modern). The higher the encryption, the harder it is to hack the document (**FIGURE 4-6**).

FIGURE 4-5 The Adobe Reader Document Properties window provides information about the security restrictions that have been placed on the document.

FIGURE 4-6 Using Adobe Acrobat, you can enable security on a PDF file that will stop users from printing or changing the document and extracting the text and pictures.

Security Options

Locking a file: You can enable security on a PDF file that will stop users from printing or changing the document and extracting the text and pictures. You will see a tiny padlock icon in the bottom-left corner if you are using Reader to view the document.

Locking a file to a computer: You can even lock the PDF file to one computer using Adobe's Policy Server.

Setting an expiration date: It's also possible to set an expiration date for the document so that the user has only a set amount of time to read it.

Personalizing a file: You can personalize a PDF file to include the purchaser's name, address, and credit card number and then embed all this information in a personalized eBook. Think of this information as a receipt that gets embedded into page 2 of the document. The user needs to know the password to open the document, so the credit card information is not on the front page and visible to everyone. Just having their personal data inside the PDF will make them think twice about uploading the document to a file-sharing service.

Assigning a password: You can assign a password to the document so that no one can open it unless they know the password.

Password

⚠ 'Secured File.pdf' is protected. Please enter a Document Open Password.

Enter Password: _____

[Cancel]   [OK]

PDF Competitors

PDF has several competitors when it comes to electronic document production such as eBooks, but some lack many features, especially the capability of rich media. Adobe has Digital Editions to display PDF eBooks, and Microsoft has Microsoft Reader for its own version of the eBook format. But Microsoft Reader is really targeted to text-only publications.

DNL Reader

DNAML's Desktop Author, an inexpensive, simple-to-use program, offers the DNL Reader. Desktop Author has really caught on in Australia for creating products such as eBrochures and promotional marketing materials. The application creates DNL files that are read by the DNL Reader. The DNL Reader has become popular in a few niche markets because the books feature flipping pages, Flash, and QuickTime rich media. The big drawback to the DNL format is that you must download the proprietary DNL Reader to view the document, or you can send the document and reader as an executable .exe file. Unfortunately, executable files are a little risky to send as email attachments because most IT departments, fearing a virus is lurking inside, will not allow them through their firewalls.

The Flash community has tried to mimic the DNL Reader with similar flipping pages and rich media, but Flash as an eBook is usually viewed inside a Web page, and the print capabilities are not as good as high-resolution PDF.

Microsoft XPS: The Real Contender to PDF

The Microsoft XPS (XML Paper Specification) format is similar in many ways to Adobe PDF and is part of the next generation of the Microsoft Windows operating system called Windows Vista. It was designed as a direct competitor to PDF, and just like PDF, an XPS document is displayed identically on every computer. The XPS Reader is available for free for Windows Vista, Windows XP, and Windows Server 2003.

An XPS file will have security, digital rights management, and signing capabilities, which were previously the exclusive domain of PDF.

Microsoft explains that the difference between the two formats is that XPS was not made for rich-media playback. Adobe, knowing that its market share for PDF might slip in the business community that uses electronic documents for billing and accounting, are enhancing the features of PDF.

When Adobe purchased Macromedia they gained a wealth of Internet-based technology that is being incorporated into PDF. One of the biggest jewels was Flash. Together as a team they have created Adobe Digital Editions, a new player for reading PDF eBooks using Flash technology. It's a light version of Adobe Reader without the fancy rich-media capabilities you will learn about in this book.

Conclusions

PDF is a trusted format backed by the entire business and publishing industry, not just Adobe. It's so secure that the U.S. government uses it for top-secret information. In fact, many government agencies will not accept any digital bid or proposal unless it is in PDF. A PDF rarely is refused by corporate firewalls, and so far the hackers who write computer viruses seem to have given PDF their blessing.

Adobe knows that Microsoft is now out to get its fair share of the corporate world that needs to file reports and transact their business electronically outside a Web page. But Microsoft still supports PDF and offers Print to PDF functions in its Office applications.

Microsoft and the Web browser application creator community now recognize that the Adobe–Macromedia merger will eventually mean the Internet will slowly transition from the always-on Web browser based on HTML to the desktop where an Internet connection is not needed after the initial download of the PDF. PDF can become the conduit for all forms of digital media.

We are just at the threshold of a type of media, based on PDF, where the term *new media* actually means something *new*.

Preparing Audio and Video for Rich-Media PDF Integration

Apple Intermediate Codec
Apple Pixlet Video
Apple VC H.263
BMP
Cinepak
Component Video
DV–PAL
DV/DVCPRO–NTSC
DVCPRO–PAL
DVCPRO HD
DVC
VC
CPR
aphics
261
263
264
JPEG 200
Motion JPEG
MPEG-4 Video
On2 VP3 Video 3.2
Photo JPEG
PNG
Sorenson Video
Sorenson Video 3
TIFF
Uncompressed 8-bit 4:2:2
Linear PCM
A-Law 2:1
AAC
AMR Narrowband
Apple Lossless
IMA 4:1
MACE 3:1
MACE 6:1
QDesign Music 2
Qualcomm PureVoice™
u-Law 2:1

The most common types of rich media you will probably want to include inside a PDF are audio and video using the Apple QuickTime, Adobe Flash, or Microsoft Windows Media Video (WMV) format. This chapter might get a little technical for the average desktop publisher who is moving into interactive PDF; however, I will be just scratching the surface of what digital audio and video is all about.

5

This digital world is complex and rapidly changing, so it's indeed a never-ending challenge to keep up with it all. You might become discouraged with the complexity of the terminology, but this chapter offers an overview of the digital video workflow; it will help you "talk the lingo" with the video production companies you might want to bring on your team and gain their respect.

If you are a digital video production company and have never made a PDF file, this chapter will provide a good overview of what PDF can and can't do regarding common types of video files. Digital video works very differently inside an Adobe Acrobat PDF.

But before getting into the nuts and bolts of producing rich-media content, it's important to understand how Adobe Reader and Adobe Acrobat present video to the user inside the PDF document.

QuickTime

macromedia FLASH ENABLED

real

Real
Mac

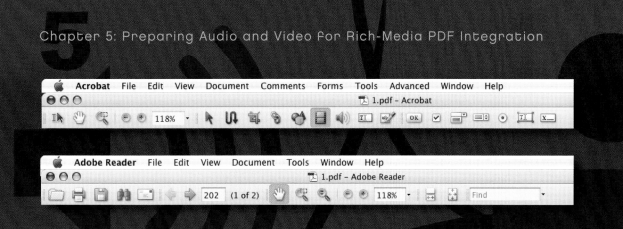

How Reader Presents Audio and Video Content

Reader only allows you to view a rich-media file; you insert the rich media using Acrobat, which of course allows you to view the rich media as well (**FIGURE 5-1**). (For the purposes of this book, when I mention the capabilities of rich-media playback in Reader, know that Acrobat can also perform the same playback functions. Acrobat and Reader are identical in every way for viewing rich media in PDF.)

Adobe Acrobat   Adobe Reader

FIGURE 5-1 Icons for Adobe Acrobat and Adobe Reader.

Adobe Acrobat and Adobe Reader are identical in every way for viewing rich-media in PDF.

When contemplating how to incorporate the multitude of digital video and audio formats inside a PDF file, the engineers at Adobe decided to take the shared approach to rich-media playback. Reader displays the text and pictures inside a PDF document using its PostScript rendering engine, but the video, audio, and animation require "helper" applications such as QuickTime, Windows Media Player, and Flash Player.

Although it would be ideal for customers to get a single download from Adobe.com that includes the latest version of Reader and a cross-platform media player such as Flash, that would make the installer quite large and would show favoritism to one patented file format. So, Reader relies on the user's installed media player to play the video and, to be fair to all formats, allows you to play audio and video in QuickTime, Windows Media Player, Flash Player, and RealNetworks RealPlayer in PDF—just not on all computer platforms, which I will address in detail in this chapter.

Since Reader relies on other audio/video software components over which Adobe has little control, it's important to understand the working interrelationships that QuickTime, Windows Media Player, RealPlayer, and Flash Player have with Reader. In some cases, new versions of the PDF specifications cause incompatibilities with media players, and vice versa.

Adobe Reader is free!
Visit Adobe.com/reader for
a free download.

Since Reader relies on other audio/video software components over which Adobe has little control, it's important to understand the working interrelationships that QuickTime, Windows Media Player, Real Media, and Flash Player have with Reader. In some cases, new versions of the PDF specifications cause incompatibilities with media players, and vice versa.

How Reader Interfaces with QuickTime, Windows Media Player, Real Media, and Flash Player

Many of you, especially if you build Web pages, may be familiar with plug-ins—tiny applications that usually reside inside the Web browser. Media players use plug-ins to play media. For example, if the Web page contains a QuickTime video, the Web browser's QuickTime plug-in tells QuickTime to play the video inside the Web page. This plug-in usually gets installed inside a browser when you upgrade to the latest versions of a media player. Along with the browser plug-in, you get a stand-alone media player that you can use to play the media outside the browser. An exception to this rule is Flash. When you upgrade the Flash Player plug-in, you do not get the stand-alone Flash Player. You need to purchase the full version of the Flash authoring application or licence the Flash Player that will operate outside of the Web browser.

On the PC, Reader uses the Flash Web browser plug-in to play Flash media. For video and audio, QuickTime and Windows Media files rely on third-party media player software components that have been installed on users' computers. When you download and install the latest version of Windows Media Player, QuickTime, or RealPlayer, the installation package contains a variety of compression codecs that are installed on your computer system during the upgrade process.

Digital Video and Audio Codecs

The video or audio compression format is the most important element of rich-media content. As defined in Chapter 2, the term *codec* is a short form for two terms: compressor and decompressor. When you capture a video to your computer, you compress and digitize the information into a specific authoring codec format that you choose to best suit your editing purpose. If you are using a MiniDV camera, the internal camera processors will compress the video using the DV codec. To capture the video to your computer using a FireWire connection, you set the digital video application, such as Apple Final Cut Pro, to capture or transfer the same DV codec to your internal drives. You are not recompressing the video; you are just transferring it in its native DV format from tape to nonlinear hard drives (**FIGURE 5-2**).

To view that digital video on your computer, you need to have the corresponding decompressor installed in the computer's operating system. In this case, the DV decompressor codec must be installed on your computer. The DV codec is mainly used for editing the video, not delivering it via the Internet. You'd need to recompress and transcode the digital video into the appropriate delivery codec to reduce the dimensions and file size so that it can be delivered via the Internet. Choosing the correct delivery codec depends on a lot of variables that you will examine later. For now, it's important to understand how the various media players handle the various file formats and delivery codecs.

FIGURE 5-2 Digital video is transfered from the camera to the computer with a Firewire connection.

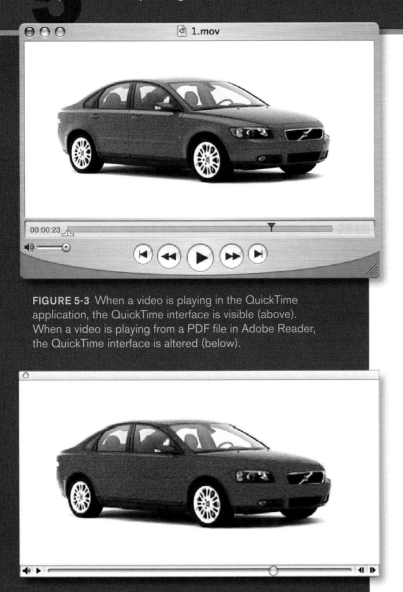

FIGURE 5-3 When a video is playing in the QuickTime application, the QuickTime interface is visible (above). When a video is playing from a PDF file in Adobe Reader, the QuickTime interface is altered (below).

Extensions are the key: QuickTime (.mov) and Windows Media Player (.wmv)

When you click on a video inside a PDF, Reader searches the computer's operating system where the decompression codecs are stored and selects the appropriate media player according to the file extension of the rich media you have chosen to play. QuickTime uses the .mov extension, Windows Media Player uses the .wmv extension, and Flash uses the .swf extension.

Let's say you have an embedded QuickTime video in a PDF, and you want to view it on a PC. Reader for Windows looks at the video's extension. If it's a QuickTime video, it will have a .mov extension. Reader will then request help from QuickTime for Windows inside the operating system to play the video inside the PDF (**FIGURE 5-3**). Reader recognizes the .mov extension and associates that video with the master QuickTime Media Player. It then looks for the appropriate QuickTime-compatible decompression codec and tells the computer to decompress the individual frames of the video using the same codec that the video file uses.

If QuickTime is not installed or if an earlier version of QuickTime is installed that does not have the latest delivery codec used to decompress the video, Reader will present a warning box that says the media player is not available, and you will be prompted to visit Apple.com/quicktime for a free upgrade (**FIGURE 5-4**). Not a pleasant experience. Bummer.

When you buy a new PC, Reader and Windows Media Player usually come preinstalled, but Quick-Time does not. The unavailability of QuickTime on many Windows PCs is one of the main reasons why many new media developers choose not to use QuickTime .mov files!

A problem that the Mac community faces is that QuickTime can't play .wmv files in a PDF. You can play .wmv files on a Mac, but only if you download the Windows Media Player for the Mac. But even then, Reader cannot play .wmv files in a PDF. This causes a big problem with cross-platform rich-media PDF development for the Mac because Reader for the Mac will use only QuickTime for all rich-media playback. As a result, no Windows Media Player and no Real Media files will play inside a PDF on the Mac. Reader for Mac does use QuickTime to play Flash SWF files, but only if it is Flash 5 or earlier and if you set the QuickTime preferences to play Flash tracks.

So, if you make a PDF that includes video in a .wmv format, it's not going to work on a Mac because QuickTime does not license the various Windows Media Player compression codecs.

Another bummer.

If QuickTime is not installed or if an earlier version of QuickTime is installed that does not have the latest delivery codec used to compress the video, Reader will present a warning box that says the media player is not available, and you will be prompted to visit Apple.com/quicktime for a free upgrade. Not a pleasant experience. Bummer.

Multimedia Player Finder

The media requires an additional player. Please click 'Get Media Player' to download the correct media player. To play the media, you will need to close and restart the application once the player installation is complete.

Get Media Player   Close

Information about download privacy

FIGURE 5-4 Reader will present a warning box that says the media player is not available.

If you make a PDF that includes video in a .wmv format, it's not going to work on a Mac because QuickTime does not license the various Windows Media Player compression codecs. Another bummer.

Multimedia Player Finder

The media requires an additional player. Please click 'Get Media Player' to download the correct media player. To play the media, you will need to close and restart the application once the player installation is complete.

Close   Get Media Player

Information about download privacy

Renditions to the Rescue

Adobe has always tried to make its PDF software cross-platform so that it will work on Macs, on Windows, and even on Linux machines. The Adobe engineers knew that the incompatibilities with video players would prove to be a disappointment among many multimedia developers, so they introduced a marvelous solution called renditions (**FIGURE 5-5**). Instead of making two versions of the PDF, one for Macs and one for Windows, you just make two versions of the video.

A rendition is a "fallback" video and audio file. You can include both QuickTime and Windows Media files in one document and then author the PDF to play one of the files using whichever media player it finds on the user's computer. If one of the media players is not installed, Reader will then use the alternate video that is either embedded in or linked to the document. The downside is that alternate embedded videos can make the PDF document quite large because you are just duplicating the video in a different format. But if you link to the video on a Web server and stream the video into the document, the file size is of little importance (**FIGURE 5-6**).

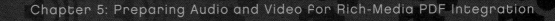

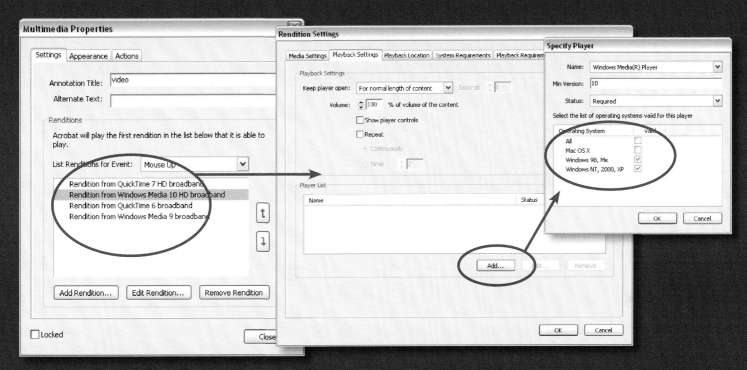

FIGURE 5-5 You can include both QuickTime and Windows Media files in one document and then author the PDF to play the file on the correct media player it finds on the user's computer.

FIGURE 5-6 Alternate embedded videos can make the document quite large because you are just duplicating the video in a different format, but if you link to the video on a Web server and stream the video into the document, the file size is of little importance.

A Real-World Scenario

Let's say you have produced a rich-media PDF sales eBrochure for a large corporation. The document includes one high-quality embedded video in the WMV format, and the final file size is just less than 5 MB, small enough to email as an attachment for the majority of people who have high-speed Internet connections. (Many Internet service providers cap their email attachments at 5 MB, but that limit is quickly rising.) You want to ensure that the video works in your client's presentation boardroom and on the PCs in the sales offices that have only Windows Media Player installed.

You know that the salespeople will be emailing the eBrochure to their clients when they request information, and some of their clients will be Mac users. You could make two versions of the PDF, one for Mac and one for Windows, but if their clients pass the Mac version along to others, it will fail on a Windows computer.

You could author the PDF to use an alternate embedded QuickTime rendition, but that would double the file size of the document's video content to 10 MB—too big to email. Or, you could provide a QuickTime rendition linked to a QuickTime video that resides on the company Web server, but the user would need an Internet connection to view the video. If the size of the PDF is crucial to its success, and you want to email the eBrochure, the latter method is a better option.

On the PC at the corporate office, Reader will recognize the .wmv video format and will make a request for the Windows Media Player rendering engine to play the video. Everything should work fine. But what happens when one user then decides to check the PDF on his Mac at home?

At home, he opens the file on his MacBook and launches Reader for Mac to view the PDF, but this time the video looks a little different. It's not as big as it was at the office. The reason for this is that Reader has been programmed to ignore the Windows Media file because the Mac cannot play it and instead use the QuickTime rendition available on the corporate Web site. To keep the file to less than 5 MB, only one video was embedded in the PDF. Since the QuickTime video would stream into the document, the producer decided to make the video a little smaller so the video could be viewed in real time over a high-speed Internet connection.

 When producing rich-media PDFs with embedded media, try to keep the file size below 5 MB if you intend to email the file.

Viewing Rich Media Offline

What makes rich-media PDF so much more convenient than a Web site is the ability to download the entire file to view the rich media offline. Once you have downloaded the PDF and the embedded video, you have instant-on, full-screen, full-motion, crystal-clear video because you avoid the constraints of a Web browser and your Internet connection speed. Users who have slow Internet connections (slower than 1 Mbps, called *high-speed lite*) can now view full-screen, full-motion video. It might take a long time to download the embedded rich-media PDF, but at least it can provide a full-screen viewing experience. And with QuickTime, you can make the full-screen video interactive, which is not possible with Windows Media Player.

Embedded Flash video was not available on the PC until Reader 8, and it's not available on the Mac as of the writing of this book.

Streaming Media Servers and Progressive Downloading

In situations where the video is just too long to download in its entirety or the video is from a live broadcast, you can stream the video into the PDF. You can use Flash video, QuickTime, Windows Media, and Real Media to accomplish this. But QuickTime is the only free cross-platform streaming format that you can use, and it is one of the best for streaming the video from a Web server.

The Real Media server software and the Windows Media Player streaming server software are not free; in fact, they can be expensive. If you want to include Flash video, the user will need to have Reader 8 or later.

The most common format for streaming video is called the progressive download format. It's like streaming video because you link the video on a Web server to the PDF, but it will progressively download to the PDF. The movie will start as soon as there is enough preloaded data to play the video to the end smoothly without interruption. The Web server setup for this process is simple because there is no special streaming software required. Just put the video in a folder on a Web server, and link to it from the PDF.

The most common format for streaming video is called the progressive download format.

Using Cross-Platform Media Codecs— MPEG Alternatives

Another solution to ensure that the rich media works on all computers is to choose a decompression codec—such as MPEG-1 for video and MP3 for audio—that will run on both platforms and in both QuickTime and Windows Media Player. The Motion Pictures Expert Group (MPEG) is an association of companies that invent and choose the "official" standards for digital audio and video codecs. The problems you face with the MPEG codecs is that many flavors of MPEG are not compatible inside QuickTime and Windows Media Player, especially the newer forms of MPEG, such as MPEG-4 H.264—the high-definition codec that is competing with Microsoft Windows Media 10 for high-definition TV.

MPEG is a file type that uses the file extension .mpg. MPEG-1 is a codec. MPEG signifies the quality of the codec based on numbers: MPEG-1, MPEG-2, and MPEG-4 are all compression codecs that sit inside the MPEG file. MPEG-1 was released in 1988. Windows Media Player and QuickTime both have licensed the rights to include the MPEG-1 codec inside their media player software to decompress MPEG-1 content. So, if you compress your video to MPEG-1, you will be able to see the video play inside the PDF on a Mac and on a PC. If you want to make the video once and ensure that it plays everywhere, your safest bet is to use MPEG-1. It's old enough that almost every computer has this codec, and it is also included in the new QuickTime and Windows Media Player installers.

However, it's not a very efficient codec for large downloads and streaming because it produces huge file sizes and is lower quality compared to the newest flavors of MPEG-2 and MPEG-4. Still, in the right circumstances (such as talking heads and scenes with little motion) MPEG-1 can provide good results at low bit rates.

The world is currently looking for a standard video codec like the standard MP3 audio codec that will play on all computers and set-top boxes, and it looks like MPEG-4 H.264 is currently being adopted by the majority of broadcast networks and DVD players in the TV world. Apple has licensed it for QuickTime 7 for the video iPod, but Microsoft has locked it out of Windows Media Player. Another bummer.

Cross-Platform Streaming Considerations

At this point, no single cross-platform codec is really efficient enough for streaming linked video media from a Web server. MPEG-1 will stream, but its dreadful quality at low data rates is just not worth it. Your best bet is to use Windows Media Video 7 for playback on the PC and QuickTime's Sorenson 3 codec for the Mac. Make one PDF file and then use the rendition function to program Acrobat to force Windows Media Player to play Windows Media 7 video on the PC and QuickTime Sorenson on the Mac. That combination will give you the best picture quality and streaming performance without having to force the user to install the latest version of its media players. Streaming video allows you to jump ahead or fast forward the video without having to download it.

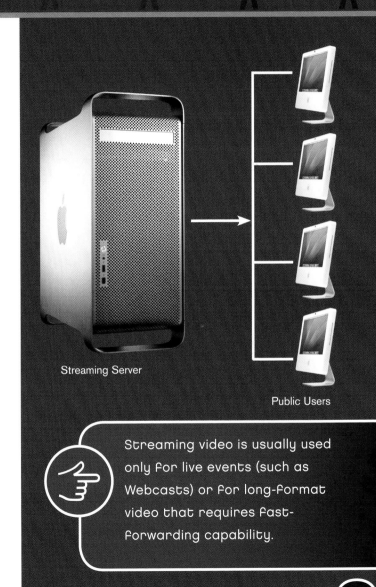

Streaming Server

Public Users

Streaming video is usually used only for live events (such as Webcasts) or for long-format video that requires fast-forwarding capability.

QuickTime versus Windows Media Player

Since version 2.0 of the PDF specification, Acrobat has provided the capability of including QuickTime video in a PDF. It was an exclusive relationship in which QuickTime was the only file format allowed until PDF 1.5 (Reader 6) was released. This long-term relationship has produced some very cool rich-media opportunities for PDF that are still available only via QuickTime.

Most broadcast and multimedia professionals will tell you that the QuickTime architecture is light years ahead of the competition.

Unfortunately, people think QuickTime is just a type of video format , but it is much more than that. Try to think of it as a multimedia operating environment. It can play (almost) any type of still picture, animation, audio, and video format.

Try not to think of QuickTime as just for Macs; it thrives in the world of PCs too. QuickTime is used for broadcast audio and TV production on the PC. Apple's latest offering of iTunes and the iPod require QuickTime to operate, and we all know that PC users love iTunes to rip and burn custom CDs.

Try not to think of QuickTime as just for Macs; it thrives in the world of PCs too.

MOVIE

.mov: How Popular Is QuickTime?

More than ten million copies of QuickTime are downloaded every month. More than 20,000 applications and content CDs include QuickTime, and more than 200 models of digital video cameras use QuickTime to capture or display their files. QuickTime is ubiquitous in the home because of the iPod and is gradually making its way into the corporate world.

Pioneering the digital media industry almost 15 years ago, QuickTime was the first software on a personal computer to take film and digitize it. It was designed from the ground up for stability, scalability, and extensibility, and it almost never crashes. It's the most powerful and comprehensive platform for developing and deploying digital media solutions. If you want to create rich media for PDF, QuickTime tools are the ones to use because they all work together seamlessly. That is why PDF and QuickTime are like two peas in a pod: They have had a long relationship, and the tools used to create desktop print materials and QuickTime are usually found on the Mac. Even if your final videos are MPEG or WMV files, QuickTime is the best multimedia environment to get you from raw content to final rich-media video.

.wmv: A PC-Only File Format for PDF

The .wmv file format is a good choice if you just want to supply good-quality video and you feel certain that most of your users are on Windows. You can embed the video into the PDF or stream it into the document from a Web server. The majority of your end users will see it because Windows Media Player is widely installed on almost every PC. It's also worth it to spend the time and energy to provide a QuickTime rendition linked to a Web server to be sure you don't leave out Mac users completely.

QuickTime Stats

- QuickTime 6 was downloaded over 350 million times. 98% were PC users.

- More than 250 digital devices include QuickTime as the media player of choice.

- Every day, more than 25,000 Web sites refer customers to Apple.com for QuickTime Player downloads.

Get QuickTime Free Download

QuickTime VR

If your production has video and virtual reality (VR) components, QuickTime is a safe bet as a one-stop shop for all of your rich-media needs.

QuickTime VR is Apple's award-winning technology that transforms still images from the flat 2D world into 3D, allowing you to pick up objects and rotate them for a 360-degree view inside a PDF.

You can place yourself in a virtual room to look straight up and down and pan from left to right. It's perfect for tours of hotels, real estate, or views of a car (**FIGURE 5-7**).

Samples on the companion rich-media PDF on the CD-ROM show you how QuickTime VR works, and I have a chapter dedicated to it later in the book.

FIGURE 5-7 QuickTime Object VRs offer the ability to control an item in a virtual space, as if it were in the palm of your hand (left). QuickTime Cubic VRs allow users to view environments without any limitations of viewing angles, from left to right and straight up or straight down (below).

67

5

Compressing Digital Video for Playback in PDF

M any digital video applications on the market will allow you to edit your digital video, but the most popular for simple editing are Adobe Premiere, Apple Final Cut Pro, and Apple iMovie. Once you have produced your final video, you then need to compress the video to reduce the file size using a codec that will suit your purposes. QuickTime Pro for the Mac and the PC allows you to compress digital video for playback inside a PDF, but applications like Sorenson Squeeze and Autodesk Cleaner can do much more.

AUTODESK CLEANER

QuickTime

Final Cut Studio

Autodesk Cleaner

Professional multimedia production companies use Autodesk Cleaner to compress Flash video, RealPlayer media, Windows Media, and QuickTime video and audio. Autodesk Cleaner can convert almost any video and audio file format to a wide variety of compression codecs. It can enhance the video in terms of brightening or darkening, enriching the colors, color correcting for unbalanced lighting, cropping the frames, and much more. The application can also analyze the video and audio tracks using a dual-pass method and then apply the optimal compression during the second pass (**FIGURE 5-8**).

The software will also allow you to compress the video for streaming or progressive downloading.

QuickTime Pro, on its own, can do some pretty amazing things, but Autodesk Cleaner offers more export options for additional file formats and compression codecs that are not licensed by Apple such as Windows Media, DivX, Sorenson Spark, and the Flash On2 Flix codec.

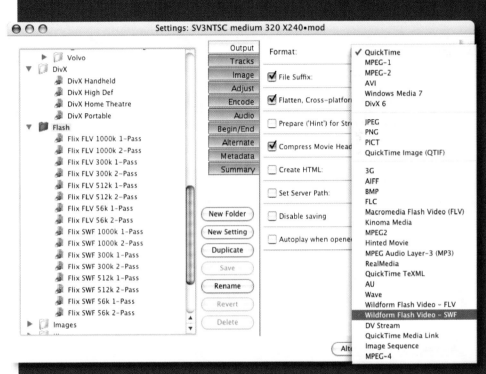

FIGURE 5-8 Autodesk Cleaner compresses Flash video, RealPlayer media, Windows Media, and QuickTime video and audio. Autodesk Cleaner can convert almost any video and audio file format to a wide variety of compression codecs.

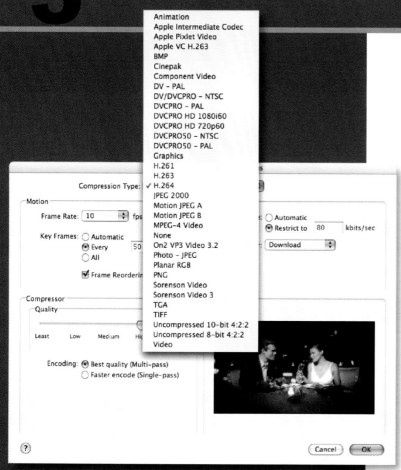

Animation
Apple Intermediate Codec
Apple Pixlet Video
Apple VC H.263
BMP
Cinepak
Component Video
DV - PAL
DV/DVCPRO - NTSC
DVCPRO - PAL
DVCPRO HD 1080i60
DVCPRO HD 720p60
DVCPRO50 - NTSC
DVCPRO50 - PAL
Graphics
H.261
H.263
✓ H.264
JPEG 2000
Motion JPEG A
Motion JPEG B
MPEG-4 Video
None
On2 VP3 Video 3.2
Photo - JPEG
Planar RGB
PNG
Sorenson Video
Sorenson Video 3
TGA
TIFF
Uncompressed 10-bit 4:2:2
Uncompressed 8-bit 4:2:2
Video

FIGURE 5-9 The free version of QuickTime does not allow you to compress video unless you upgrade for $30 to QuickTime Pro.

QuickTime Pro

The QuickTime file format comes with many open standard codecs, and additional codecs are available from third-party companies. Quick-Time Pro can compress video using single- and dual-pass methods just like dedicated compression software such as Sorenson Video Developer Edition, which provides slightly better quality dual-pass video compression. There are essentially two types of QuickTime codecs:

- **Authoring codecs** are known as lossless codecs and are high quality and large in file size (for example, M-JPEG, Photo-JPEG, and DV DVC Pro). They are used during capturing and edit-ing and are not used as rich-media content for PDF. Authoring codecs are used for "intermediate" production and storage. You can edit digital video in these formats.

- **Delivery codecs** (for example, Sorenson, MPEG-1, MPEG-4, AAC, and MP3) are used for the final rich media that will be inserted into PDFs and presented to viewers.

The free version of QuickTime does not allow you to compress video unless you upgrade for $30 to QuickTime Pro (**FIGURE 5-9**).

Do not re-edit or recompress files that have been compressed into a delivery codec because this decreases quality and in some cases renders the file useless.

Interactive QuickTime Movies Using Wired Sprites

One subject that is a constant concern throughout this book is the file size of your final document. You will want to keep it as small as possible for two reasons: so you can email it to others and so you don't scare away people who are afraid of downloading large files.

The QuickTime format allows you to create simulated full-screen video at extremely small file sizes. You can achieve this using QuickTime sprites, which are small graphics that can be animated. QuickTime allows you to add a Flash track to your .mov file right alongside the audio and/or video track and then provide everything from navigation buttons to full animations, but with the release of QuickTime 7.1.3 Apple disabled that capability unless you manually enable Flash playback via the QuickTime preferences window. Unfortunately the end user will not know how to do this, so using Flash inside QuickTime is not recommended for rich media in PDF.

You can easily bring a static, flat PDF page to life by embedding interactive QuickTime content or wired sprites and layers. For example, a wired sprite can be a still graphic placed over a small video that is then placed over a full-screen still-image background. The result appears to end users to be a full-screen video. As a track type in a QuickTime movie, wired sprites can become interactive hot-spot layers of graphics that allow you to animate portions of the movie (**FIGURE 5-10**).

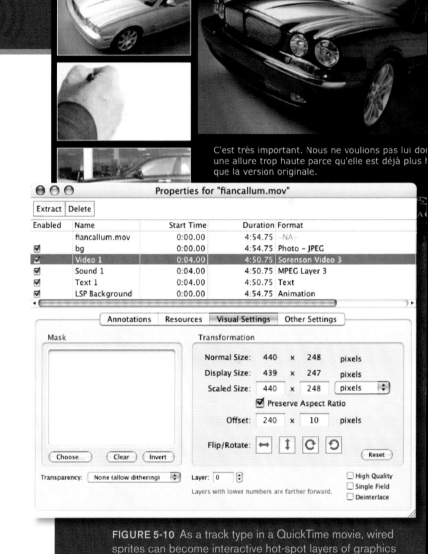

FIGURE 5-10 As a track type in a QuickTime movie, wired sprites can become interactive hot-spot layers of graphics that allow you to animate portions of the movie.

QuickTime Codecs

QuickTime can utilize the following native codecs:

3DMF (MacOS 9 & Windows)	Cubic VR	M3U (MP3 Playlist files)	SDP
3GPP	DLS		SDV
3GPP2	DV	MPEG-4	SF2
AIFF	FlashPix	MQV	SGI
AMC	FLC	M4A	SMIL
AMR	GIF	M4V (iTunes video)	Targ
Animated GIF	GSM		Text
AU	JPEG	PDF (Mac OS X)	TIFF
Audio CD Data	Karaoke	Photoshop	TIFF Fax
AVI	SWF (Macromedia Flash 5)	PICS	VDU (Sony Video Disk Unit)
BMP	MIDI	PICT	VR (Virtual Reality)
CAF	MPEG-1	PLS	Wave
	MP3	PNG	
		SD2	

Tip: The settings in QuickTime 7.1.3 disable Flash tracks from playing within QuickTime Player. This feature can be enabled in the QuickTime preferences window.

QuickTime Codecs

What really sets QuickTime apart from its competitors is its movie file format, .mov. Structured as a versatile and scalable "container," it can hold a variety of media types. This is what makes QuickTime preferable over Windows Media because many more codecs are available for interactive uses inside one self-contained video file.

I often use the following delivery codecs in Quick-Time movies:

- Animated GIF
- Cubic VR
- GIF
- JPEG
- MIDI
- MPEG-1
- MP3
- MPEG-4
- M4A
- M4V (iTunes video)
- PDF (Mac OS X)
- Text
- Virtual Reality (VR)

As you can see, this is a pretty impressive list, and the cool part of QuickTime is that you can mix a variety of codecs and file types in one QuickTime .mov file and make them interactive. To do this, you use a QuickTime authoring application such as Totally Hip's LiveStage.

For example, you could take a series of nearly full-screen JPEG images and make a slide show with narration and music supplementing the pictures. The last picture could hold its image, and you could place a smaller video in front of it. Besides the movie, you could have text that changes in sync with the narration. To the user it will seem like the whole picture is a video. But in fact, it's actually four elements all running in sync to the audio track inside one QuickTime container .mov file.

The advantage of this "convergence" method is that combined tracks will result in smaller file sizes. Instead of bandwidth-intensive, full-screen, 30 frames per second video, the still-image JPEG slide show will take up very little space, the text track will be negligible, the audio track will be a small MP3 file, and the only bandwidth-intensive track will be the tiny video that plays at the end of the slide show. This scenario is perfect for producing a rich-media PDF that is small in file size but contains media that has large, almost full-screen, playback dimensions.

Flash can also export to QuickTime, which will allow you to combine still images, video, and Flash into one self-contained file; however, it will not play inside a PDF unless the user enables QuickTime to play Flash tracks (**FIGURE 5-11**).

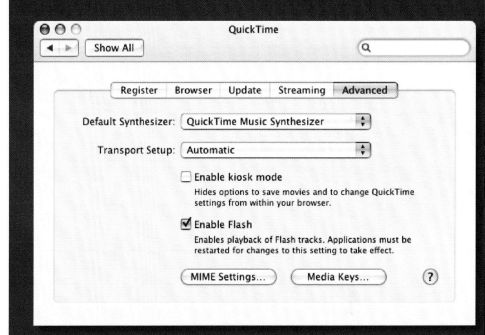

FIGURE 5-11 Enabling Flash 5 playback in QuickTime Player.

To enable Flash playback on the Macintosh, you must select the "Enable Flash" checkbox in the QuickTime preferences under the "Advanced" tab.

QuickTime

A Brief History of QuickTime Codecs and Capabilities

QuickTime 4—Interactive!

Introduced in June 1999

This was the first version that introduced interactivity to the format. You can add Web links, and QuickTime effects are rendered upon playback, so you can use text tracks, sprites, and more for cross-platform titles. If you want to make your video interactive, it's a safe bet that people will be able to see it.

QuickTime 5—Supports Flash

Introduced in April 2001

Support for MPEG-1 playback, both local and streaming on Macintosh and Windows. It also supports QuickTime VR 360-degree cubic movies, real-time audio and video streaming, the high-quality Sorenson 3 codec, and Flash 4.

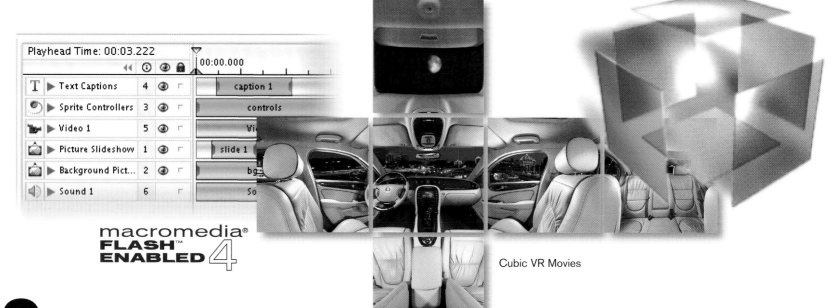

Cubic VR Movies

macromedia®
FLASH™

QuickTime 6—AAC iPod Audio

Introduced in July 2002

QuickTime 6 is the most widely installed version of QuickTime, and it includes the basic version of MPEG-4 high-quality AAC audio used for the iPod, and the JPEG2000 still-image codecs. Flash 5 support was the last version licensed by Apple. Make sure your Flash files are saved in Flash 5 or earlier and your QuickTime preference settings allow for Flash playback.

AAC Audio

QuickTime 7—MPEG4 H.264

Introduced in April 2005

QuickTime 7 includes the high-quality MPEG-4 H.264 codec that has become the MPEG standard for high-definition DVD and high-definition digital television.

Use the MPEG-4 H.264 codec if you know the intended playback computer can support it, or if you can provide an alternate rendition of the video that uses an earlier codec such as Sorenson or MPEG-1.

For a short, full-screen commercial, to ensure your QuickTime video can be viewed by the widest possible audience, it's best to make two renditions, one that uses the latest MPEG-4 H.264 high-definition codec and a second that uses the Sorenson codec available in QuickTime 5.

QuickTime Version Decisions

So, with all these available options, which QuickTime codec do you choose for your PDF? That depends on how many people you think have upgraded to QuickTime 7 or later, which includes MPEG-4 H.264.

The iPod has really sped up the adoption of QuickTime 7 to the PC, so many young users probably already have it; however, many others have not yet upgraded their earlier versions of QuickTime, so it's important you do not rely on the QuickTime 7 codec, MPEG-4 H.264, for your QuickTime movie if you want to ensure the widest possible audience. It's best to make two renditions, one that uses the latest MPEG-4 H.264 high-definition codec (for a short, full-screen embedded commercial) and a second that streams the Sorenson codec available in QuickTime 5.

If you are delivering the rich-media PDF on CD-ROM, you can use the latest codecs available. Just supply the latest QuickTime Media Player installer on the CD. It's free from Apple.

If you are embedding the media in a PDF, the new MPEG-4 H.264 quality is beautiful and the file sizes are very small, but they can be processor intensive. For viewing 640 x 480 standard definition (SD) H.264 video on a Windows computer, you need a 1.5 GHz Intel Pentium 4 or faster processor with at least 512 MB of RAM and a 64 MB or greater video card.

Audio-Only Considerations

The world of audio is a whole new subject; however, it's a much simpler topic than video; there is a lot less to worry about. MP3 is a very safe codec to use because it works well on both computer platforms; both QuickTime and Windows Media Player will play it.

You can use iTunes to create an MP3 file, but it's best to use a professional encoder to compress your audio files to the MP3 format. Professional-level encoder/ripper applications, such as Autodesk Cleaner, include an advanced, dual-pass MP3 encoder created by the Fraunhofer Society research organization, the inventor of the MP3 format.

Computer Generated MIDI Files

MIDI stands for Music Instrument Digital Interface, and is a file format that allows you to play sound effects and music using a computer. MIDI files are created using a music sequencing program, such as Apple Logic Pro. Instead of playing digital audio files, the sounds are synthesized by the media player. The benefit of MIDI files is that they are extremely small in size and if produced well, they are very high quality—perfect when you have to email your PDF and want to include sound effects and music.

Attaching Audio Files to the PDF

For the iPod, Apple uses the latest AAC codec, using the .M4A extension. Since Apple uses this format for its iPod, the AAC codec is a wise choice when you are attaching audio files to the PDF for transfer to the iPod. Apple iTunes is a free application that can create high fidelity iPod-ready audio files.

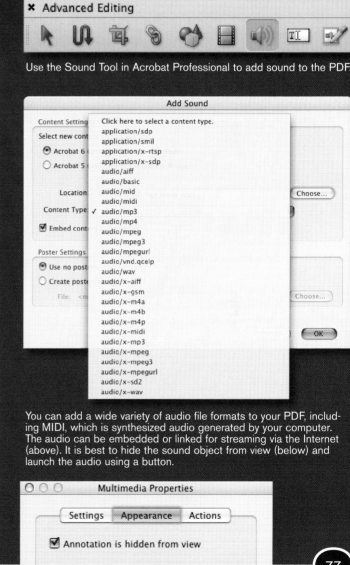

Use the Sound Tool in Acrobat Professional to add sound to the PDF.

You can add a wide variety of audio file formats to your PDF, including MIDI, which is synthesized audio generated by your computer. The audio can be embedded or linked for streaming via the Internet (above). It is best to hide the sound object from view (below) and launch the audio using a button.

Final Cut Pro

iDVD HD

Mac Mini

Making the Right Choices

ven though Real Media video was a real contender in the past, the multimedia industry has abandoned it now that Flash video has grown into a decent medium for video playback on the Web. Although you are starting to see a lot of Flash video on the Internet inside Web pages, it will be some time before Flash video finds a good home in PDF. Flash video, as of the release of this book, does not work on the Mac. QuickTime and WMV work much more efficiently for large, full-screen video playback, and that's where rich-media video in PDF really shines.

At this point, if you are going to make a PDF with video and want it to play on all computers, you really have to use the cross-platform codec, MPEG 1, or offer QuickTime video and WMV in the same PDF. This is simple to do if the videos are linked to the PDF.

Your PDF will be small in file size if you plan properly, and you'll also be able to email it, which is the bonus of PDF.

Choosing the right compression codec for your rich media will most likely be the hardest decision you will make during the project planning stages. You have many variables to consider, such as media player incompatibilities, the target market of your audience, and those nasty bugs that are present in some previous versions of Reader or QuickTime.

Choosing the right tools to produce the content is just as important. QuickTime used to be a negative word to many PC users, who believed it would work only on a Mac. Until recently, before the widespread adoption of broadband, it was a pain to download QuickTime because of the long wait.

But with the ubiquity of broadband and the iPod in the marketplace, Apple is once again at the forefront of inventing cool products, and consumers now see that Apple offers much more than computer hardware. QuickTime is the preferred rich-media authoring format for professionals and for amateurs, so no matter whether you are thinking of getting into the multimedia business or this is your hobby, you might want to add an iMac or a Mini to your computer collection. Apple is also making great inexpensive professional audio and video software that comes preinstalled on Macs.

QuickTime and Final Cut Pro are also changing the workflows for TV and movie production studios in Hollywood because they are now being accepted by editors who are experienced with the standard editing workhorse, the Avid editing system. These new workflows are all based on QuickTime, an open file format that can move digital data from the audio studio to the special effects department and then to editing, broadcast TV, feature film, and of course the Internet. It's interactive—perfect for bringing static PDF pages to life.

Conclusions

The advantage of PDF is that you can get the PDF outside the browser to provide a TV-like experience. Think full-screen video now that the computer is moving into the living room via Intel's Viiv and Apple's wireless reciever with Front Row technology.

Imagine a world in the not too distant future where you download a PDF file to your computer. Inside that PDF is an attached video for iTunes or renditions of video that link to a Web server in various media player formats ready for viewing full screen on your widescreen TV via Viiv. (**FIGURE 5-12**).

The iPod family of products

FIGURE 5-12 Interactive PDF ready for viewing in full screen on your widescreen TV.

From Print to Interactive PDF

When desktop publishing was first invented, a whole new service industry developed to help the print designers who wanted to do it all—create the layout, typeset the page, edit the graphics, and deliver the final film to the printer. This all became possible using relatively inexpensive home computer equipment with the aid of a service bureau. The service bureau had the expensive laser image setter that could output the film to printing plates. Today, that process has been replaced by digital PDF files that load directly into a digital printing press.

As the "disruptive" PDF technologies become mainstream, some companies fight to keep the new forms of media from invading their turf. However, other companies adapt to the new opportunities for print shops, print publishers, and Web and TV producers to become involved in rich-media PDF production by adding digital video, audio, and animation to their list of services.

Flash developers who are knowledgeable about databases such as the open source MySQL and about Adobe ColdFusion servers can now offer their services for electronic publishing in PDF. This opens up a whole new opportunity for ecommerce via a PDF file instead of a Web page.

In this chapter, you'll learn how to repurpose traditional printed materials for the computer monitor and look at the various ways you can present the materials using interactive elements.

Photo top: Courtesy of Xerox Corporation

6

Where Do You Begin?

If your background is in print publishing and you have decided to explore the next phase of interactive publications, you might want to test the market by producing electronic versions of your past print projects. If this works out well for you, perhaps your client will pay for the electronic versions. Print brochures become eBrochures, print books become eBooks, and so on.

In my company's situation, almost all of our business was television and interactive CD or DVD production. We first had to learn the tools designers use to create printed materials and then had to redesign the print content to meet the look and feel of the clients' brands. Then, once we had a page the client was happy with, the easy part was to add the rich media.

In television production, you are always working in a 4:3 or 16:9 aspect ratio. In print production, you are working on page spreads. The challenge is merging the two for viewing on a computer monitor.

Viewing PDFs Inside Web Pages

Even though PDF documents have been widely adopted, most people find them hard to read onscreen unless they are somewhat experienced with the Adobe Reader navigation tools. If the PDF originates on a Web site, it will most likely open in the same browser window via the Reader plug-in and become even harder to read because there is less display space for the actual document. The browser's menu and the Reader toolbar will take up a third of the computer monitor, leaving little space to read text if it's formatted in traditional magazine columns. Scrolling up and down becomes cumbersome, so the user will try to fit the page in the window, making the text too small to read.

Most print publications are produced for reading text on an 8.5 x 11-inch page in portrait format using small type. The computer display is a hybrid of the movie theater screen, which was designed to display breathtaking scenic landscapes (which is where the term landscape display comes from). When desktop publishers create versions of their printed magazines for their Web sites, 99 percent of these PDFs are difficult to read on a computer monitor, and therein lies the perceived problem with PDF.

In situations like this, consumers have given PDF a negative rating. You will often hear this complaint: "It's almost impossible to read a PDF on a computer. That's why I never choose to open PDF files on Web pages." Even though this is mostly true, it is surprising to see sizable numbers of PDF downloads in our clients' server tracking reports. Usually, 20 percent of visitors to a Web site will view a PDF file if it is available.

The main reason for the number of downloads is that visitors want to take something away with them; they want to own part of the Web site by downloading and printing large portions of it as PDF. Most of our clients like the capability of emailing a PDF file for direct-marketing purposes.

There are a few simple ways to ensure that the end user will not have trouble viewing the PDF. If a PDF is only a few pages in length, it's best to have the Webmaster launch a new full-screen browser window with hidden browser toolbars, set the PDF document to Fit to Width, and make sure the PDF tools are visible above the document. Users will have much more screen space to read the document, and the toolbar will allow users to print and save the file to their computers if they decide to do so.

Remember the following important advantages that PDF has over a Web site. I will refer to them often throughout the book.

- **You can't print a Web site:** You can print pages, but not the whole site in one click.
- **You can't download a Web site:** Well-designed PDF electronic documents are perfect for downloading to view outside the browser.
- **You can't email a Web site:** You can email a link to a page but not a whole Web site.

With PDF you can do all these things.

Think Cross-Media When Producing Printed Material

Few desktop publishers think far enough ahead to see a new opportunity—they're only concerned about the printed product. They focus on the text font, the branding, and the client logo. Unfortunately, they can't see the writing on the wall as their printed product is slowly being phased out by interactive Web pages. Webmasters are not making it any easier for the desktop publishers; they would love to have the print budget reassigned to them. I often hear from the Web department: "We have decided to do a version of these brochures in Flash. We can use the same pictures and text and then put together a real interactive experience. Look here! See how we can make the pages flip just like real turning pages?" Flipping pages does seem to get the attention of marketing managers, but for consumers the awe quickly wears off, especially when they try to print the brochure.

Print publishers should take a few hints from Flash Web developers who create entire sites in Flash. These Webmasters have passed the splash screen stage of their careers and have moved on to creating Flash movies that you don't have to scroll like Web pages; instead, you "flip" the Flash pages. These masters of Flash have learned from their previous Web page design experience that when text and graphics appear "below the fold" at the bottom of the computer monitor, it will often not be read—or clicked. You never see long, scrolling Flash documents, do you? So, follow their lead, and try not to make PDF files that the user needs to scroll in order to read the text.

Design a Document for TV Viewing

We promote rich-media PDF as a new new-media format; call it Internet 2.0 if you'd like—it's downloadable media convergence that works like a Web site, but better. The PDF replaces the Web browser and can provide everything a Web page can. A rich-media document usually contains video, so try to approach the design of the document from a TV point of view. Instead of using portrait layout, design the document in landscape display, and set the aspect ratio of the page to fill the screen of the computer monitor from edge to edge. If you simulate a TV viewing experience, content such as video and virtual reality photography can appear on the page or float above the page in full-screen mode.

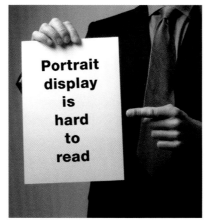

Adobe InDesign:
Rich-Media Page Layout
with Interactive Tools

There are many rich-media tools you can use to create document content, but the ideal page layout program is InDesign. If your background is in the print industry, you will probably be well versed with QuarkXPress. It's a great application for creating print materials, but it is less than ideal to use for rich-media production.

InDesign has made inroads into the print publishing industry, and besides being a great application for printing, it has everything you need to do the following:

- Embed or link rich media such as video and animation inside the PDF

- Create interactive rollover buttons for launching the rich media

- Create buttons to navigate through the pages of the document **(FIGURE 6-1)**

- Hyperlink words to launch Web pages

- Export the document directly to PDF without using Adobe Acrobat Distiller **(FIGURE 6-2)**

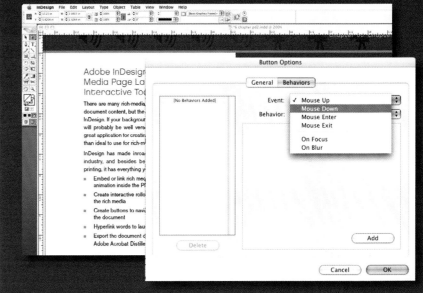

FIGURE 6-1 InDesign can create buttons that allow you to navigate through an interactive PDF.

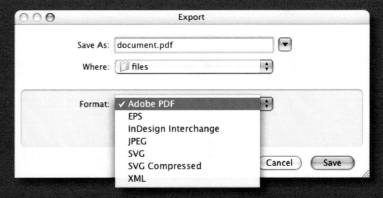

FIGURE 6-2 InDesign can export documents to a number of different file formats, including directly to PDF without the need for Acrobat Distiller.

Adobe Acrobat, JavaScript, and Flash Features

InDesign is perfect for adding rich media to the document and it does provide some basic navigation tools, but working with JavaScript in Acrobat can give you so much more. Acrobat allows you to insert JavaScript to create pop-up menus **(FIGURE 6-3)**, create search buttons, create print functionality, change the document display to full screen, and add forms for database connectivity. Virtually everything a Web site can do, a PDF can emulate using Adobe JavaScript for page navigation and using Flash with database servers.

Web sites will often use Flash or JavaScript rollover drop-down menus to allow users to get a quick glimpse of the categories and contents of the site. JavaScript pop-up menus provide the same capabilities for PDF documents. If you launch a PDF document to full screen for a TV-like experience you will need to supply your own navigation buttons for users to control the document, as the Reader toolbars at the top of the screen will be hidden.

Connecting PDF and Databases via Flash

Many Web sites are database driven, meaning their content comes from database tables. Instead of using a Web design application such as Adobe Dreamweaver to add content to a Web page, you can use a Web browser to upload text and graphics to a database. News sites, message boards, and blogs use databases to store information, and that information can be altered using a Web browser.

Flash can also talk to a database—ColdFusion database servers are set up for this specific purpose. News sites, message boards, and blogs can also be created in Flash using a database, and instead of a Web page, the database information can be displayed in a PDF file. This allows the content inside the downloaded PDF to be updated from an external source, provided an Internet connection is present. For example, you can get the latest news inside a PDF from an external RSS news feed.

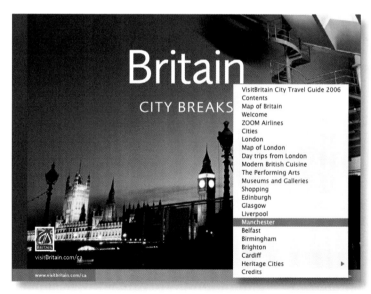

FIGURE 6-3 Adobe Javascript pop-up menu.

Including More Than One Video Format

InDesign and Acrobat have similar tools for embedding rich media, but Acrobat has many more features. Acrobat allows you to provide multiple renditions of the video. These features come in handy when users don't have the necessary media players installed on their systems. For example, you could place two or more formats of a video inside a PDF at the same place in the document. You could compress one video in the Apple QuickTime format and the other in Windows media. Using Acrobat renditions **(FIGURE 6-4)**, you could program Reader to use the QuickTime movie for both Mac and Windows computers, and if the Windows computer does not have QuickTime, Reader will then choose the alternate rendition, which is the Windows Media file.

Controlling the Playback of an Audio or Video Track

You can use Adobe JavaScript to control the playback of an audio or video track. For example, you could transcribe text from a 30-minute video and place the text in a PDF document. The text headings can then be hyperlinked to the video to allow the user to move the playback of the video forward or backward to the specific timeline of the video that contains the corresponding text **(FIGURE 6-5)**. In addition, you could program the time track from the audio or video to turn the pages in sync with the video. I have provided a sample eBook, called *The Evil Governor*, on the companion CD-ROM that demonstrates this process. In Chapter 13, you will explore the process of timing audio to PDF pages.

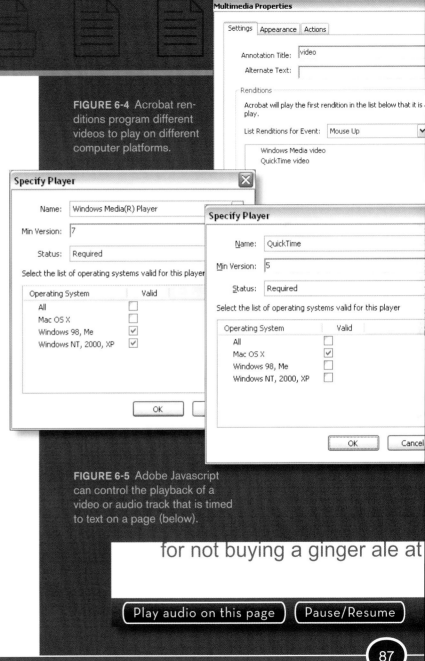

FIGURE 6-4 Acrobat renditions program different videos to play on different computer platforms.

FIGURE 6-5 Adobe Javascript can control the playback of a video or audio track that is timed to text on a page (below).

87

Interactive Form Fields

PDF documents can contain form fields used to hold data entered by the user. For example, the name, address, telephone number, and more can be entered into a PDF form.

Adobe Reader 7 and earlier allowed you to print only a completed PDF form, which was then usually faxed or mailed back to the sender. Adobe Acrobat 8 Professional introduced the capability to enable the free Adobe Reader 8 to save information that is entered into a PDF form for later viewing. This was a major turning point for the world of electronic forms, because the information now remained in a secure digital format and paper, and in many cases fax machines, were no longer required.

A form can contain fields that calculate mathematical equations. An electronic registration form can be filled out, saved, and returned by emailing the PDF.

Select Conference Options:
- [ ] Session 1 ($100)
- [ ] Session 2 ($300)
- [ ] Session 3 ($150)
- [0] Total

From Print to eBrochure

To read text onscreen, the font size should be large enough for users to view comfortably on a 12-inch portable computer. The trend these days is to make the text small, in many cases smaller than 8-point type. It's called the fine print.

With a well thought-out plan, you can produce compatible media formats. In cases where clients have planned properly and have approached us well ahead of print brochure design, we mention that if they produce their printed product in landscape display, and with a text font that is readable in print and onscreen, it will save them a lot of money because they will be designing for two forms of media—print and electronic PDF.

When print material is used as content to make an eBrochure, drastic changes are often required to make the page legible. One page in the print brochure often becomes three pages in an eBrochure because the font size must be increased so viewers can read it on a computer screen. An 80-page print brochure can easily turn into 240 eBrochure pages, especially if you decide to enlarge the pictures. As a result, the eBrochure can easily grow to more than 5 MB, which is too big to be emailed.

Travel eBrochures often run more than 80 pages and are filled with information. All too often, users are presented with tiny pictures and reams of text with disclaimers for fuel surcharges, taxes, blackout periods, plus a host of other items that could be revealed using a button or a pop-up menu.

PDF Overlay Windows

The ideal design for travel eBrochures or any publication where the pictures sell the product, is to provide large, almost full-page pictures. We all enjoy big glossy landscape-formatted coffee table books don't we? When hunting for travel information, consumers want to see big pictures of the bedrooms, the pool, and the beach, but the travel vacation company is often on a tight marketing budget and sets a limitation of one page per hotel. The pictures are small, and the text becomes almost microscopic. Acrobat form fields and hidden layers can provide a perfect solution to this problem.

A PDF page can contain layers that you can show and hide using button actions to set the layer visibility. You can create these layers using InDesign and use Acrobat to program them to be visible or invisible depending on how you want to present the document to the user **(FIGURE 6-6)**. For example, in one PDF document, you could have two or more text layers for languages and one layer for pictures. On the first page, an introductory splash screen, similar to those found on Web pages, could allow users to choose their preferred language via a drop-down menu; the user's menu selection would tell the document to show one language text layer and hide the others. You could reuse the same pictures, logos, and graphics for all the languages to make efficient use of the data. PDF text data creates small file sizes; it's the pictures and logos that dramatically increase the document file size.

FIGURE 6-6 Acrobat layers can be hidden with Javascript commands. This is useful for creating a document with multiple language layers (above). The Button Tool action can easily change the layer visibility to show or hide the desired layers (below).

You could also use JavaScript to show or hide form field areas of the page that are controlled by rollover buttons. This feature is generally used to change the display state of the button, but it can also show pictures or pages of text in PDF **(FIGURE 6-7)**. For example, you could set up your page so that when the user rolls the cursor over an info box, specific text and graphics appear in front of a background image. Just think of this feature as a big rollover button of PDF text. Just like layers, these fields can be initially hidden and then displayed when requested by the user.

In this design process, you hide the text and provide a menu to display it inside boxes or fields that will overlay on top of the page. This allows you to have big beautiful pictures, and the fine-print text becomes visible only when users request it. You can hide details like the prices, room amenities, restaurant menus, and disclaimers, and then show them using a drop-down menu or button. Unlike printed brochures, which can quickly become dated, updating text overlay fields is a simple procedure. You don't have to redesign the layout of the page to accommodate the additional text because it appears in front of the background page design.

If you decide to use pictures inside fields, the file size of the PDF will grow dramatically, so I don't recommend using bitmapped graphics if file size is an issue. PDF text has the advantage of remaining small in file size because the computer generates the text. When you enlarge the eBrochure to a full-screen display, the overlay PDF text box will enlarge in proportion to the background image, and the text will remain crystal clear.

The "show and hide" field capabilities are all available using Reader 4 and newer, so you can provide a very compelling interactive CD or Web-like experience to a wide audience. That viewpoint is the key. Get out of the static printed page mindset, and try to provide a better interactive experience than Web pages currently provide. Enlarge the pictures, headings, titles, and branding logos; provide the important details that catch the reader's eye; and hide all the other information that is distracting to the page. When users want additional information, they can click a word or a menu, and up pops a whole list of topics appearing in front of the background images.

FIGURE 6-7 Pop-up menus can reveal extra detailed information sitting in hidden overlays on the page.

Conclusions

In the early days of the desktop publishing industry, workflows were developed and altered to take advantage of the new tools that became available, and rich-media publishing is taking a similar course. With the release of Adobe 8, advanced Flash scripting can now make PDF a truly living aimated document via direct two-way communication with databases (**FIGURE 6.8**).

A good rich-media PDF is one that is easy to read and navigate, so the desktop publisher needs to think more about how it will display on a computer screen instead of paper. Think landscape. Don't allow the PDF to open in the user's main browser window. Launch a new window and hide the browser navigation menus so you can fill the screen with PDF instead of the browser chrome. Better yet, force the PDF to download to to the user's computer for launching full screen, outside of the browser. Think TV or interactive CD-ROM.

You don't have to show everything at once on a page. You can hide text and pictures and have them display only when you want more information. The use of Adobe JavaScript will not only provide navigation between the pages but also within the page itself.

Don't expect that the end user will have the latest versions of the software required to play the PDF or the rich media. Provide several different versions or renditions of rich-media file formats so that the PDF and the rich-media can play back on a Mac and a PC.

FIGURE 6-8 A PDF file can contain Flash files that connect to an online ColdFusion database. Message boards, calendars, shopping carts, and even e-commerce are available with the combination of Flash and a database.

macromedia®
COLDFUSION®

Adding Interactivity and Rich Media to PDF Documents

7

Until a few years ago, Adobe Acrobat was the only tool that allowed you to add rich media to a PDF file. Today, you still need Acrobat to program the document for advanced functionality, but for adding video and simple buttons to launch audio and video playback, Adobe has added rich-media features to Adobe InDesign, which makes multimedia PDF creation so much easier.

If you are familiar with QuarkXPress, you might find InDesign a little overwhelming at first. It's not a clone of QuarkXPress; InDesign is a combination of Adobe Illustrator for vector drawing tools and palettes, QuarkXPress for layout, Adobe Photoshop connectivity for quick edits and alpha channel compositing, Acrobat for interactivity, and Acrobat Distiller for export option settings. If you are familiar only with QuarkXPress it may take a bit of time to get used to the InDesign interface, but Adobe has tried to make the transition easy for you. If you can save your QuarkXPress files in the Quark 4 format, you can import them directly into InDesign.

7

Achieving Successful Rich-Media Playback

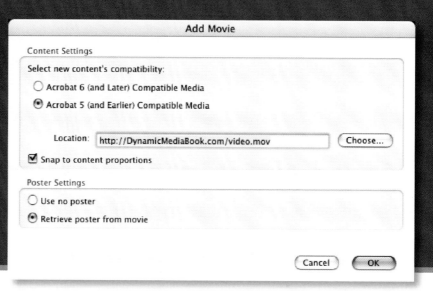

When adding media clips to an Adobe PDF document, you need to consider which version of Adobe Reader users will have on their computers. When you add a movie or sound clip to a PDF document, you choose whether the clip will be available in Acrobat 6 or later or in Acrobat 5 for linked QuickTime movies that reside on the Internet. If you select Acrobat 6–compatible media, you can provide your audience with embedded movie clips in the PDF document. However, viewers must use version 6 or later of Acrobat or Reader to view the media files.

PDF documents will play all video and sound files that are compatible with Apple QuickTime, Windows Media Player, Adobe Flash Player, RealOne, and the built-in Windows player, but viewers of the PDF document must have the necessary hardware

and software to play the media files. There are three hurdles that you must jump over if you are using a Mac to create your PDF documents. First, you cannot embed or play Windows Media files. Second, you cannot import Flash files newer than version 5 into the document. To embed Windows Media Video (WMV), you will need a Windows computer, which can embed both QuickTime and Windows Media files. Third, and most important, if you are using Acrobat 8 to author your documents, you will need to have a very fast Mac to accomplish the task. Acrobat 8 is very processor intensive. Reader 7 performs very well on most Macs, but Reader 8 has been optimized to run on Intel processors. If you are targeting a Mac audience, don't overbuild your production! You might experience our *Dynamic Media* companion eBook running very slow using Reader 8 on low-end PowerPC Macs.

If you are making your PDF document available on a Web site, make sure you provide information on the Web page that describes the type of media inside the PDF and the media players the user will need to view the rich-media content. Once the document is downloaded, if the user does not have the proper media players, Reader will alert the user with a pop-up message and direct them to the appropriate site to download the associated media player and to get the latest version of Reader.

Downloading Embedded and Linked Rich-Media PDFs

There is no general rule for the size of a PDF file that the average user will download. In the movie industry, it's not uncommon to download entire feature films that are more than 500 MB. If your PDF presents interesting in-demand content, a 100 MB PDF file that contains video is not extraordinary. If you want the video to be large and crystal clear, embedding the video inside the PDF is a wise choice because you know it will play perfectly once it arrives on your viewers' computers, provided they have the correct media players.

If you link to a video that resides on a Web server, make sure the video can stream smoothly without interruptions. It can be a feature-length film, but you need to keep the data rate of the video small enough that the average high-speed connection can play it without pausing and dropping frames. If you plan on emailing the PDF, linking is the preferred method.

If you are thinking of linking to video that resides on a CD or DVD, don't. It is best to embed the video inside the PDF. If users decide to copy the PDF to their hard drive, they will never have to worry about losing or breaking the links to the video.

Placing Rich Media Using InDesign

After you have created a nice-looking document using InDesign, you then need to add the rich-media content. You "place" the content the same way you place still images in the page. People in the video and new-media industry may think this placing method is a little strange because they usually import the content. As you can see, Adobe has sided with the print publishers to make it easy for them to integrate rich media within documents.

Once you place the media clip on the page, you can resize it just like you size the still images by dragging the corners of the bounding box. It's important to preserve the aspect ratio; if the video is stretched out of proportion it will cause poor playback. A nice trick is to align the video perfectly in front of the background image or frame. When the video launches, the still picture turns into a motion picture, just like magic. It's simple but quite effective. Try keeping all the rich media in a separate layer because it is easier to manage in multiple versions of the document. Remember, not everyone will have the latest version of Reader to view the rich media, so it's a good idea to make a version of the PDF that can stand alone as text and pictures.

FIGURE 7-1 Media files can be placed sitting in a document, floating above it, hidden (for sound files), and can be presented in full screen. The controller bar can be visible or hidden, depending on the desired effect of the rich-media file. Looping can be enabled for moving elements on a document, such as a logo or VR object.

Presenting Rich Media

Double-click on the movie to set the playback settings. The Movie Options window will pop up and it is here you will decide how the video will present itself (**FIGURE 7-1**). Whether you choose to link or embed the video, you still need to decide how you want to present the video on the page. It will be either in front of the background image or in a floating window above the page. If you choose to present the video flat on the page, the video will resize proportionately if the page is enlarged to full screen. Take this into consideration when you compress the video and when you first size it on the page.

If the video floats over the page, it will display by default at the same size as when you created it and will contain options to enlarge the video. Launching the video full screen requires users to change their security settings for full-screen playback.

You can also choose to show or hide the video playback Controller, have the video close when it reaches the end or when you turn the page, or have the playback loop. Looping is beneficial when you want to simulate the rotation of an image on the page, such as a spinning globe.

The final option is to choose a poster frame or a still image for the video when the page first displays. You can select a frame from the video called a *poster frame*, or you can hide the video altogether. If you are using the high-resolution image for the background and the video is in register with that picture, you do not need to have the poster frame visible. You can use an invisible box for the interactive "hot" area of the screen where the user can click to play the video.

Exporting the PDF for Testing Playback

One drawback to placing rich media with InDesign reveals itself when you want to see how the video will work. You first need to export the page as a PDF and then view it in Reader. The PDF export settings may be daunting, since they're covering the print world, where there is a lot to consider (**FIGURE 7-2**); for rich-media playback, you should compress the graphics for computer display using a setting between 72 and 150 dots per inch (dpi). Choose the suitable compression settings to reduce the file size to your preferred acceptable picture quality. Keep in mind that when you enlarge the document to full screen, the pictures might display some compression artifacts. Before you export the document, check the Include: Interactive Elements option and the "View PDF after Exporting" check box if you want to save some time during your testing phase. This will automatically launch Reader and load your most recently exported document.

To check to see whether the video works, just click the video's picture, and in a few seconds you should see the video play. If you have hidden the video control bar, you won't be able to stop the video unless you add interactive buttons to control the video; fortunately, this is fairly simple to do.

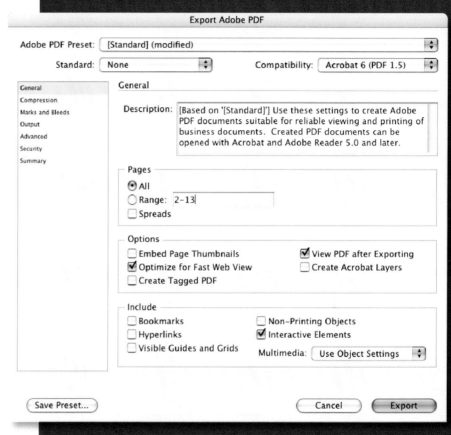

FIGURE 7-2 InDesign's PDF export settings may be daunting since they're covering the print world. Make sure you select the Interactive Elements check box to export the rich-media inside the PDF. If you have hyperlinks in the document, make sure to check the Hyperlinks check box.

Using the Button Tool

To add interactive buttons to your pages, you will utilize InDesign's Button tool, located in the toolbox; its icon displays a little finger on a button. Just select the tool, and draw a square box somewhere on the page. You can fill it with a color just like other boxes and then add programming to show the different selected states of the button. To show the States palette, select Window > Interactive > States **(FIGURE 7-3)**. The States palette has layers that allow you to change the look of the button for the Up, Rollover, and Down states—that is, when the cursor isn't near the button, when the cursor passes over the button, and when the button is clicked.

Choices for the style of the button's look are Bevel, Drop Shadow, and Glow, but you can also create your own custom buttons for each state of Up, Rollover, and Down. Just use Photoshop to create an appealing button and perhaps bevel the edge, emboss some text into the button face, and so on. Each state of the button should look a little different so that users can receive some immediate feedback when they roll over it on the page with their cursors. To insert the new graphics into the button, just select each button layer in the States palette, and choose "Place content into state" from the States palette drop-down menu. You now have an interactive button that you can use to control the video, turn the page, jump to a page, and so on.

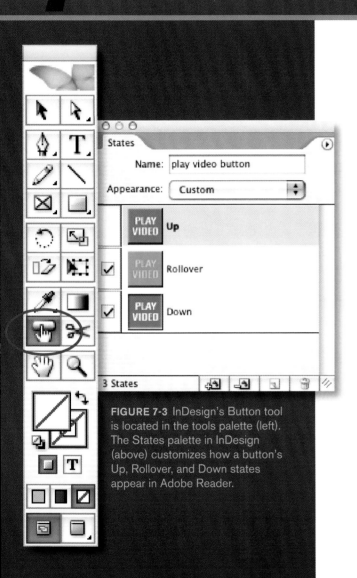

FIGURE 7-3 InDesign's Button tool is located in the tools palette (left). The States palette in InDesign (above) customizes how a button's Up, Rollover, and Down states appear in Adobe Reader.

Button Options General Window

To program the button, just double-click it to display the Button Options window. In the General area, you name the button, describe what it is used for, and set the display of the button. For example, the "Display but doesn't print" option is perfect for people who like to print PDFs; in other words, you do not need to enable a button to print if it is not important to the printed page.

Button Options Behaviors Window

In the Behaviors area, you program the button to control the rich media or to provide navigation throughout the document **(FIGURE 7-4)**. From the Event menu, select what mouse activity will cause the interactivity to occur. If you have used the States palette to create your button, it's already semi-interactive; when you move your cursor over the button or click it, it will change or highlight, so the appearance is all taken care of for you. You just need to select the "On mouse up" event to trigger the action and a behavior that you want the button to do. The term *behavior* has been adopted from the Macromedia interactive programming language, which basically is an easy way to provide code to the document without writing it manually. You choose a behavior, and InDesign writes the underlying code for you.

To control the movie on the page, you first select Movie from the Behavior drop-down menu. That will load a list of additional movie options into the same window. Then select the movie (if there is more than one movie on the page, you will see a list of all movies) and the Play options for that movie, such as "Play." Just click the Add button to add your behavior to the list of behaviors. The behavior list allows the button to perform several functions such as playing one video and stopping another video on the same page. Just repeat this same process to make additional buttons that will pause, resume, and stop the movies.

A wide variety of additional behaviors are available to allow the user to navigate the document, such as turning to the next page, etc., but for advanced navigation, I suggest you use Adobe JavaScript if you can write the code or use the Hyperlinks palette in InDesign to accomplish this task.

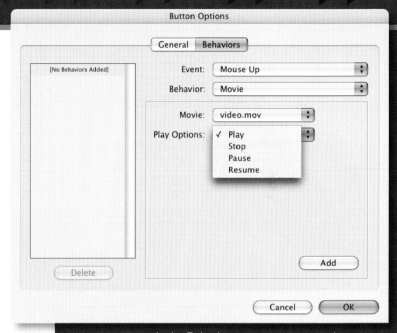

FIGURE 7-4 In the Behaviors area, you program the button to control the rich media or to provide navigation throughout the document.

For advanced navigation, I suggest you use Adobe JavaScript if you can write the code or use the Hyperlinks palette in InDesign.

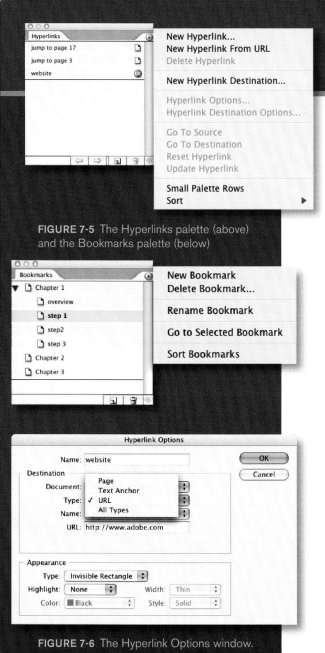

FIGURE 7-5 The Hyperlinks palette (above) and the Bookmarks palette (below)

FIGURE 7-6 The Hyperlink Options window.

Using the Hyperlinks Palette: Advanced Navigation and Connections to the Internet

InDesign's Hyperlinks palette provides advanced navigation to the document to allow users to jump to specific pages in the PDF document and to Web pages.

To open the Links palette, select Windows > Interactive > Hyperlinks. That opens the palette with two tabs: one lists all the hyperlinks you will add to the document, and the other contains your anchor bookmarks (FIGURE 7-5).

You can use the Text tool to create and select text fields that you associate or link to a PDF page or a Web page. Just as on Web pages, you might highlight and change the specific words to blue (or another color) to show users that there is additional information waiting for them on the Internet or on another page if they click the colored text.

To program these words, use the Text tool to select the text and then in the Hyperlinks palette, select the Create New Hyperlink icon. A new hyperlink listing will appear in the window, labeled with the words you have selected. It's a good idea to name the hyperlink for the Web site or the page to which you are jumping. Double-click the listing to open the Hyperlink Options dialog box (FIGURE 7-6), which allows you to select the destination for that hyperlink. If it is a page in the PDF, you can select a page number; if it is a Web link, you can type the URL of the Web page.

That pretty much covers the starter course for the rich-media interactive features in InDesign. It's a great application for laying out the document, adding the rich media, and providing Web links. Its greatest advantage for this job over other page layout applications such as QuarkXPress is that it allows you to export the document with all your rich media and programming intact. If you have to make a change to the document, InDesign reflows the text, pictures, video, animation, and interactive hot spots of the document.

Adding Interactivity and Rich Media via Acrobat

If you decide to use a different application, such as Microsoft Word, QuarkXPress, or Illustrator to create your document, you will need to use Acrobat to add rich media to the document.

In this process, you "print" the document to PDF and then open the page inside Acrobat to program the page using various tools that are similar to those in InDesign. Acrobat uses hot spot *fields* on the page for interactivity, which you draw on the page manually. If you make changes to your original document and then print it to PDF, it is possible to replace the PDF page and keep the interactive field areas. If the new underlying hot-spot text area or movie location changes, you will have to realign the fields on the page to match the new locations. For this reason, InDesign is a real time-saver when you need to revise the document because the links and the video are embedded in the page during export.

Acrobat's main function in the rich-media PDF workflow is to provide an additional layer of interactivity and control over the handling of the rich media. Whereas InDesign can embed only video and Flash animation, Acrobat can embed **(FIGURE 7-7)** or link to video, animation, and audio in multiple versions called *renditions* (refer to Chapter 5 for more information). Another function of Acrobat is to provide JavaScript programming to control the rich media and the pages in ways that are not possible using InDesign. You will see some of these advanced features later in the case studies and in the video tutorials in our eBook.

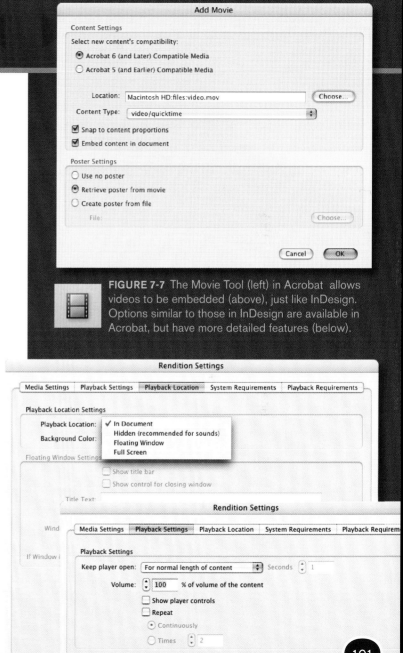

FIGURE 7-7 The Movie Tool (left) in Acrobat allows videos to be embedded (above), just like InDesign. Options similar to those in InDesign are available in Acrobat, but have more detailed features (below).

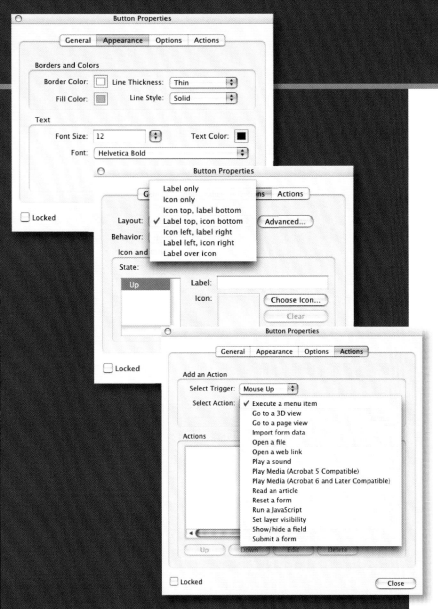

Using Various Acrobat Tools for Interactivity

The interactive capabilities of Acrobat are impressive. Acrobat provides many ways to make a PDF document interactive. For example, if you launch the PDF in full-screen mode, the Reader toolbar will be hidden, so you will need to include buttons or hotspots to allow the user to close the document, print, quit the program, and so on. You accomplish this by creating a button that executes a menu item using the "actions" function in Adobe Acrobat.

The Acrobat Button tool is similar to InDesign's Button tool. You select the Button tool, draw a button on the page and double click on it, which brings up a Button Properties window. Here you can set the appearance of a default button, choose options to further customize it to add graphics, set rollover functions, and apply actions that will execute a menu item, jump to a page, hide a field, add JavaScript, and much more **(FIGURE 7-8)**.

You can set a trigger to play a movie or sound when the page opens. This is called a "page open" command. You can add interactivity using other tools, such as the Form tool, which creates forms that the user can fill out and then use to submit information right from the PDF file. You can also use the Form tool to play and pause a video. You can use the Link tool to launch rich media, to open other PDF files, to create links to open Web pages, and more **(FIGURE 7-9)**.

FIGURE 7-8 Acrobat's Button Properties adjust settings for the button's appearance (top), options (middle), and actions (bottom).

Once you have mastered the Button tool, go ahead and try these other tools to perform the same functions provided by the Button tool. For example, you might want to create documents in which the buttons are embedded graphics and are part of the master PDF page. In this case, you do not need the Button tool; you could use the Link tool to create a hot spot area instead.

Most print publishers and Web developers have no idea of the power lurking behind Acrobat's user interface, which up until now they have mainly used to print PDF files and to make comments in the document. Acrobat is a powerful, complex tool for PDF programming that is only now seeing its potential recognized as a robust multimedia authoring system.

Conclusions

InDesign is the preferred tool for creating rich-media PDF documents. It has all the capabilities to add the rich media and make the document interactive. Acrobat cannot lay out a page like InDesign, but it provides all of the rich-media functionality and interactivity. Acrobat is needed when you want to program advanced interactivity to the PDF pages and have more control over the rich media. Once you get experienced with these two programs, you will probably create your own workflow because there are so many tools and different ways to get to the end product. I use InDesign to create the document, to add the rich-media and Web hyperlinks, but everything else is accomplished in Acrobat Professional.

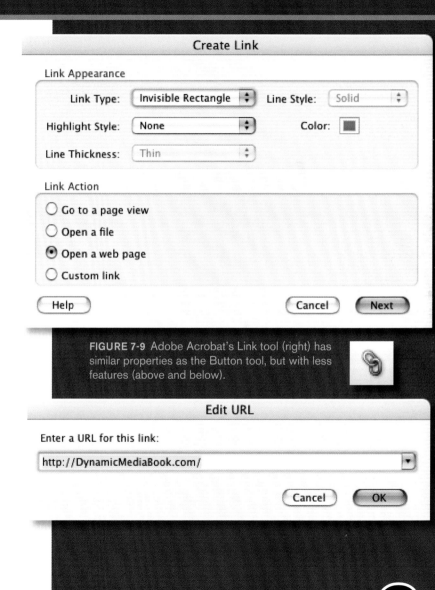

FIGURE 7-9 Adobe Acrobat's Link tool (right) has similar properties as the Button tool, but with less features (above and below).

Why PDF? The Proof Is in the Printing

8

An interactive PDF offers many benefits over HTML Web pages, but the most obvious is its printing capabilities. I try to point out to prospective clients that Web sites are good for text-based information, but when it comes to graphics and photographs, there really is no comparison; PDF is the best format. In addition, although clients can print individual pages of a site, they can't print the whole Web site in one shot. But by downloading a version of a site in PDF form, they can print one or all of the pages with one click.

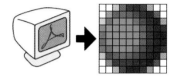

Web page pictures are usually highly compressed JPEG images, which means they display quickly in the browser. These low-resolution images at 72 dots per inch (dpi) are good enough for screen display, but when you print the page, the pictures often become blurry, with noticeable compression artifacts producing jagged edges. PDF, on the other hand, was designed for printing. The pictures in a PDF page are not resolution dependent on a 72 dpi computer screen display. Even though the pictures may look the same on a Web page and in a PDF file, the resolution and image quality of a PDF can be much higher. It's perfect for printing.

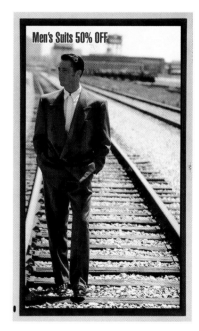

For example, when you export PDF pages from your page layout program, you can set the resolution of the pictures to be greater than 72 dpi. Often, we will output PDF eBrochures at 120 to 150 dpi to allow for higher-quality printing and also for sharp, artifact-free images when the PDF is enlarged to fill clients' computer screens. The clarity of the higher-resolution image will look spectacular on large, widescreen, high-resolution computer monitors such as Apple's two-page Cinema Display and the large plasma monitors that are becoming popular for signage in stores and shopping malls.

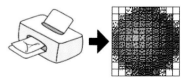

8

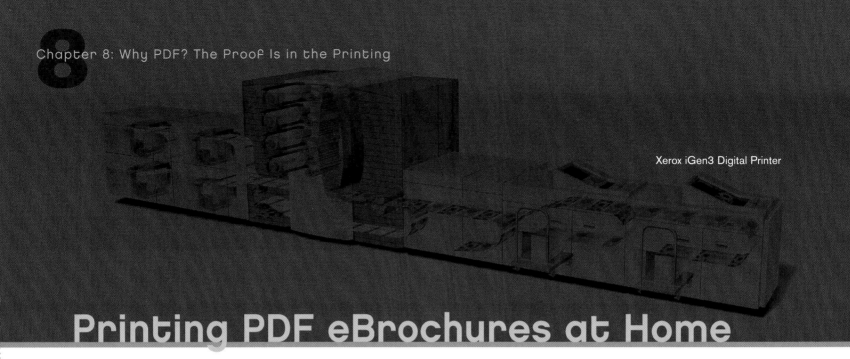

Xerox iGen3 Digital Printer

Printing PDF eBrochures at Home

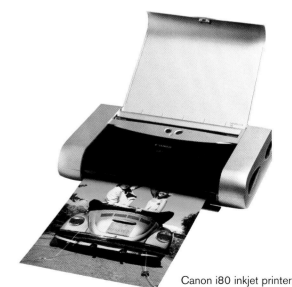

Many people now have digital cameras and high-quality photo inkjet printers that produce glossy 8 x 10 photographs. The pictures produced on consumer-grade printers will often rival the prints from professional photo labs. PDF has special printing features that allow even consumer-grade printers to provide comparable results. This capability has started to worry the commercial printing houses because consumers are now downloading PDF eBrochures and printing only the pages they need.

Another trend is variable printing on demand. Instead of printing thousands of brochures, consumers are customizing their brochure from the company Web site. Vendors such as Xerox offer high-resolution digital printers, such as the iGen3 with which one brochure can be printed on demand using PDF technology and then mailed. The consumer can also download the customized PDF eBrochure to print on their home inkjet printer.

Canon i80 inkjet printer

The company that provides the information as an eBrochure is happy because it saves on postage, handling, and printing costs. Consumers are happy because they receive the information within a few seconds without waiting several days for the mail. Basically, everyone is happy except the offset commercial printer and in some cases the advertising agency.

Quite often, the ad agency or the brochure designer will quote a price for a brochure in which the profits are weighted to the actual printing of the brochure. Large printing plants might have designers on staff, or they might own shares in print design companies; in this case, they will have a vested interest in keeping their printing plants busy and their clients in the dark as to the cost effectiveness of PDF eBrochures.

In cases like these, the printers will argue that the print quality of the PDF eBrochure will never match the commercial printing press and that consumers expect much more. They will point out that home users just do not know how to configure the print settings of their home printers to match their computers. The colors are not the same, the paper stocks and the bleed of the ink will provide poor results, they will claim. These are all valid points, but the consumer will ultimately decide what is "good enough" for them.

We too had great concerns about promising our clients too much in regard to color reproduction—that is, until the Benjamin Moore paint company approached us to create an eBrochure to supplement its printed brochures.

| manchester tan **HC-81** | gold dust **PT-270** | crushed velvet **2076-10** | deep caviar **2130-20** |

| nantucket gray **HC-111** | abingdon putty **HC-99** | ivory white **CC-130** | endearing pink **PT-170** |

Case Study: Producing Benjamin Moore eBrochures

W hen people decide to paint the interior of their house, they often visit a local paint store to select an assortment of paper paint chips containing the colors they think will work for a particular room. They'll take the chips home; hold them against the wall, the couch, the drapes, and so on; and agonize over what the whole room will look like painted in a particular color.

If you are familiar with Benjamin Moore, you know that the company creates printed brochures that contain a wide selection of paper paint chips glued into each print brochure. Each paint chip contains the actual paint color and a corresponding color code that is used to mix the paint.

Colours for your home

Printing and Color Issues

Creating a Benjamin Moore paint sample brochure is not a simple task. Text and photographs of sample room settings are first printed on large foldout card stock. White placeholder boxes are used to position the 50 colored pieces of painted chips that will be glued into the brochure. It is a time-consuming, not to mention costly, procedure.

Benjamin Moore wanted to deliver electronic versions of these brochures so consumers could download them from its Web site, view them interactively on their computers, and then print them on their home printers. The company's biggest concern was how close the actual colors would match the commercial versions.

For most graphic design companies, this sounds like a job from hell, because clients often are particular about the "brand color" of their logos. Designers often lose sleep worrying that the wrong Pantone color will be used for an advertiser's logo. In this case, we thought the client might expect too much from the PDF digital medium.

We were up-front with Benjamin Moore and said, "We are dealing with many variables here that are out of our control, and we can't guarantee the printed home consumer product will exactly match the commercial printing house. There are issues such as metallic paint chips, and the fact that many home users won't print on glossy cardboard stock."

But to our delight, Benjamin Moore seemed to understand all these issues and really just wanted the brochure to look as good

as it could on computer monitors. The color on the screen had to closely resemble the printed brochure so the consumer could see the color suggestions beside the photographs of painted rooms containing furniture. The company wanted the consumer to get a feel for warm and cool colors and to see how they work within the room images also included in the brochure. Once the consumers made up their minds, they could print the page of that color, hold it up to their couch or drapes, and then head off to the paint store to see the true color of that paint.

Benjamin Moore pointed out that even then, the commercially printed paint chip color would look different when the customer brought it home. For instance, if you hold the paint chip up in the store, the florescent green lighting makes it a lighter color. Take it outside in the direct sun, and it again looks different. Take it home and look at it under halogen or regular lightbulbs, and it will have a warmer color. So Benjamin Moore was well aware of the phrase "good enough." Working under those conditions, the task seemed doable.

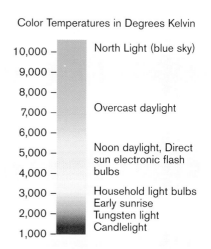

Color Temperatures in Degrees Kelvin

10,000 — North Light (blue sky)

9,000 —

8,000 —

7,000 — Overcast daylight

6,000 —

5,000 — Noon daylight, Direct sun electronic flash

4,000 — bulbs

3,000 — Household light bulbs
Early sunrise

2,000 — Tungsten light
Candlelight

1,000 —

Collecting the Content, Color Matching, and Building the Brochure

The content for this project consisted of a QuarkXPress file that was used to print the brochure and a copy of the final brochure that contained the reference paint chip colors. We imported the QuarkXPress file into Adobe InDesign to redesign the double-sided, eight-page foldout into single pages that could be launched full screen on the home user's computer monitor.

The QuarkXPress files did not contain any color information for the paint chips, just empty white boxes. The paper painted chips would be glued over the top of the white areas of the image.

For our first attempt to create the colors, we decided to scan the final printed product brochure on a flatbed scanner and sample the color using Adobe Photoshop's Eyedropper tool. The RGB color values could then be typed into the object area boxes inside InDesign. Unfortunately, that approach backfired, as several paint chips had metallic finishes, and the reflections of light from the scanner resulted in colors that were way off.

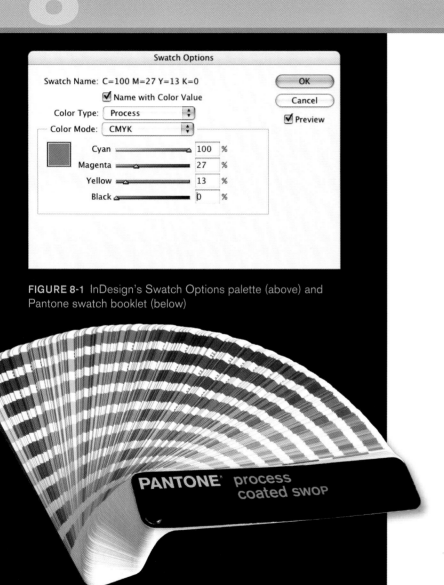

FIGURE 8-1 InDesign's Swatch Options palette (above) and Pantone swatch booklet (below)

What we ended up doing was comparing a Pantone swatch booklet to the brochure's painted chips, and we then typed the closest Pantone color into the object box color specification. That gave us a pretty good approximation, and all that was required was to hold up the brochure to the monitor and adjust the color by hand using InDesign's Swatch Options (FIGURE 8-1). We had to export the document to PDF several times and then check and recheck the colors on several monitors, especially PC monitors, since they often display darker than Macintosh displays. Noticeable problems were dark purple colors that became black, and metallic browns that looked a bit reddish, so we then had to overcompensate for brightness. Surprisingly, the final printed product on our inkjet printer provided a close match for the colors that were within the printing spectrum of the printer, as long as we printed on glossy stock.

What the client liked most about the results was the immediacy of product revisions. Using Adobe Acrobat 7 or later, you can provide "commenting" privileges in each document, so that anyone with the free version of Adobe Reader 7 can mark up the document with their comments and revisions. We could email the client the eBrochure, she would mark up her concerns and then email it back for us to tweak. No couriers, no PMT proofs—just digital files sent to and fro until everyone was happy.

That was almost four years ago, and we have now produced four Living Brochures for Benjamin Moore.

Conclusions: Is It Good Enough?

Benjamin Moore continues to produce high-quality print brochures but thinks the PDF eBrochure is an entirely new form of media that provides an alternative to consumers who want to download, view, print, and email Benjamin Moore's marketing tools to friends and family. It's information users can take from Benjamin Moore's Web site, keep for their own, and forward on to others. The full-screen interactive PDF brochure is also much more compelling to look at and a lot easier to navigate than a Web page. Benjamin Moore's use of PDF for accurate color reproduction is certainly a sign that the print industry is now coming to terms with consumers who are willing to forgo waiting for a high-quality printed brochure in the mail for the sake of having a "good enough" rendition delivered to them within a few seconds via the Internet.

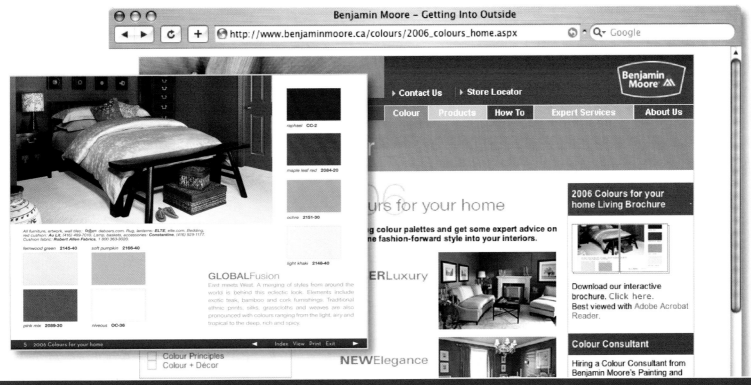

Design Issues: Converting Printed Documents to Interactive PDF

9

One complaint that you will often hear about multipage catalogs, brochures, or magazine PDF documents is that they are too big to download. This is true if you do not use the proper methods of creating and compressing a file for Internet delivery. If you choose the wrong type of graphic file format and amount of compression, you could end up producing unreadable text and dreadful artifacts in photographic images.

This chapter examines best practices for converting large printed documents so they are easy to read, navigate, and download as interactive PDFs.

You'll learn about the ideal fonts, page sizes, and number of columns to use, and, more specifically, you'll learn about the challenges of converting tall print publications to the landscape format.

Page Display Considerations

Almost all print publications that feature photography are based on a two-page layout, or *spread*, but with interactive PDF, the computer monitor is often too small to display the design for easy reading. For that reason, most electronic PDF documents on the Web are just print documents converted to PDF and include some interactive links to Web pages. As a result, readers have to use the rudimentary navigation tools that come with Adobe Reader–fitting the page to the width of the screen to see the whole thing, zooming in to read the text, and using the Hand tool to move the page on the screen. It's not an ideal reading experience.

FIGURE 9-1 To launch a PDF automatically to full screen mode using Acrobat, go to File > Properties and select the Initial View tab. In the Window Options select the Open in Full Screen Mode check box. This can also be accomplished using Adobe JavaScript.

Really, this type of PDF is created for downloading and then printing to paper. If you intend to design an interactive PDF longer than a few pages that's to be read on a computer screen, you need to get out of the printed page mind-set and think more like a TV producer. Think of your page in landscape format, not portrait. You might want to program your document to automatically launch in full screen mode **(FIGURE 9-1)** or hide the toolbars. The objective is to fill the screen with text that users can read comfortably, without scrolling or zooming. The text needs to be large enough to read on a portable computer, so you need to utilize a font that works well in small point sizes.

If you are starting from scratch and have total control over the look and feel of the PDF page, your job is fairly simple. If you are handed a printed piece and asked to make an electronic version of it that is easy to read onscreen, there are a few limitations that you need to consider if you want to keep the look and feel or integrity of the publication.

Page Sizes

Setting the size of the page is one of the most important parts of the production. Even though you can't make the page bigger than the size of the computer monitor, you need to think about the people who might want to print it out. Except on a widescreen display, the average aspect ratio of a computer monitor is 4:3 (4 units wide by 3 units tall). Try to utilize as much of the display space of the screen as possible, especially if you know users have 12-inch screens on their laptops.

For most of our eBrochure products, we use a page size that's 10 inches wide by 7.5 inches high; these dimensions will match the 4:3 aspect ratio of the computer monitor in full screen mode. Many people choose to use 11 inches by 8.5 inches to match the common paper size for printing, but that will affect the relationship between the computer screen and printed font display size.

The larger the page, the smaller the font will display on your screen. For example, if you create a page for a coupon book that is 3 inches wide and 2 inches high using 10-point type, that font will expand to almost 30-point type when the page is enlarged to fill the screen. It will print in 10-point type, but screen size has no relationship to print output. In full-screen mode, the screen display size set for your monitor also doesn't affect the size of the font. If you change your monitor setting to 800 x 600 or 1024 x 768, the size of the font will remain the same.

When you create eBooks, it's quite common to mimic the look of a paperback book and create a page that is 9 inches high by 6 inches wide using 10-point type. In this case, users will see black borders at the sides of the book when viewing the eBook in full-screen mode. In a regular page display with the visible Reader toolbars, two facing pages will fit nicely on the screen, and it will be easy to read on a computer.

Columns Indicate the Type of Media

In the print world, the page size often determines the format of the publication. A large, tall page with long, narrow columns is usually for a newspaper. A single 8.5 x 11-inch page with a single column is a flyer. If it is more than 30 pages, it becomes a magazine or brochure. The physical dimensions of the publication and thickness of the paper convey the type of media content it contains. But with electronic documents, you can't use the size of the page to imply content; therefore, you must rely on the design within the page to provide the "image" of the document.

It's the number and width of the columns that often indicate the type of media the electronic document contains. If you are creating an electronic newspaper, you most likely have several narrow columns across the page—possibly four columns. A newsletter or a book, such as a training manual, might use a single column.

Although this may not seem important, your clients will care that you're presenting their publication correctly. Magazine publishers often remind me that an electronic magazine is not an eBrochure. Even though they are the same size and the content could be similar, publishers hate the word *brochure*. Brochures are free; therefore, they have no commercial value. If you are going to convert a printed magazine to PDF, you will need to simulate a design that has a perceived value to obtain subscribers and sponsored advertising. If your client wants you to use the same fonts and font sizes as in their print product, the number and width of the text columns will be your biggest concerns.

Advertising Fit

Advertising in a print publication can become a problem when sponsors place their advertising beside articles that relate to their products. A half-page print advertisement with an article at the top of the page becomes a full page for the advertiser in a landscape eBrochure. A full-page print advertisement becomes a vertical electronic advertisement taking up two-thirds of the page. A two-page spread advertisement is a full page. Incorporating Flash banner advertising used on Web sites can be a good solution for Web links and animation, and the dimensions are much more suited to displaying onscreen. Skyscraper banner advertising works well in a landscape PDF.

Typographic Attributes

Adobe Acrobat will *rasterize*, or render, the fonts to appear onscreen as accurately as possible, but you need to be aware that there are limits to how small certain font type faces can be reduced and still maintain their unique characteristics. Some fonts are more legible in smaller sizes than others. Sans-serif fonts usually work better in smaller sizes than do serif fonts.

Fonts and Sizes

You should try to use font sizes that are at least 9 point.

Here are a few examples of sans-serif and serif fonts:

Berthold Akzidenz Grotesk

- The quick brown fox jumps over the lazy dog: 14-point, sans-serif.
- The quick brown fox jumps over the lazy dog: 11-point, sans-serif.
- The quick brown fox jumps over the lazy dog: 9-point, sans-serif.

Adobe Caslon Pro

- The quick brown fox jumps over the lazy dog: 14-point, serif.
- The quick brown fox jumps over the lazy dog: 11-point, serif.
- The quick brown fox jumps over the lazy dog: 9-point, serif.

Font Attributes

Font attributes can also play a part in a font's legibility onscreen. For example, if you plan to set portions of your text in italics, you may have to increase the overall point size of the type to accommodate such attributes.

Here are a few examples of font attributes:

- The quick brown fox jumps over the lazy dog: 14-point, sans-serif, regular.

- *The quick brown fox jumps over the lazy dog: 14-point, sans-serif, italic.*

- **The quick brown fox jumps over the lazy dog: 14-point, sans-serif, bold.**

- ***The quick brown fox jumps over the lazy dog: 14-point, sans-serif, bold, italic.***

- The quick brown fox jumps over the lazy dog: 9-point, sans-serif, regular.

- *The quick brown fox jumps over the lazy dog: 11-point, sans-serif, italic.*

- **The quick brown fox jumps over the lazy dog: 9-point, sans-serif, bold.**

- ***The quick brown fox jumps over the lazy dog: 11-point, sans-serif, bold, italic.***

- The quick brown fox jumps over the lazy dog: 14-point, serif, regular.

- *The quick brown fox jumps over the lazy dog: 14-point, serif, italic.*

- **The quick brown fox jumps over the lazy dog: 14-point, serif, bold.**

- ***The quick brown fox jumps over the lazy dog: 14-point, serif, bold, italic.***

- The quick brown fox jumps over the lazy dog: 9-point, serif, regular.

- *The quick brown fox jumps over the lazy dog: 11-point, serif, italic.*

- **The quick brown fox jumps over the lazy dog: 11-point, serif, bold.**

- ***The quick brown fox jumps over the lazy dog: 11-point, serif, bold, italic.***

Column Widths

Try to stay away from creating body text that runs from one side of the page to the other. Two or more columns make reading much easier.

Here are some examples:

- Example 1: This line of text is too wide because it runs from one side of the page to the other. This format makes it difficult to read on a computer monitor and on a printed page. It is best to use two or more narrow columns.

- Example 2: This is a more comfortable width for reading because your eyes can easily follow the ending of the line to the next line below.

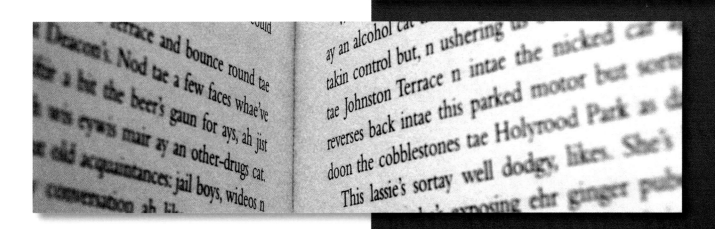

Case Study

"Britain City Breaks" Living Brochure

Every year, the British Tourism Authority produces more than a dozen print publications that focus on the many tourism aspects of England, Ireland, and Scotland. England is world renowned for having a robust print industry, but the British Tourism Authority discovered that the Internet is now the number-one resource for tourists who want to plan trips. So, they decided to reduce the number of printed brochures and instead redirect its marketing funds to Internet-related products such as interactive PDFs.

One of its most popular travel print publications is a pocket guide called *Britain City Breaks* that was specially produced by publisher Lonely Planet. It's very durable and

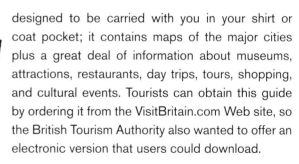

designed to be carried with you in your shirt or coat pocket; it contains maps of the major cities plus a great deal of information about museums, attractions, restaurants, day trips, tours, shopping, and cultural events. Tourists can obtain this guide by ordering it from the VisitBritain.com Web site, so the British Tourism Authority also wanted to offer an electronic version that users could download.

The British Tourism Authority hired a direct marketing company called BrainTrain Inc. to create a campaign with a contest to promote the availability of an electronic PDF version of the pocket guide. BrainTrain Inc. chose my company to convert the print product into an interactive PDF "Living Brochure."

Nightlife

London is often thought of as a series of interconnected villages, and each has something different going on. Why not pick the one closest to you and seek out it's quiet pubs, live music venues, cinemas and theatres? You'll find something surprising and different everywhere you turn. The theatre scene, opera, ballet and classical music are all of international quality and are performed in beautiful, historic venues across the city.

Pick up a copy of the listings magazine *Time Out* for more details.

Three Kings of Clerkenwell (020 7253 0483; 7 Clerkenwell Close EC1) Eccentric décor and great food, the place for a warm summer's evening.

Princess Louise (020 7405 8816; 208 High Holborn WC1) Spectacularly decorated Victorian pub, a perfect meeting place or cosy evening hang-out.

Captain Kidd (108 Wapping High St E1) One of London's finest riverside pubs and a historic setting given that this was once the grisly execution spot for miscreant pirates like the eponymous Captain Kidd. Caters to a professional crowd during the week and is a great family spot at weekends given its fine beer garden and excellent restaurant.

Crown & Goose (100 Arlington Rd NW1) One of our favourite London pubs. The square room has a central wooden bar between British Racing Green Walls studded with gilt-framed mirrors and illuminated by big shuttered windows. More importantly, it combines a good-looking crowd, easy conviviality, top tucker and good beer.

Lamb & Flag (33 Rose St WC2) A popular historic pub and a great Covent Garden 'find'. It was built in 1623 and was formerly called the 'Bucket of Blood'.

Cow (89 Westbourne Park Rd W2) A superb gastro-pub with outstanding food and a jovial pub-is-a-pub atmosphere. Seafood is a speciality and the staff are much friendlier than you'd expect from somewhere so perpetually hip.

Ronnie Scott's (020 7439 0747; 47 Frith St W1) Familiar to aficionados as the best jazz club in London. The food, atmosphere and acts are always spot-on.

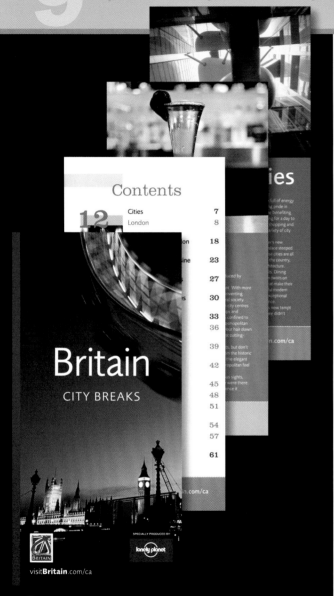

The Challenge of Nonstandard Print Publications

The 72-page printed pocket guide designed by Lonely Planet was very tall and narrow to allow it to be carried in your pocket. The dimensions were 8 x 3.75 inches, most of the text was 7-point type, and the many pictures were extremely small. It was a wonderful production and true to the Lonely Planet brand because it contained a wealth of well-researched information.

Since the printed guide was narrow, it consisted mainly of one or two columns of text in a sans-serif font. The brochure had a nice selection of pictures throughout, but the images were often less than 1.5 inches wide.

The designers at Lonely Planet used QuarkXPress to lay out the printed guide, and they delivered copies of the files to us on DVD to reformat for the interactive PDF. We imported the Quark file into Adobe InDesign, and fortunately everything came across in the translation. The result was a long, narrow document, but at least it was all together in one application; all the fonts, pictures, line art, and logos were there for redesigning purposes. It's a real pain when you are missing portions of the content because of data corruption; you then have to return to the client to ask for the master file. That can set back the project several weeks in some cases.

The next step was to create a new InDesign document using an ideal page size for onscreen display. We have become comfortable with 10 x 7.5-inch page sizes, and at this point we were only concerned with fitting one page of printed information from the guide into one page of the interactive PDF. The goal was a direct page-for-page translation using the same fonts, text, and pictures. To accomplish this task, two print columns of text and pictures from the guide became three columns in the PDF, with some variations to that design depending on other elements such as maps and advertising.

Converting the document to landscape display was merely a copy-and-paste procedure; we took text information from one document window and flowed it into the columns of the other document window. Because we were working with high-resolution pictures, we could enlarge the photographs to fill the pages where necessary.

Handling Vector Graphics

EPS maps created with an application such as Adobe Illustrator can cause some headaches in interactive PDFs. Highly detailed maps are often large files and display very poorly in earlier versions of Reader, such as version 4; in addition, when the text is smaller than 7 points, it becomes very difficult to read. If your PDF contains EPS vector maps, logos, and EPS advertising, your final PDF file can quickly bloat in size.

The map of Britain supplied to us as an EPS file contained so much detail on a single page that we decided to divide it into two pages **(FIGURE 9-2)**. We also converted the EPS map into a PSD file so that it would display properly in earlier versions of Reader. You'll encounter a trade-off when converting EPS to PSD. When working with EPS maps, it is nice to zoom into the map to get a close-up view, but zooming into a PDF document that is launched full screen can be challenging to navigate because you lose your navigation buttons at the bottom or top of the page. So we prefer to rasterize a close-up view of the map and have it appear as a pop-up overlay on a bitmapped graphic.

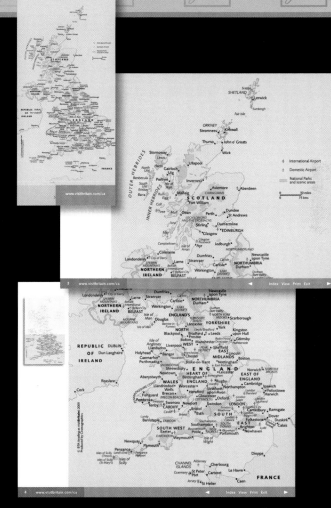

FIGURE 9-2 Highly detailed maps are often large files and display very poorly in earlier versions of Reader. We converted the EPS map into a rasterized file so that it would display properly in earlier versions of Reader, and we divided it into two pages.

9

FIGURE 9-3 The client wanted the full-page ad (right) to remain a full-page ad in the eBrochure so they supplied us with a redesigned ad to fill the electronic page (below).

Cautions with Advertising Redesign

Advertising agencies take great pride in their creative advertising design. In the past when we have tried to alter the design of an advertisement to fit the page layout, we've found it best to leave the ad as it was. It seems that we get a lot of leeway from the ad agencies with the page design, but they don't want us to mess with the ad. That is sacred ground.

The "Britain City Breaks" guide contained a full-page advertisement on the back page, and if we just plopped it on the last page as a tall narrow graphic, it would sort of leave the document with lots of white at the sides of the page. We asked whether we could move the advertisement to another page so we could create a final closing page with credits, and the client agreed this was a good idea. We were surprised to hear that the client also wanted the full-page ad to remain a full-page ad in the eBrochure; they supplied us with a redesigned ad to fill the electronic page **(FIGURE 9-3)**. Publishers are not usually in the business of redesigning advertising for their clients, but they sold a full-page ad, and it needed to be redesigned to be a full page. If only more publishers would go the extra mile to reformat the advertising, I am sure this would surely speed up the adoption of the interactive PDF.

Adding the Rich Media

The final 71-page living brochure was 6.7 MB in size, and the client was very pleased with the end result. We suggested that we insert some video into the document, knowing they had stock footage "B-roll" that they used for television stations. They suggested we edit four video clips of cities and place them in the related parts of the eBrochure.

After thinking carefully about the end user who would want to visit Britain, we decided to keep the final file size as small as possible. In the end, we decided to go with Windows Media, knowing it would not play on Macs. We could have chosen the MPEG-1 format for the videos, which would have provided Mac playback, but the additional four videos in an MPEG-1 format would have increased the file size well beyond the 13 MB that we could obtain by using Windows Media. For this client, file size was a concern, so we made two versions of the document: a standard version without video, which would run in Reader 4 and a full-video version, which would run in Reader 6 or later.

A Web page was created for the client that described the contents of the living brochure, and both PDF documents were hosted on a third-party server **(FIGURE 9-4)**. You will find that sometimes the client wants to host the eBrochures, and in other cases the client prefers not to fiddle with their corporate Web site. BrainTrain had a complete campaign that included a microsite, a contest, and Web serving, so in this case it was best to keep the technical issues under one roof.

Britain - City Breaks Living Brochure

Britain · City Breaks Living Brochure

Features of this 71-page Adobe PDF eBrochure:
- Works like a CD-ROM
- Displays full screen on any computer
- Interactive navigation
- Easy to read, print & email to your friends
- Features colorful photos & graphics
- Full version contains embedded videos

Britain CITY BREAKS

Select your version below:

Standard Version: (no videos or VR).
Minimum requirements: Adobe Reader 4. **Mac & PC compatible.**

Download Now
6.9 MB PDF

Full Version: featuring new Adobe Reader Embedded Multimedia Technology. **PC compatible only.**
Minimum requirements: **Adobe Reader 6**

Download Now
12.9 MB PDF

Internet connection not required after download of PDF file. Videos are embedded in the PDF file.

 Get Adobe Reader
Adobe Reader is free.

Trouble downloading the eBrochure?
Right-click here and select save target.

CLOSE WINDOW

FIGURE 9-4 A Web page was created to allow for the downloading of the Standard and Full versions of the eBrochures. PHP scripts were utilized to force the PDF files to download outside of the Web browser so they would open in full-screen mode.

Lessons Learned

One challenge you'll face when designing a layout for an electronic interpretation of a print production is keeping the original look and feel. If you try to fit a lot of text on a page, don't choose smaller than 9-point text, or the text will be too hard to read on a portable laptop. Also, use san-serif fonts because they are the most legible at small font sizes. Unfortunately, that may change the look and feel of the publication if it originally used serif fonts, as most print magazines do.

Another challenge you'll face is keeping the file size small enough to download. The final "Britain City Breaks" 71-page electronic PDF was just under 7 MB in size. With four additional videos, the size only grew to 13 MB, and every page contained big, beautiful photographs. InDesign did an excellent job of compressing the photography to very small file sizes, but with a little help from you, it can work even better. Specifically, when final file size is important, keep an eye out for large EPS files that can bloat the document; in some cases, it is better to render vector graphics and EPS files to the JPEG format. Also, use efficient video compression codecs, like Windows Media 7 or later.

In addition, advertisers are often touchy about someone else redesigning their advertising to fit the landscape format of the PDF page, so make sure you notify the client well in advance that there could be some potential problems with ads.

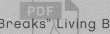

Conclusions

Large, multipage catalogs, magazines, and even pocket guides are a good source of content for rich-media publications. The hard part is coming up with an original design for pages so they convey the type of media that the electronic version emulates. In addition, if you use font sizes smaller than 9 point, the user might have to strain to view the text in full-screen mode on a 12-inch portable computer screen.

Finally, don't just hand your client a final PDF file expecting that they will be able to present it properly on their corporate Web site. Go the extra mile. Create a Web page or, even better, a microsite that will allow visitors to learn about the eBrochure and enter their name and email for permission to download the PDF and to get a chance to win a trip to paradise.

Audio eBooks in Education

10

In this chapter, you'll explore how interactive rich-media audio in the form of spoken narrative can bring the printed page to life. You'll also look at various ways to make a PDF document interactive such as adding buttons to control the playback of the audio and hyperlinking to other pages using buttons or highlighted text. Finally, you'll learn how you can incorporate interactive PDF forms into the electronic document for testing purposes.

Challenges of the Printed Word

I have a close friend who is the principal of a secondary school, and we often talk about the challenges she faces every day of educating students in a world dominated by the media, from television to video games.

Her students are mainly immigrants who learn English quickly just by listening to the radio and watching television. But reading and writing in English has become a serious issue. "Kids just do not want to read anymore. We live in a world of interactive video games, music TV stations, and iPods. Textbooks are just too boring for them," she sighs.

This disconnection from the written word seems to be a growing problem in the educational system. The sales of textbooks are declining each year, and student dropout rates have become alarmingly high. Some teachers believe our children have become overstimulated by the mass media available to them and that schools lack the tools to compete for their attention.

Many parents buy their children portable computers so they can use them in school for writing assignments and at home for online learning courses offered by universities and private schools. Online courses are popular with students who want to learn a foreign language because they create their own schedule and can control the pace of the lesson. It's interactive just like the video games they have grown up playing.

We know it is much easier for a student to learn to read when the words are pronounced or read aloud. An English as a Second Language (ESL) course usually starts with narrated audio and text in short phrases and then moves on to full sentences, paragraphs, and finally short stories. That formula works for learning a language, but the moral of the story is sometimes lost. Students get so caught up trying to understand the words that they do not grasp the important message the story is trying to impart.

In the traditional school system, students are given books to read as homework assignments, and then in a classroom setting, students analyze the story by providing their thoughts and interpretations. In addition, the student writes a book report or takes a test to enable the teacher to grade them. But a downloadable rich-media eBook could provide students with similar experiences and more.

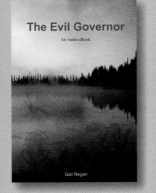

The Evil Governor Rich-Media Audio Short-Story eBook

Gail Regan is one of the main principals on the board of governors for Cara Operations, a large restaurant and food service company. In her earlier career, she was a successful schoolteacher, and it was there she noticed students were being taught generalized subjects but were not learning how to make decisions that would affect their careers in the long term.

Knowing that the youth of today would become the entrepreneurs of tomorrow, Gail wanted to explain how to hold the board of directors of a company accountable for decisions and to introduce the concept of responsible governing. To accomplish this goal, she decided to utilize her roots as a teacher, but this time she would use the latest technology available—an interactive, audio PDF eBook titled The Evil Governor. The free eBook could

be downloaded by anyone who wanted to study the politics of running a company, to learn about western culture, and possibly to learn the English language at the same time. The entire eBook would be narrated to allow the reader to listen and learn.

She hired a writer to help her create a fictional short story about a powerful woman who worked her way up the corporate ladder and tried to stay there using evil methods. She wanted the interactive eBook to introduce the reader to a set of morals that would differentiate the good and bad ways of governing a company or even a family. To accomplish this task, the book would use interactive icons and hyperlinked text to jump the user to excerpts from a larger and more in-depth body of her work available for purchase as a long-format, DVD audio drama.

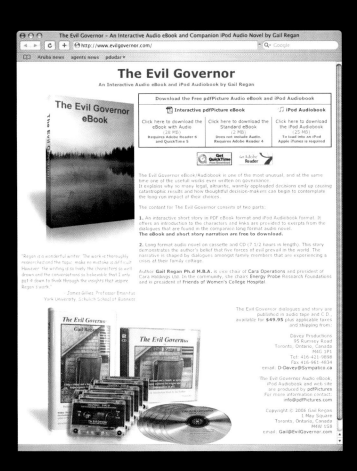

FIGURE 10-1 *The Evil Governor* Web site is used to promote the audio cassettes, CDs, DVDs, and digital eBook.

Collecting the Content

Gail commissioned two versions of *The Evil Governor*. One, targeted to an older audience, was a long-form audio drama featuring several cast members and would be available only as an audio CD or DVD. My company's job was to produce the second version, an interactive audio eBook with a single narrator that was a condensed version of the audio drama. It was targeted to junior-high students. The eBook would be available as a free download from Gail's Web site, www.EvilGovernor.com (**FIGURE 10-1**).

The style of writing for the short story was intended for all ages, but the eBook would include hidden hyperlinked information targeted to a more mature, intellectual audience. Users could just sit back and listen to the story, or they could interact with the eBook to gain deeper meanings from the story.

To narrate the story, Gail provided the script as a Microsoft Word document, and the audio consisted of a replicated CD that was sold with the long-form audio DVD drama.

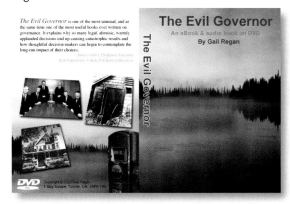

Creating the Document

Using Adobe InDesign, we decided to lay out the document so it would display a single page of text to resemble a standard paperback book. Since we weren't sure of the ages or reading skills of the users, for the text we chose a 15-point Arial font that would be legible even on a 12-inch portable computer screen. If the eBook was used to learn English, the large, single-column text would make it easy to read while listening to the corresponding audio.

To differentiate it from other available eBooks, several paragraphs of the book featured colored text and icons to indicate to the user that there was additional information for those topics. If a user clicked these symbols (**FIGURE 10-2**), the eBook would jump to reference pages that provided detailed information about the morals of the story, including syndrome mixing, narcissism, vested interests, patriarchy, and inequality. A pop-up JavaScript menu (**FIGURE 10-3**) allowed users to jump to a particular chapter or portion of the book that was significant to the story.

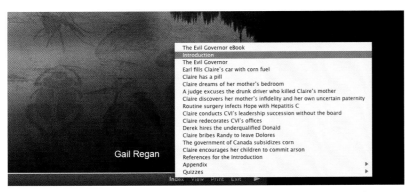

FIGURE 10-3 Pop-up JavaScript menu used to navigate to important topics.

interests. Poison ivy is green, occurs in Muskoka and hurts those careless enough to touch it.

Gold symbolizes royalty, so I have used it to indicate the ideal of patriarchy. The roach is an ancient Egyptian symbol and a Muskoka cottage pest, so I chose it as patriarchy's symbol.

Red is the color of romantic love so I use it to indicate sexual issues and their symbolization in wealth and power. I chose the snake as the symbol for excess sex because snakes are symbolically used this way in the bible and sometimes they frighten visitors to Muskoka.

When the print in the story is blue, syndrome mixing is happening and you should decide whether it is in its normative or bad form. When the icon of the mosquito is shown, it is a signal to link to an excerpt from the dialogues and its references to social and management science. Similarly, purple with its icon the zebra mussel indicates narcissism, green and poison ivy show alignments, gold and the roach mean patriarchy, red and the snake signal sexualization. In all cases, I encourage you to contemplate whether you are seeing a normative force of evil or bad faith behavior.

FIGURE 10-2 *The Evil Governor* eBook consisted of a single column of text that included icons hyperlinked to in-depth reference materials.

FIGURE 10-5 The correct answers could be activated via JavaScript buttons to show or hide the correct answers

Quiz | 171

Quiz 1

The categories are coded as follows:
1a. Normative syndrome mixing
1b. Bad syndrome mixing
2a. Normative praise seeking, blame avoidance, distancing
2b. Self destruction
3a. Normative alignment of vested interests
3b. Bad alignment of vested interests
4a. Normative patriarchy
4b. Bad patriarchy
5a. Normative sexualization of wealth and power
5b. Casual sex

Select one of these events in the story to the appropriate category above.

1) Faith Chapman's affair
1a___ 2a___b___ 3a___b___ 4a___b___ 5a___ b✓

2) Judge's sentencing of Billy Duncan, the drunk driver
1a___b___ 2a___ b___ 3a___b___ 4a✓b___ 5a___b___

3) Municipal hospital stocks contaminated blood
1a___b___ 2a___b___ 3a✓b___ 4a___b___ 5a___b___

4) Claire renovates the office to attract Derek
1a___b___ 2a___b___ 3a___b___ 4a___b✓ 5a___b___

5) To please Claire, CVI board appoints Derek
1a___b✓ 2a___b___ 3a___b___ 4a___b___ 5a___b___

6) Derek hires Donald as OFO
1a___b___ 2a___b___ 3a✓b___ 4a___b___ 5a___b___

7) Claire bribes Randy to leave Dolores
1a___b___ 2a___b___ 3a___b___ 4a✓b___ 5a___b___

8) Government matches corn subsidy
1a✓b___ 2a___b___ 3a___b___ 4a___b___ 5a___b___

9) To handle her feelings, Claire takes pills and drinks wine
1a___b___ 2a___b✓ 3a___b___ 4a___b___ 5a___b___

10) Earl adds ethanol to gasoline
1a___b✓ 2a___b___ 3a___b___ 4a___b___ 5a___b___

Show Answers   Hide Answers   Reset

Index   View   Print   Exit

Taking the Test

As a former teacher, Gail understood the importance of tests and examinations and wanted to allow students to test themselves using an interactive mini-quiz at the back of the eBook. We used InDesign to lay out the text for the quiz and Adobe Acrobat to make the quiz interactive. Acrobat allows you to insert blank check boxes into a PDF page that the user can select to make active. We placed hidden form-field text boxes (**FIGURE 10-4**) over the correct answers, which could be activated via JavaScript buttons to show or hide the correct answers (**FIGURE 10-5**). Acrobat 8 allows you to create and enable a form that can be used as a test. Using the free Reader 8, students can fill in the answers, save the test and submit it via an email attachment or via the school's network to a database for grading.

FIGURE 10-4 Hidden form-fields over quiz answers.

9) To handle her feelings, Claire takes pills and drinks wine
1a___ b___   2a___ b___   3a___ b___   4a___ b___   5a___ b___

10) Earl adds ethanol to gasoline
1a___ b___   2a___ b___   3a___ b___   4a___ b___   5a___ b___

Show Answers   Hide Answers   Reset

Adding the Rich-Media Audio

All the audio was prerecorded in a professional studio, so all we had to do was convert the content into a highly compressed format to allow it to be included in a downloadable eBook.

The narration was supplied on three CDs that were also sold with the audio DVD drama. Since they were in Compact CD Redbook audio format, we had to rip and burn the three CD tracks into three master .aiff files, which we accomplished with Apple iTunes. To combine the three files into a single seamless 80-minute digital audio track, we decided to use Apple Final Cut Pro, which is commonly used for video editing but is perfect for simple audio work too.

Audio Compression

Audio compression is critical in long-form audio eBooks because you want to maintain the fidelity while producing the smallest file size you can possibly obtain. Using the superior dual-pass capabilities of Autodesk Cleaner, we compressed the single stereo .aiff file to a mono .mp3 file, which resulted in a file that was only 25 MB.

This audio file was embedded into the book using the Sound tool and attached to the document using the attachment window. The user can transfer the attached file to a portable .MP3 player such as the iPod.

The Attachment button allows you to add removable files, such as audio, to PDF documents.

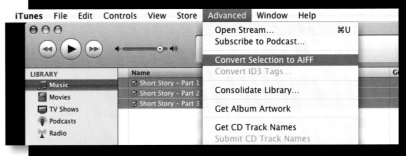

Apple iTunes conversion from Redbook Audio to AIFF

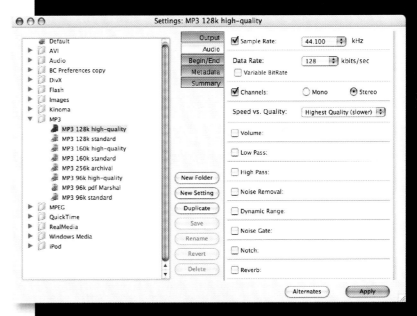

Autodesk Cleaner compression settings window

Timing via Acrobat and JavaScript

Many countries do not yet enjoy the always-on, high-speed broadband connections we have grown accustomed to, so it was important to allow the book to be read and heard anywhere without an Internet connection.

To allow the user to download both the eBook and the audio in one self-contained package, we embedded the audio into the document using Acrobat's Sound Tool, then timed it using JavaScript functions so that the book's pages would be in sync with the audio track.

For example, if a user turned to page 20 in the book, a "play audio on this page" button would jump the audio to the first paragraph on that page. Clicking the Pause button would pause or resume the audio track. This time-sync feature is possible by timing the number of seconds from the start of the audio track and recording the values reached with each new page. When you click the "play audio on this page" button, the JavaScript code looks at the page number and cross-references it to the number of seconds the audio file must play in real time to get to that page. It then moves the audio ahead and plays at that corresponding position on the page. The audio track will also turn the page at the appropriate time to keep the narration and text in sync.

This is a good example of how JavaScript can control both the PDF and rich media, but you have to consider many factors if you are making a hybrid PDF that can play rich media on both Mac and Windows computers because the timing function operates differently for QuickTime Player and Windows Media Player.

If you time your audio track to the pages using the QuickTime format and force it to play on Mac and Windows computers using QuickTime, you won't have any audio sync problems. You can use whatever codec you want such as MP3 or AAC.

If you think your Windows audience might not have QuickTime installed on their computers, you will then want to use a common codec such as MP3 and force Windows Media Player to play the MP3 file. In this case, you must use separate timing functions for QuickTime and Windows Media Player because they use different time references.

Our JavaScript programmer placed the code to control the pages and the audio in the Document JavaScript Window. The JavaScript code will first determine the type of computer users are on, either a PC or a Mac. Then it will take the appropriate timing information you have supplied and use it to keep the audio and text in sync. On a Mac it will use the QuickTime page reference times, and on the PC it will use the Windows Media page reference times.

Final Products

We decided to make several versions of the project so it could be enjoyed as a simple eBook, a rich-media audio eBook, and an audio-only file that could be transferred to an MP3 player such as an iPod. The eBook by itself was 2 MB, the audio eBook was 28 MB, and the stand-alone MP3 audio file was 25 MB.

If you want to experience it for yourself I have provided the entire short-story audio eBook on the CD-ROM that comes with this book.

The Future of Rich-Media Audio eBooks

Audio PDF eBooks have a great potential to catch on in the near future because they are fairly simple to produce and their small size can be compressed quite a bit. In fact, you can provide almost half an hour of audio in a 5 MB file, which makes it practical to email as well.

Of course, the story content is critical to the success of any book, but this form of rich media requires only a professional voice or the author's voice and a small home studio to produce a professional product. In fact, not every word in the book has to be narrated. A few chosen quotes from the author or the person you are writing about can make the static text come alive. In other words, quoted text can become actual spoken text.

In every area and profession, a reservoir of valuable print content is just waiting to be combined with the spoken word to create rich-media eBooks.

Don't be surprised if you soon start to see hundreds of audio PDF eBook versions of books that are now out of print showing up in Google's new eBook category.

If you are just starting to create rich-media audio, you can take the sponsored approach by giving away your audio eBook for free. Just find a company that wants to get its information into the hands of a group of people interested in its products. eBooks with topics such as health, finance, and religion are perfect examples. In addition, motivational speakers will find that audio eBooks are great promotional tools to get their voices heard.

Researchers and writers should consider the amount of audio content that sits on the shelves of talk-radio stations. Historically significant interviews with musicians, movie stars, politicians, and other famous (or infamous) people have all been archived. This content is just waiting for the day when innovators will realize that there is a new form of publishing revenue available to them.

Further, journalists who have relied on small tape or digital recorders to capture their interviews are in a perfect position to exploit this new form of media. Even the iPod has several microphone adapters that will allow you to capture spoken word directly to the iPod in a final compressed digital format.

Finally, textbook publishers can now provide rich-media audio eBook versions of their printed products. University professors can record their lectures and embed their comments into companion home-study materials. Via downloadable interactive PDF audio documents, the whole world can subscribe to long-distance learning courses that can teach, talk, and test.

Conclusions

In the educational system, audio eBooks are a great way to make learning fun. When spoken word accompanies the written word, the story takes on a whole new dimension as the narrator pauses or adds emphasis to sentences. The user is drawn into the story by the emotion in the voice.

For ESL students, learning to read and spell is simplified because the words are pronounced as they're being seen onscreen. Hearing and practicing the syllables that form the words can help readers minimize a foreign accent.

Hyperlinks in the eBook can direct users to a much larger body of knowledge that can reside either in the eBook or on a Web page. Book authors often research on the Internet for facts to support their content, so readers can just click a highlighted word to read the actual source of the information online.

Offline interactive tests that accompany the book can provide students with immediate feedback and a glimpse of the final exam. The interactive tests can also be submitted to a database to allow the teacher to monitor and mark a student's performance.

Although it's been challenging to get people to pay for eBooks, Apple has had success with iTunes "audiobooks," which are audio-only files at this point. The good news is that people seem willing to pay for audio, so if you can provide an eBook with attached iPod audio, it will only improve your chances of commercial success.

The Evil Governor
An Audio eBook

Gail Regan

141

Adding Rich-Media Audio Ambiance to Your PDF

11

Imagine watching a feature film without background music and sound effects—it would seem stark naked. Now imagine a *National Geographic* eBook where a photograph of a jungle or stream takes on an added dimension through the use of a sound track. The sounds of a running stream as well as birds and perhaps a frog or two can help you imagine what it would be like to be sitting right there in a canoe.

Sound effects can have a profound effect in rich-media PDFs. The soft tone of a cuckoo clock or the tick of an antique grandfather clock can certainly provide a mood and enhance the page. Rare sounds from living creatures such as the communication of whales underwater, the unnerving sound of a rattlesnake, or the beating of a human heart can induce a definite emotional response. More dramatic examples might be the sounds of thunderstorms, lightning, tornadoes, or the eruption of a volcano. Essentially, music and sound can make your PDF come to life with very little effort.

In this chapter, you'll explore the preferred cross-platform audio file formats used in rich-media PDF documents, and I'll offer a few examples of how they can enhance the printed word.

Rich-Media Audio in Education

As many teachers and parents will acknowledge, today's students need to be entertained or they will just tune out. Sound effects most certainly add to learning an entertainment component that's most often found in the video games that students play. Through *edutainment* (learning that is designed to educate and be fun too), students are much more likely to focus on the subject matter and concepts being taught.

Take, for example, most military history books. They are just too boring for today's video-game generation. The average textbook that just states the facts of a battle makes it hard for students to recall the important details of the battle. The text usually reads something like this: "At Franklin, Tennessee, on November 30, 1864, General Hood's Confederates lost more than 6,000 of 21,000 effectives, most of them in about two hours. Six Confederate generals also died there."

If you can find the right sound effects for the pictures, the book can take on a game-like experience. For example, to enhance archival photos of the Civil War, "soldiers" could speak about their experiences. Imagine a picture of a field hospital ward where you can hear the "thoughts" of each patient when you click his face or body while ambient sound effects of a distant battle play in the background. Students could hear the thoughts of dying patients: "I see the light. It's wonderful, so peaceful. I pray to be buried here at my home in Franklin, Tennessee." Or they could hear another patient's thoughts: "November 30, 1864. It's my birthday today, and I'm only 16. If I live, I will defect from these crazy Confederate generals. Six of them just died in battle. They can't even save themselves."

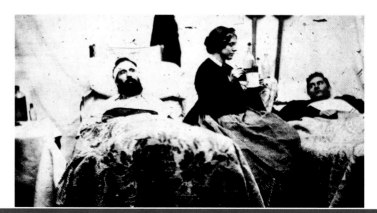

For a more compelling audio narrative, you could use the "thoughts" of General Hood reflecting after the battle. Students could just click the picture of General Hood, and the rich-media audio would play: "What a blunder I have made. I lost a quarter of my men in just two hours. Six thousand brave souls." The thoughts of the soldiers and commanders could be based on the text in the book, and all it would take is a bit of clever writing to interpret history into a first-person narrative.

Reformatting Television Programs for eBooks

The secret to this edutainment process is to follow a similar route as the Public Broadcasting Service (PBS) when it produces award-winning Civil War documentaries that consist of archival photographs–the "Ken Burns" approach. Ken zooms, pans, and dissolves still photographs to make them come alive, creating a compelling video experience. An educational book publishing company could purchase the interactive rights to similar documentaries to create an eBook using the still pictures from the show, the closed-captioning track for text, and the audio for the narration.

General Hood

Documentary film producer Ken Burns

"Paperback" eNovels

Many people like to read a good novel at the beach, the park, or some other place that provides a bit of background ambiance. Some like to read at home by the crackling fire, listening to relaxing music with sound effects such as a river with natural wildlife.

The majority of the population likes to read in the comfort of their bed, and if they have a portable computer to read a rich-media eNovel, they can experience all the locations where the story takes place in crystal-clear stereo (using headphones so they don't disturb their sleeping partner).

When producing an eNovel, the ideal situation is to provide a quiet sound effect track that enhances the story line. For example, let's say you are reading about the Titanic. The story starts at a busy harbor as people are boarding and the ship is getting ready to depart. As you read the text at your own speed, you can hear the ambient harbor in the background. That audio loops until you turn to a page where the story is set in a different location.

You then board the ship and enter the dining room. You can hear the sounds of clinking dishes and violins. This carries on for a few

pages until the scene changes to the front deck of the ship. Now you hear the waves splashing against the bow of the ship, the foghorn blowing, and then the ship crashing against the iceberg. Since you are "turning" the pages, you control the audio track.

The Impact of Music

Ambient music can also bring the page to life. If you have ever searched the Web for island travel destinations, you may have come across a few sites that provide a Caribbean song on the home page. A travel eBrochure that offers a wide selection of countries and cultures of the world could provide a much richer experience using relaxing background music while the user reads about the customs, events, and amenities that the tour has to offer. Turn the page, and a new song plays to support that particular destination.

In the next section, you'll look at a rich-media PDF project that was created for a travel wholesaler that wanted to add video and music to liven up its static PDF pages.

Merit Travel's Cross-Platform eBrochure

2005 - 2006 departures

a collection of unique travel experiences

um
uniquely**merit**

For a detailed itinerary visit www.uniquelymerit.ca   Index View Print Exit ▶

Michael Merrithew

M ichael Merrithew operates an upscale travel company that specializes in custom vacation packages. His clients are often corporations that want to provide their staff members with a completely different travel experience, and Merit Travel tries its best to tailor an itinerary to its clients' needs.

To introduce these services, Merit Travel's marketing representatives decided to contract our company to produce a travel eBrochure that would include a 30-second personal message from Michael, the company's president.

FIGURE 11-1 We redesigned the brochure's portrait pages into a landscape format to allow for full-screen display on a computer monitor.

One of the limitations to MPEG-1 video files is that they require standard playback dimensions using 4:3 aspect ratios. If you crop the video to a vertical format, they tend to stutter and jerk when played.

Collecting the Content

The QuarkXPress files of the original printed Merit Travel brochure were sent to us on several CDs. We saved them as Quark 4 files so that we could import them into Adobe InDesign, our preferred page layout application. We then redesigned the brochure's portrait pages into a landscape format to allow for full-screen display on a computer monitor (**FIGURE 11-1**).

Adding Video

We shot the testimonial by Michael in our studio on a DVCAM camera and edited the video using Apple Final Cut Pro. The client wanted to make sure the video would play on as many computers as possible and feared that QuickTime might not be installed on its clients' computers since most would be in corporate offices. We exported the master video as a QuickTime DV file and then compressed it as an MPEG-1 file using Autodesk Cleaner.

In this case, we chose to use the MPEG-1 video compression codec because it would allow for playback on all computers; QuickTime would play the MPEG-1 file on a Mac, and the Windows Media Player would play the file on the PC. Now, MPEG-1 is not the most efficient codec, but it is a high-quality universal decompression codec found in most media

players. One of the limitations to MPEG-1 video files is that they require standard playback dimensions using 4:3 aspect ratios. If you crop the video to a vertical format, they tend to stutter and jerk when played. Another limitation to MPEG-1 is that the final file size can become quite large. It's just not a very efficient codec for the Internet, but in this case, MPEG-1 video was perfect because it was just a tiny clip of a talking head with little motion in the video.

We added the video to the introductory testimonial page and positioned it beside the signature of the president (**FIGURE 11-2**) using Adobe Acrobat Professional for Windows. It's not possible to use a Mac to insert video into a Mac PDF file unless it has a .mov extension, and the extension for MPEG is .mpg. Don't get me wrong— a Mac will play MPEG-1 video; you just can't insert it. (It's one of those Mac/PC things you just have to accept.)

Adding Interactivity

We used Acrobat Professional for the Mac to author the PDF for interactivity such as the page turns, the pop-up menu, and the print and exit functionality. Everything worked as it should, and we delivered it to the client for approval. The effect of the president popping up to welcome the viewer really amazed the client. On the PC, you can launch the video to fill the screen by double-clicking the image.

I suggested inserting videos of all the countries the company listed in its eBrochure because I had a large stock-footage library of destinations. But it would have made the eBrochure quite large in file size, so instead the client suggested an alternative—music.

exploring new destinations, I never tire of sharing stories with friends and fellow travellers with hammerhead sharks in the Galapagos Islands is one of many reasons for the creation The enclosed itineraries range from a cruise down the Yangtze River to hiking in the (inclusive vacation, but definitely a travel adventure to remember.

We pride ourselves in offering a truly unique vacation experience, available exclusively to broaden horizons with destinations and itineraries that offer you a world of experienc *vacation itinerary to fit any group.*

Our Uniquely Merit brochure showcases some of our most popular vacation itinerarie any of our Merit Travel locations. Along with these pre-set itineraries, we specialize Our most recent success story is an eight day Holland Liberation tour. This trip was so time. Just tell us what kind of travel experience you are looking for and let us do the re

Whichever Uniquely Merit journey you choose, you can travel knowing that your tri *based on our knowledge and expertise. We assure you a truly memorable and er*

With Merit you won't simply visit the country to which you travel, you will gain insight ar and people.

Bon Voyage!

Michael Merrithew
President & CEO

a collection of unique travel exper

d itinerary visit **www.uniquelymerit.ca**

FIGURE 11-2 Michael Merrithew's testimonial video was embedded into the introduction page.

If you program the MPEG file to use Windows Media Player for playback, you can launch the video full screen by double-clicking on the video.

FIGURE 11-3 The Page Properties window with optional Actions from Adobe Acrobat 8.

Adding Music

The client thought that after the initial impact of the video, the rest of the pages were too silent and wondered if we had music in the stock-footage library that could bring the pages to life—different songs to fit the various destinations. Using iTunes we exported a variety of songs from music CDs to the MP3 format and then sent them to the client's office for them to choose.

After the client found the appropriate music for each destination, we inserted all the audio using Acrobat Professional for the Mac. A Mac can do this via the Sound tool; it allows you to insert audio files that are not QuickTime. The tricky part is authoring the PDF to turn on the sound when you turn the page, keep it on for a range of pages, and then turn it off for a new travel section while starting the next song for the next range of pages.

Acrobat's Page-Based Format

One of the frustrations multimedia producers have when using Acrobat for the first time is that everything is page-based. Multimedia programs such as Director and Flash are timeline-based, and Acrobat uses a very different method for controlling the interactivity and media within the document. You can do this with JavaScript, but the language is difficult to learn, and the page-based format that Acrobat uses is nontraditional for multimedia applications. The simple way to automatically start and stop audio is to embed the audio in the page using the Sound tool and then control it using the "On page open" and "On page close" commands found in the Page Properties window (**FIGURE 11-3**).

Download Ready

Once we combined the audio and video into one cohesive product, the client was happy and posted the eBrochure on its Web site for download. After a few consultations with their Webmaster as to the correct method to "force download" the file so that it would open full screen on users' computers instead of the Web browser, everything was good to go.

Compatibility Issues

When dealing with simple, short audio files, you do not need to be concerned about Mac/PC compatibility if you are using MP3 files for audio. Adobe Reader will tell Macs to use QuickTime to play the MP3 file, and on Windows, Reader will use Windows Media Player or the default MP3 player set by the user to play the file. Therefore, when producing your first rich-media PDF, using audio only is a good starting point because MP3 files are cross-platform.

The iPod uses the next generation of audio file format, known as AAC (Advanced Audio Codec), which is also the audio part of the MPEG-4 standard. Those audio files are small, and the quality is near perfect. But AAC is a little overkill for rich-media PDF eBooks that are meant to be played through computer speakers. MP3 audio files are now widely used throughout the world, so if you want to ensure that you target the biggest audience and the file will work everywhere, including in the corporate boardroom and in the home, then play it safe and use MP3 for rich-media audio.

As noted earlier in the chapter, if you plan to add video, MPEG-1 is a great video codec to use if you want to ensure that the video and audio will play on the widest variety of computer operating systems. It's not the most efficient codec because it's more than 15 years old and the industry has had many advances since then, but it's still the best codec to use for cross-platform compatibility. However, file sizes are quite large, and the quality is poor compared to newer codecs such as MPEG-4.

So far, Apple is really the only big player in the MPEG-4 market, and Microsoft does not want to support the industry-standard MPEG-4 H.264 format (yet).

Unfortunately, MPEG-4 has its compatibility problems too, and it's just starting to be adopted by the industry.

In the near future, as Quick-Time gets ingrained into the public conscious-ness and installed on PC users' machines via iTunes and the iPod or the video iPod, cross-platform compatibility utilizing the latest MPEG compression technology may no longer be an issue.

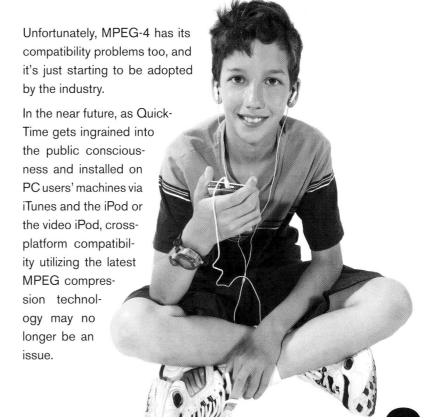

Lessons Learned

From eBooks to eBrochures, your rich-media PDFs can include sound effects that profoundly affect the feel of the project. By considering these guidelines you can successfully create an audio-enhanced product that people will enjoy:

- **Use appropriate music:** Rich-media background music files will work best in productions when the music supports a theme. It's important to choose music that is not distracting and can be turned off if the user starts to get annoyed.

- **Embed audio files:** Digital audio files can be quite small, and in many cases the audio can be seamlessly looped after running for a minute or so, providing a perfect opportunity to embed the audio inside the PDF. No Internet connection is needed after the initial download.

- **Include sound effects:** If you want to get a little adventurous, you can also have embedded background sound effects playing while triggering additional tracks of audio such as narration. It's possible to play more than one audio track at the same time.

- **Give the user control:** Let the user take control of the sound in a PDF. It's the added interactivity that will make your electronic audio book a success.

Conclusions

Audio is the easiest form of rich media to add to a PDF. There are hundreds of inexpensive stock music and sound effect libraries that you can buy and use as rich-media content for your PDF. Consider the number of self-help books available in which you read about how to calm your mind, relax, and de-stress. Now consider the amount of meditation music used as a soothing background for your evening read. Why can't they both be merged into a PDF file? Buy the eBook, and the bonus is the audio track. Or if the audio file is attached to the PDF, you can extract the audio and put it into your iPod or burn a CD. Then the eBook is a bonus.

Digital Music Booklets

12

The Apple iPod is a worldwide, runaway success with more than a billion song downloads from the Apple iTunes Music store. Most record companies, after some initial resistance, have decided to accommodate a public that prefers on-demand digital downloads over CDs. The music industry has taken the "if you can't beat 'em, join 'em" approach and continually tries to find ways to get artists listed in the iTunes Top-10 list, which is a sure path to gold or platinum sales for an artist. The Billboard Top 10 is slowly losing its position of power and prestige!

When scouting for the next up-and-coming talent, the major labels are paying attention to the independent artists who are hot downloads on iTunes.

But many musicians and their fans have long been disappointed with the absence of cover art and the printed materials that once accompanied vinyl records, cassette tapes, and CDs. They claim iTunes has now eliminated an important connection to the essence or personality of the band: Fans don't have anything physical to hold in their hands or hang on the wall. But Apple has taken these critics to heart and has provided a digital alternative to remedy this situation: PDF digital booklets.

In this chapter, you'll explore what PDF digital booklets can do, and I'll walk you through how to create them.

12

Digital PDF Booklets

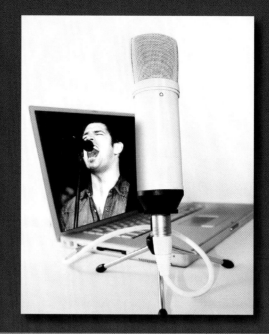

To entice consumers to purchase more than one song, Apple has facilitated the delivery of PDF *digital booklets* of music artists, which are now offered for free if you buy every song on an album. The PDF digital booklet and the digital audio files are packaged in one download that ends up inside your iTunes Library. It all started with U2's digital "box set," which includes 446 songs, live cuts, unreleased tracks, and a complete digital booklet featuring cover art, track listings, and band commentary.

Carry Underwood, one of the winning vocalists of the *American Idol* TV show, now offers a simple four-page PDF digital booklet that you can view in Adobe Reader if you purchase the entire collection of songs from her *Some Hearts* album. This digital booklet consists of four full-screen 10 x 7.5-inch pictures of her

that seem to be perfect for printing and framing. No text, no interactivity—just pictures.

Even though Apple does not actively promote iTunes' ability to store a library of interactive PDFs inside iTunes, you can try it for yourself. Drag any PDF document to iTunes, and double-click it. On PCs, this will launch Reader; on a Mac, it will launch PDF Preview.

A Giant Step into the Future

The current offerings of iTunes digital booklets are pretty basic, but they do have the potential to become full-blown interactive rich-media record albums. Consider a future where you download songs for your iPod and along with those songs you receive a PDF digital booklet that contains a highly interactive virtual tour through the group's home-recording studio, where Flash animations bring the page to life, and where you listen to exclusive streaming audio interviews with members of the band. To regain the physical element that's missing from the digital domain, you'll be able to print high-quality pictures of the band and read the song lyrics. And everything will reside in a rich-media PDF.

In addition, bands without a current record contract will have a perfect medium to get noticed by record companies and talent scouts who prefer to discover music not yet in the mainstream.

In the following section, you'll look at the workflow for producing a rich-media digital booklet that can be emailed, delivered over the Internet via iTunes or via a Web site that you may have to promote your music.

Chris Seldon Interactive Music PDF

Singer/songwriter Chris Seldon has vast experience in digital music production. In addition to writing his own songs, he consults for many professional recording studio executives and artists. His experience with Digidesign Pro Tools digital audio–recording software and his working knowledge of the Mac computer as a multimedia workhorse have allowed him to become an innovator in the music industry.

In conjunction with Chris, my company embarked on a project to create a DVD containing a music video with 5.1 Dolby Digital surround sound and an interactive rich-media digital booklet of his band.

For my company, this was the ultimate convergence project. Fans could see the music video on a music TV station, on a DVD, and inside a PDF.

Working within the constraints of a limited budget, we decided to take a documentary approach and shoot the promotional music video in the studio while the song was being recorded and then later add a few outdoor scenes to get away from the confined spaces of the studio.

We also needed the recording and mixing studios to have experience with surround sound and to help finance part of the production in exchange for some promotional consideration. Specifically, the studios would be prominently featured in the music video and in the digital booklet via Apple QuickTime VR photography. Fortunately, we found several studios that wanted to participate.

"Jaded" Music Video & iPod Audio

Chris Seldon

Chris Seldon pdfPicture Music Video Album

Index   View   Print   Exit   ▶

Creating and Collecting the Content

We shot the recording-studio scenes live at Umbrella Sound Studios in one day using Sony PD 150 and D30 DVCAM cameras while the band was recording the song. An audio tap from the mixing console to the cameras made it relatively simple to get the reference audio we'd need to keep the video in sync with the final music during post-production video editing.

The studio's engineer exported a rough stereo mix immediately after the recording session and converted it to an audio CD for playback on a portable-music boombox. I used this for audio playback for the outdoor locations, which required two additional days of filming.

After recording the music, the engineer exported the 24 individual master audio tracks to an Apple FireWire drive for transporting to Up Is Loud, the studio chosen to mix the song. Up Is Loud is a Mac-based, feature-film mixing studio that has experience with Pro Tools 5.1 surround sound and QuickTime video interlock. I figured if we used the compatible QuickTime format for all the audio and video production, the media would stay in sync during the music mixing, video editing, and final compression process.

One page in the digital booklet was to be dedicated to a VR tour of the studios. So while the group was recording and mixing the music, our photographer took still pictures and VR photography of the studio's control rooms using a wide-angle fish-eye Nikon lens.

After viewing the first rough cut of the video, the group wanted additional scenes of Chris singing in a controlled lighting environment using a green-screen key wall. So we used Adobe After Effects to composite Chris's vocal close-ups with him in front of several different backgrounds, and used Apple Final Cut Pro software to edit the footage.

Unfortunately, digital video cameras produce a detailed, clear, hard-news look that is often unflattering to actors. So to obtain the look of 35 mm film, we processed the entire video with DigiEffects CineLook plug-ins to soften the image and to add film "grain."

Digital Booklet

The digital booklet features several pages' worth of pictures of Chris, a video of the band playing live in the recording studios, an attached MP3 audio file of the song for transfer to an MP3 player, and to allow the band's fans to get a personal, behind-the-scenes, 360-degree view, we included a QuickTime VR tour of the recording studios.

VR Photography

Photographers use wide-angle lenses to shoot VR photography because they are the best way to capture a 360-degree scene in a minimum number of shots. They also create a dramatic look as a raw image. The lens has a wide focal length, which keeps an object that is a few inches from the camera in sharp focus. Once the band saw the photographs for the QuickTime VR, they fell in love with the look and suggested we also use a fish-eye picture of the recording studios for the credits page. Because we had a good selection of photos that the band uses for its promotional material as well as the additional studio shots, we had plenty of images from which to choose.

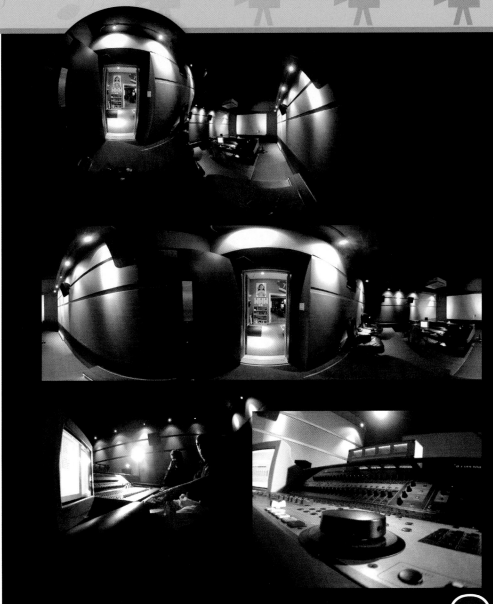

161

InDesign Layout and Interactivity

Our designers laid out the digital booklet's pages using Adobe InDesign. One of the nicest features of this application is its ability to insert links to Web pages so users can obtain additional information. As you reflow the document's pages, the text Web links remain intact. Our programmer used the Link tool to connect the recording studios' names, which were underlined in blue on the credits page, to their Web sites for more information about each studio.

The QuickTime VRs of the studios were embedded into the page (**FIGURE 12-1**) and buttons were created to launch them in floating windows. If the PDF is in full-screen mode, the QuickTime VR does not expand with the page if you use floating windows to present your rich media. It is important to know that you will not see the rich media in floating windows on a Mac if the user is viewing the document in Adobe Reader 6, although it works fine on a PC. It's a bug that was fixed in Adobe Reader 7.

FIGURE 12-1   QuickTime VR in floating windows.

InDesign also allowed us to place the pictures and embed the corresponding rich-media video and graphics into a separate registered layer. The photograph for the page that launched the video showed the mixing studio and prominently featured a wide video screen used to mix feature films. To users, it looked like they were actually watching the video inside the studio with the band.

Instead of floating the video above that page, we wanted the video to play in the page. To make the video appear and play seamlessly in register to the background image, the first frame of

the uncompressed video was exported from FinalCut and saved as a .PSD file. InDesign allowed us to place the digital video and the printable .PSD poster frame image in exactly the same position inside the center of the studio's video projection screen (**FIGURE 12-2**). Click on the Play Video button and the picture on the screen comes to life like magic.

FIGURE 12-2 InDesign allowed us to place the digital video and the printable .PSD poster frame image in exactly the same position inside the center of the studio's video projection screen.

I wanted to include the song's lyrics in the booklet and felt that a pop-up window overlay would be a good way to present the text. To accomplish this we created a small single PDF page of text with a transparent background using Adobe InDesign. Acrobat's Button tool can be used to create an area of the page that can contain overlay graphics. Buttons can be very large, and in this case we made a button that covered almost half the page. Usually, pictures are placed inside of buttons, but in our case we used PDF text. Acrobat was used to place and program the button to show and hide the PDF page of lyrics on top of the final PDF page.

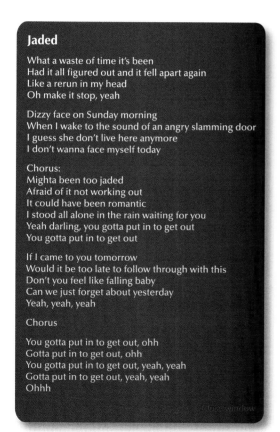

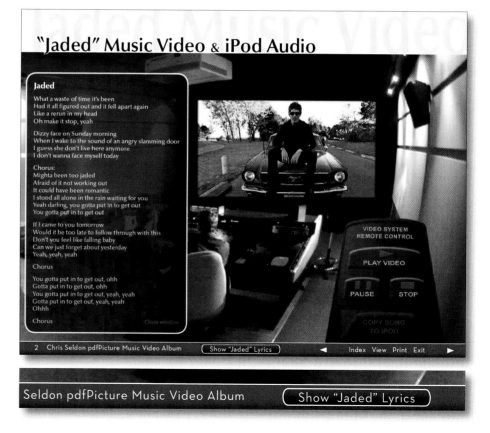

To control the video playback, we used Photoshop to create graphics for a handheld video remote controller and its interactive buttons. The controller buttons would highlight when the mouse rolled over them and would remain highlighted if selected. Once again, the Button tool was used to create the hotspots and to show or hide the highlight graphics for the Play Video, Pause, Stop, and Copy Song to iPod buttons. Acrobat's "*action*" tool was used to program the buttons to control the video and to open the attachment window containing the MP3 audio file of the song. The user would need Adobe Reader 7 or later to remove the attached file. To attach the MP3 audio file to the document, we used Acrobat's Attachments tool (**FIGURE 12-3**).

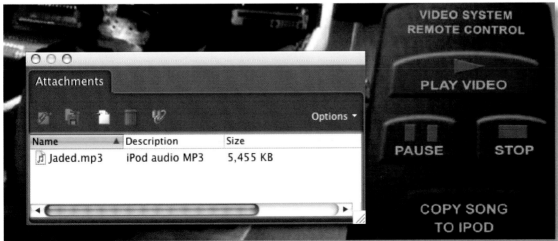

FIGURE 12-3 Acrobat's Attachments window allows you to remove the MP3 file from the PDF to transfer to an iPod or other MP3 player.

Q

QuickTime

Final Products

We selected one rich-media format for the entire digital booklet: Quick-Time. All the VR, video, and audio used this media player, which ensured playback on both Macs and PCs. Since this product was targeted to the iTunes/iPod demographic, we felt sure everyone would have QuickTime.

The hybrid DVD video provided the large, widescreen playback of songs in 5.1 surround sound and also contained the PDF digital booklet. The band could sell this DVD at live performances and send it to record companies and music TV stations.

Chris also wanted to be able to email the PDF to record companies and other individuals. But if the video were embedded in the PDF, it would be too large to email; therefore, we made two versions. The "enhanced" version included linked video that resided on a Web server, and the "full" version included embedded video for the DVD. The linked video flowed into the document from an external Web server using QuickTime's progressive download method, which prevents the video from starting until there is enough data preloaded into the cache to play smoothly. It's important that the streaming video not be too large in size because that would prohibit the video from streaming into the page in real time without a long wait.

We compressed the rich-media audio and video using Autodesk Cleaner, and chose the Sorensen 3 codec to ensure playback on QuickTime 5 and newer versions. Because the video was located outside the PDF, the final file was small, just under 1 MB, which permitted the digital booklet to be emailed easily.

Attaching the Audio File

Using Adobe Reader 7 or newer, it is possible to remove any attached file from a PDF, and in our case, the file attached was an iPod-friendly high-quality MP3 music file. Users were able to remove the attached file from the PDF, transfer it to iTunes, and then transfer it to their iPods.

The full version of the digital booklet included all the embedded media, including the video, the QuickTime VR, and the attached music file—a whole promotional package all inside one rich-media PDF that could be emailed, downloaded, and included on the DVD video.

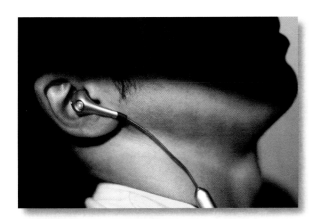

Adobe Acrobat's attachment window allows you to add and remove attachments from a PDF document.

Lessons Learned

With every project you complete, you will learn new techniques. Keep these tips in mind when you produce your projects:

- **Image compression:** Fans love to print pictures from digital booklets to put on their walls, so don't compress the pictures too much. If you are using InDesign or Acrobat, you have several choices for PDF export image quality. The compression settings are Minimum, Low, Medium, High, and Maximum. Use the Low or Medium compression setting, and set the output to 150 pixels per inch. If you are creating a version to email, try to keep the final file size to less than 5 MB.

- **Web links:** We found that one of the most appreciated features of the digital booklet were the links to the studio's and Chris's Web sites. Not only did the studio benefit from the exposure of the QuickTime VR tours, but it also got immediate referrals from the PDF right to their site. If you are trying to raise funds to produce this type of promotional material, try to think like movie producers who usually get sponsored locations, cars, computers, and more for free in exchange for credits or product placement in their films.

- **Video compression:** Everyone likes to look at big video, especially music videos that have lots of color and fast motion in the picture. To keep the quality clear, don't compress the video at too low a data rate, or the video will look blurry. However, the trade-off is that the file gets quite large. The only way to get a good result is by trying different compression settings and testing the final video on various computers. If you are linking to a video on a Web server, be careful; a four-minute video can grow to be more

than 20 MB. Even though you are progressively downloading the linked video, it might frustrate users if they have to wait several minutes for video preloading before they can view it. Just like with a Web page, it is wise to let the user choose a small, medium, or large format—whatever best fits with the speed of their Internet connection.

If you embed the video, you can make the size as big as you want—even full screen—because the downloading takes place in advance of playback. It's not unusual for kids who have grown up using file-sharing services to download music and movies that are more than 100 MB to burn a CD or even a DVD. Just be aware that not all computers are powerful enough to play the latest high-definition codecs, such as MPEG-4 H.264.

Conclusions

A band doesn't have to be signed to a record company to take its music to market. You don't need to have a deal with Apple to distribute your digital booklet via the Internet. In addition to a promotional Web site, think about creating an interactive PDF that includes various types of rich media. Instead of embedding the songs inside the PDF, which will make the document large in file size, stream the songs into the document—then you and your fans can email the whole album to others who may be interested in your music. If your fans like what they hear, a link in the PDF can direct them to a Web site where they can buy your "full version" digital booklet and, in this case, attach the music files so you can provide the capability of removing the songs for burning a CD or transfer to an iPod or another MP3 player. Apple's motto is "Think Different," and this is one way to make any band stand out from the crowd.

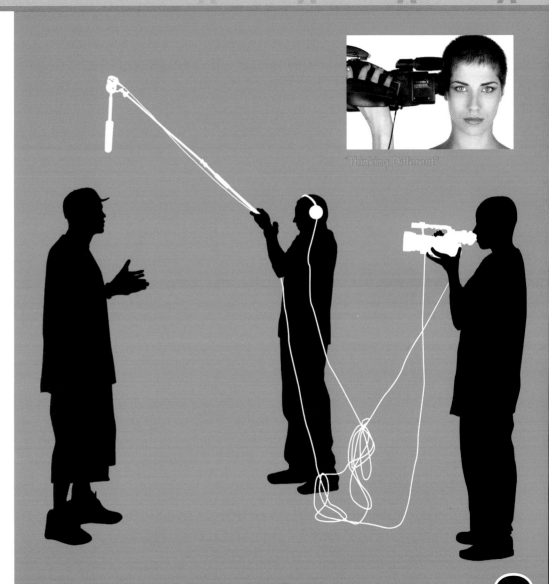

"Thinking Different"

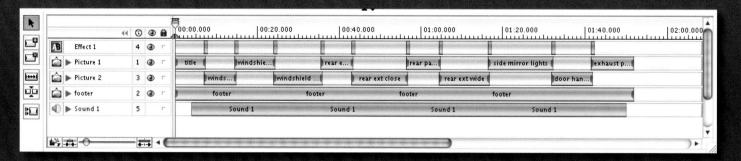

Rich-Media Slide Shows

One of the biggest concerns that prospective clients have about rich-media PDFs is that the files can become quite large in size, especially if they include full-motion video. The ability to email the PDF is especially appealing to direct-marketing companies, but many Internet service providers cap email attachments at 5 MB, so it's important to plan ahead to avoid that limitation.

If the video resides on a Web server outside the PDF and streams into the document, you really have no constraints in file size. But if you plan to embed the rich media inside the PDF, your choice is short video clips or an alternative that I actually prefer–Flash or Apple QuickTime slide shows.

13

Slide Shows versus Video

We have conducted focus groups using several different options for rich media to judge what consumers prefer to see in travel eBrochures. When we compared small quarter-screen video to full-screen slide shows, the big-picture effect won every time. If your video includes little motion, such as simply dissolving from the beach to the pool to the golf course, you could create the same effect using a series of pictures instead of bandwidth-intensive video at 15 or 30 frames per second.

For example, a large 30-second video might contain six scenes, each of which displays for five seconds. If you show five seconds of the beach and then dissolve to the pool for five seconds, and so on, the resulting video file would average about 5 MB in size.

An alternative is to use six still pictures in QuickTime or Flash, where the application will hold each picture for five seconds and then dissolve each picture. The QuickTime movie or Flash file would be about one-tenth the size of the video. Instead of 30 seconds of video, you could now have a five-minute slide show with music and narration. This method is often used for rich-media advertising in Web pages, but in our case inside a PDF it would contain full-screen images.

But to produce high-quality, accessible, rich-media PDFs, you have to consider a couple of other factors as well: compression and integration.

Compression Issues

One issue you must consider when producing rich-media PDFs is the performance of the computer that will play the rich media. Not every home user has a fast processor, which is needed to play large, full-screen, highly compressed video. But playing full-screen Flash or QuickTime slide shows is not a problem.

The compression artifacts in video can be quite noticeable, but when using JPEG still images, the clarity of the picture can be astounding. If the video you are considering in your project doesn't rely on motion to demonstrate a point, keep in mind that many people prefer to see a large, near-full-screen narrated slide show using beautiful photography (**FIGURE 13-1**) than a small, one-eighth-screen video clip (**FIGURE 13-2**). The key is to make the video as large as possible while keeping the file size within reason if downloading is required.

Content Integration

Another factor you need to consider is the content for your rich-media integration. If you are starting from scratch and can shoot the material, you ideally can combine video and still photography to provide the moving image for situations such as interviews and testimonials and to dissolve to the still slide show, allowing the narration to continue in sync with the pictures. It's possible to mix multiple data streams inside one QuickTime container file using Totally Hip's LiveStage (www.TotallyHip.com). This application gives you the ability to design interactive videos where several media tracks are playing at the same time. These Quick-Time wired-sprite media tracks are capable of providing a compelling rich-media presentation at extremely small data rates and file sizes.

FIGURE 13-1 Slide show using still images.

In the next section, you'll look at a successful example of mixing video and still images in an eBrochure my company created for the Volvo car company.

FIGURE 13-2 15 fps video clip.

Converging the Volvo Accessories Brochure and DVD

The Volvo line of cars is well known for safety and the numerous accessories available to consumers. In fact, Volvo distributes printed catalogs of racks, cargo holds, trailer hitches, stereos, iPod adapters, and many more items via mail after a car is sold. Volvo owners are like Mac owners—they just love their cars and will often keep upgrading them as the years go on.

Each year Volvo creates a new glossy accessories catalog and companion DVD in which customers get a pretty good idea of what a new gadget actually does without seeing it demonstrated at the showroom. For instance, the DVD might demonstrate how easy it is to remove a bike from a roof rack. Volvo's dealerships distribute thousands of DVDs so customers don't have to travel to the dealership to see a demo in person.

The high cost of printing the brochures and DVDs, the mailing and handling charges, and the wait time involved to get the product into the hands of their customers got Volvo thinking about alternative delivery methods via its Web site.

Because Volvo had great success with its downloadable rich-media PDF "living brochures" of its individual cars, it again turned to BrainTrain and my company to create a rich-media version of its accessories brochure. But in this case, the final brochure had to include 72 videos from the DVD and be small enough to allow for a reasonable download time from its Web site—a seemingly impossible task, we thought when first presented with the challenge.

FOR YOUR ENTERTAINMENT

Though highly enjoyable just as it is, your Volvo can be transformed into a virtual mobile entertainment centre.

- Speakers
- Subwoofer
- Volvo digital juke box
- Volvo iPod adapter
- Volvo FM transmitter for iPod
- 10 Disc CD changer
- HU 850 Radio
- 6 Disc in dash CD player
- RSE (Rear seat entertainment system)

To produce this rich-media brochure, we would have to compress a 3 GB DVD to less than 40 MB, which was the required target. To download the document, we figured it would take an average home consumer with a high-speed Internet connection about two to five minutes, a duration that most people have become accustomed to when downloading music and software upgrades. More than 40 MB might scare away the consumer.

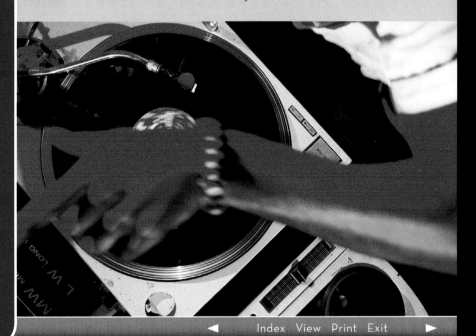

Index   View   Print   Exit   ►

175

Collecting the Content

On reviewing the DVD video, we saw that most of the scenes consisted of either still pictures transferred to video or scenes that had little motion. They were mainly scenes of the interior of the car, such as the radio or speakers, or scenes of the exterior, such as the trailer hitch, and so on, at various angles and degrees of close-up photography. The cars were usually parked, and a model demonstrated how to use the accessory.

We were able to re-create each accessory video by using still images exported (or *frame grabbed*) from the video and then dissolving the pictures together in a slide show using QuickTime. The effect would be to have the pictures in the PDF turn into a slide show. Customers could click the picture in the brochure, and the slide show would start perfectly in register with the background

image. Since we kept the slide show's width and height relatively small to fit perfectly in register with the document's pictures, we would not exceed the project's 40 MB limit.

A master copy of the DVD was supplied in BetaCam SP format, which we digitized onto a Macintosh computer using Final Cut Pro. Each accessory video was then exported as a single self-contained video using the DV codec for archiving purposes in case full motion digital videos were required one day in the future.

We then opened each video in QuickTime Pro. Using the player's timeline controller, we selected and exported a series of still images that provided a good demonstration of each accessory. This process, sometimes called *frame capturing*, gave us thousands of pictures that we then imported into Totally Hip's LiveStage QuickTime authoring application to create the slide shows.

We also exported the audio track from the master videos using QuickTime Pro to the .aif format, which we then imported into LiveStage to allow for sequencing and syncing of the still images to the appropriate part of the audio narration.

For the few videos that required full-motion video to demonstrate the accessories, we kept the frame rate to 15 frames per second and used the Sorenson 3 codec for compression.

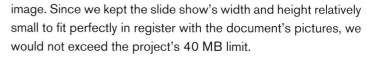

Tip: We try to use FireWire drives and the DV codec whenever possible because it provides a very good storage medium and picture quality, and the video can be viewed on any computer without special hardware cards for playback using QuickTime.

Why Not Use Flash?

Exporting and saving movies as QuickTime is probably one of the most misunderstood steps of the rich-media PDF workflow. I am often asked, "If you are working with still images, why do you export and save your movies as QuickTime? Why not just use Flash? Can't the Mac and PC play Flash files? Won't QuickTime make the files huge?"

The confusion lies in not understanding that Quick-Time and QuickTime video are very different.

A Flash slide show and a QuickTime slide show are pretty much the same. They are not video; they are just a series of pictures that dissolve. Hold the first slide for five seconds. Hold the second slide for four seconds, and so on. If you have five slides, the final file size is the sum of those five slides.

And it's true that if you set the frame rate at 30 frames per second, QuickTime video can be very large, but in this case we were not setting a frame rate. When you set a frame rate to 30 frames per second—30 pictures in just a second!—five seconds of video will generate 150 frames. QuickTime is a file format. The final file size all depends on which codec you have used to export the file and what frame rate you used to play it.

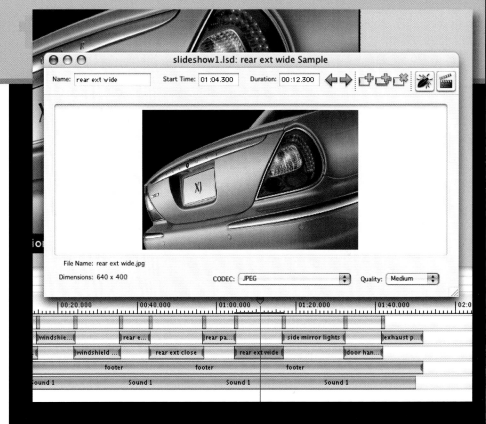

Our preference is to use LiveStage to create the QuickTime slide shows, but you can use Flash, which allows you to export a series of images as an .swf file. Once the .mov file is embedded inside the PDF, the .mov extension will tell Adobe Reader to use the QuickTime Player installed on the Mac or PC to play the series of "still image wired sprites" inside the .mov file.

Flash files inside a PDF work perfectly on a Windows computer, provided the user has Adobe Reader 8 and Flash installed.

Flash files do not work on a Macintosh computer using QuickTime 7.1.3, unless you adjust the QuickTime preferences to enable Flash playback.

For cross-platform compatibility, save your slide shows using the QuickTime format... NOT Flash!

Flash Playback on a PC

I am also often asked, "Why do you use QuickTime to play a slide show on a PC? Can't PCs play Flash files using Flash Player?" To that I say that on a PC, only Reader 7.0.7 or newer will allow a Flash file to be played if it is embedded in the PDF document. So, for cross-platform compatibility, it's best to use QuickTime to play the slide show. The .mov extension for the embedded file will tell the PC to use QuickTime to play the slide show inside the QuickTime file.

Flash Playback on a Mac

Another important point to remember is that if you embed an .SWF Flash file in a PDF, it will not play back on a Mac, unless you adjust the QuickTime preferences to enable Flash (if it recognizes an .SWF Flash file, Reader tells the Mac to use QuickTime to play it). Even if you have the latest version of Flash Player installed on your Mac, Reader tells the computer to ignore the Flash Player and use only the Flash playback capabilities of QuickTime. The big disappointment for everyone is that QuickTime will play only versions of Flash 5 or earlier. Another limitation is that the Flash file cannot have any programming that requires the user to enter information to initiate interactivity. On the Mac, Reader disables keyboard control to linked or embedded SWF and QuickTime movies. However, the mouse still works. Adobe is currently working on a solution to have SWF playback on the Mac using the Flash player just as it does on the PC.

Reaching a Decision

So, after considering all the limitations of Flash, we exported 72 QuickTime .mov slide shows from LiveStage, our preferred QuickTime-authoring tool, using the JPEG codec and the dimensions from the pictures in the PDF living brochure.

Creating the eBrochure

Volvo delivered the files for the printed brochure, in addition to several copies of the final printed product, on two DVDs. Volvo supplied two versions, French and English, in the QuarkXPress Passport format, which we converted to Adobe InDesign.

Once our designers had the text, logos, and pictures in our preferred page layout application, they had to redesign the page layout to convert the portrait format to the landscape format to allow the final

eBrochure to display full screen on a computer monitor. They set the page dimensions to 10 inches wide by 7.5 inches high and spent about a week altering the design so that some two-page spreads would be single pages, the font size would be increased to allow for easy reading, and the pictures would be either cropped or expanded to allow for the videos to be matched in register and in position.

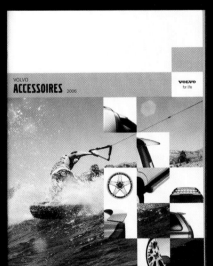

Before: vertical layout

After: horizontal layout

| S40 | V50 | S60 | V70 | XC70 | S80 | XC90 |

BIKE LIFT CARRIER

Volvo's bicycle lift carrier contains a gas strut that allows effortless lifting and lowering of most types of bikes. No need to remove the wheels when loading or unloading. Load bars (not included) can accommodate two lift carriers.

FIGURE 13-3 Full-motion 15 fps video is embedded into the document in register with the background picture.

Nontraditional Aspect Ratio for Video

Clients will often remark about the seemingly magical effect that takes place when the still image from the document turns into a video when the user clicks it. To create a smooth transition so that the movie dissolves over the top of the picture, you need to create videos that have the same aspect ratio as the pictures in the document.

If the eBrochure is launched full screen on a monitor set to its highest resolution, say 1024 x 768, the slide show video will need to have enough resolution to expand and enlarge along with the document. In this case, we had to create a larger video (about 30 percent larger than the original dimensions of the background poster frame created in InDesign) and then reduce it to place it into the document on top of the background image. When the final PDF is automatically launched to full screen, the video picture quality will still be clear, because at full screen it displays and plays at the original full-screen dimensions and resolution.

Some of the videos required full motion to demonstrate the product (**FIGURE 13-3**). Others needed only a few still images to convey the operation of the accessory.

In most cases, our programmers use Adobe Acrobat to insert one or two videos or slide shows, but since the Volvo living brochure had more than 70 slide shows, it was more efficient to embed and program the videos using InDesign, export the document, and then add the interactivity for navigation in Acrobat to create the rich-media PDF (**FIGURE 13-4**). If I had to make changes to the text or pictures of the original document, I could then just re-export the document or a range of pages to PDF and then replace those pages using Acrobat. All the rich media and the interactivity would remain intact for the replaced pages if the JavaScript programming were not contained inside the individual pages. This method is called document-level JavaScript.

At first we wondered whether there was a limit to how many videos one could put inside a PDF file, but after exporting the raw PDF document and checking it on both a Mac and a PC using Reader 6 and 7, it seemed that all the embedded video was working as it should. The final PDF file size was less than 40 MB, even though it contained pictures with a resolution of 120 pixels per inch (ppi) for printing purposes.

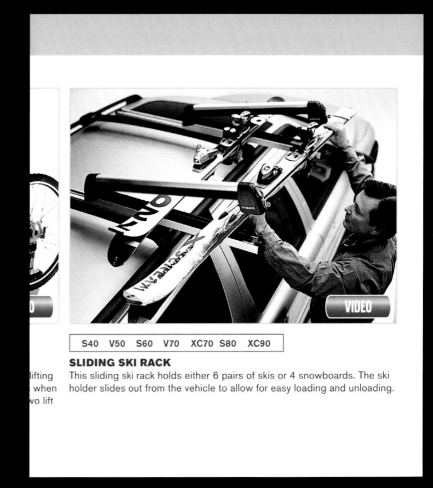

SLIDING SKI RACK

This sliding ski rack holds either 6 pairs of skis or 4 snowboards. The ski holder slides out from the vehicle to allow for easy loading and unloading.

FIGURE 13-4 The still-image slide show is embedded into the document in register with the background image.

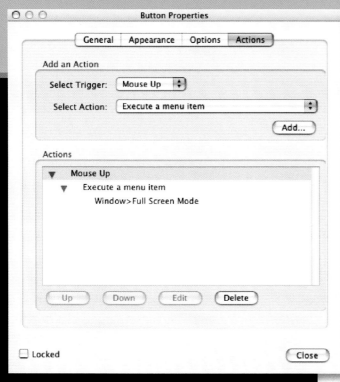

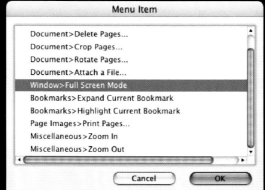

FIGURE 13-5 The Menu Item actions are available using the Button Properties dialog box in Acrobat.

Adding Interactivity

The videos were programmed to "play video" using InDesign, and the document was made interactive using Acrobat Professional. This involved applying the interactive code to the navigation bar at the bottom of the page. The text areas became interactive hot spots to allow users to alter the view (from full screen to the default view that displays the Reader toolbars), to turn the pages via the left and right arrows, to print, to escape, and to quit the document. To quickly navigate through the document, users could select options from a drop-down menu; specifically, they were able to jump to a particular page using a cascading menu to choose a category first and then select an item within that category.

You can use many different methods to program the document for interactivity. You can write JavaScript code and paste it into the buttons, or you can use Acrobat's Button tool and create a menu action without writing a line of code.

Adding interactivity with the Button tool is simple:

1. Draw a button on the page using the Button tool.
2. Double-click the button, select the Actions tab of the Button Properties dialog, and add a new action with Mouse Up selected as the trigger.
3. Click Add, then select any menu item; that menu item will be copied into the button.

If you select File > Print, for example, your button will open the Print dialog box when clicked. If you select Window > Full Screen Mode, clicking the button will cause the document to display in full-screen view. To have the button turn the page, choose View > Go To > Previous or Next Page. You can add multiple menu items as actions for your button (**FIGURE 13-5**).

Lessons Learned

Although it was quite a time-consuming procedure to re-create 72 videos to turn them into a slide show format, this case study proved it is possible to make a relatively small rich-media PDF document that quite clearly demonstrates how to use the Volvo accessories without full-motion video.

You can produce streaming QuickTime movies for cross-platform playback on Adobe Reader 5 and newer. If you know that the end user will have a PC and Reader 8 or newer, it is safe to use Flash files.

Conclusions

Consider the number of half-hour "how-to" TV shows that could be turned into "do-it-yourself" rich-media PDF eBooks. You would need only the closed-captioned text track from the TV program to use for text (with some additional information if needed). For the page layout you could extract the pictures for the eBook directly from the video and place them into InDesign. And thinking of this from a content point of view, you could create a printable interactive rich-media eBook, with all the content coming from one TV show.

For the rich-media video portion of the eBook, you could stream video into each picture from the TV station's Web site. To allow for smooth, continuous streaming, you would have to keep the dimensions of the video quite small if it were full-motion video. Or you could also provide a full-screen video-like version by following the same procedure as we did for the Volvo brochure. Just create full-screen slide shows using the frame grabs, and stream the files from a Web server into the document. As long as each video frame appears for a few seconds, you would have no problem streaming the pictures and the narration via the average home user's broadband connection.

Interactive
Virtual Reality
3D Rich-Media PDF

14

When you think of 3D, you might envision the blue-green or polarized paper glasses you wear in a movie theater to transform a two-dimensional image into a three-dimensional picture by providing depth of field. But in interactive rich-media PDFs, you have several ways to present a similar interactive experience where a user, via a mouse, can manipulate VR objects embedded in the pages.

In this chapter, I'll discuss the various file formats and methods to produce object VR photography and how the pictures can be programmed to become a VR object movie. I will also discuss a new format, U3D, which became available in Adobe Reader 7, and you will learn how you can use this type of rich media for product catalogs, training manuals, and much more.

Object Virtual Reality Photography

Object VR photography allows companies to present their products to a worldwide base of customers without physically shipping the product. The product can be animated to demonstrate how it works, and "hot-spot areas" of the object can link to a Web site to provide additional information. Object VR photography inside a PDF is redefining the traditional product brochure where a product shot is confined to one angle. Now, a customer can examine a product in three dimensions with the click of a mouse.

An object VR image can appear as a digital sequence of images presented from an image file format such as QuickTime VR, Adobe Flash, or animated GIF. The source images comprising the sequence are captured in specific intervals within a 360-degree rotation usually consisting of 12-shot intervals—one shot every 30 degrees. To view an object for higher- or lower-angle views, you move the camera to a positive or negative angle in relation to the landscape latitudinal view. The object can also be computer generated using data from a 3D modeling application where each frame of the object is rendered to produce a photograph.

QuickTime 3D Virtual Reality Objects

Although you can present VR objects in a PDF file in several ways, the oldest and most popular format is QuickTime VR. You'll usually find this format on CDs and Web sites that display products such as toys, museum pieces, or automobiles from different angles. Any object that can be photographed from the front, side, and back can be converted into a QuickTime VR movie; however, for the best effect, it is preferable to shoot a series of shots from the top and bottom of the object to get the full 360-degree effect. These sequential shots simulate the rotation of an object to provide an immersive image under the control of the user.

Creating a VR Object

You can create a photographic VR object from a series of photos shot at even steps around an object's center point. High-end digital cameras such as the Phase One camera are often employed so the pictures of the object also can be used for print and lower-resolution electronic media files.

Kaidan Magellan 2000/2500 Object Rig

Most digital still cameras can be connected to a TV monitor or computer to allow you to immediately see the captured image. The Nikon D1 series includes great cameras for image capture, and many consumer-level cameras, even digital video cameras, can produce professional results.

To maintain a visual consistency to the overall sequence of images, you must pay attention to the lighting for each captured interval. You can use either strobes or hot lights, although most photographers favor hot lights because they can view the glare and flares produced by the model on a computer or TV monitor before the shot is taken.

If you want the user to be able to see the bottom and top of your model, you need to shoot additional rows of images. The camera should be raised and lowered from the center point and the object rotated on a turntable while the camera captures the upper and lower portions of the image. An object turntable looks a lot like a pottery wheel. A low-tech method is to purchase a lazy Susan and manually index the turntable. You can also automate this whole photographic procedure by using motorized turntables and robotic arms that house computer-controlled digital cameras. Kaidan is one company that specializes in manufacturing a wide variety of turntables and object rigs that automate this process.

If you shoot an object against a well-lit blue- or green-screen background, you can also automate the removal of the background key color so the only touch-up work is the cropping of the support that holds the actual object.

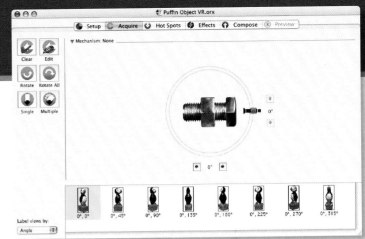

However, the resulting photographs captured using this method will require a great amount of post-production work to remove the unwanted background that will be visible in each frame. By cropping the image closely and then placing it on a white background, you can simulate the illusion that the object is rotating on the white page.

You then import the photos into a QuickTime VR–authoring application that places the pictures in a row of frames and seamlessly loops the images together. It works just like frames of film, but the QuickTime Player software allows you to grab a frame and shuttle it forward or backward. As you move your mouse from left to right to display a single image, it looks like the object is rotating. When the user moves the mouse up or down, the player skips to find a picture in a frame that corresponds to the view of the same side of the object, from a lower or upper row of images. This method simulates the rotating object floating freely in space.

The more views you have, the more realistic the virtual world becomes; of course, the number of total images will increase the file size of the overall image. You should always be aware of the careful balancing act between image quality and file size. It's important to compress the image with the correct JPEG settings, or it will look pixilated when it expands to fill the screen. Setting the image quality to Low should do the trick. If the VR is embedded in a PDF, the final size of the file can become quite large if there are many angles of view. In fact, it's not uncommon to see object movies that are more than 2 MB in size. It's important to plan for a reasonable target file size considering the dimensions of the object, the number of pictures, and the compression used to export the file. Also, will the object require top and bottom viewing? If not, you may want to include more horizontal views of the object to make the rotational motion smoother.

The Future of QuickTime VR 3D Inside Rich-Media PDFs

QuickTime VR object movies are pretty rare on the Internet. You will often find them on automotive Web sites or on Apple.com, but the widespread adoption of this technology has been slow. One reason is that the file size can become quite large if you want to make a smooth 3D simulation of more than 11 views of an object, which will provide only one horizontal row of pictures—no top or bottom shots. When viewing QuickTime VR object movies on Web sites, the user needs to wait until all the images have been downloaded before they can view and interact with the model.

With the wide adoption of broadband Internet connections and the Apple iTunes software, which requires QuickTime, you can now also embed QuickTime VR inside a rich-media PDF. This has opened a whole new realm for QuickTime inside digital publications that feature products and electronic catalogs. Imagine a PDF fashion catalog where you can rotate the model to view the clothes from the front, side, and back. Automobile eBrochures can provide a full 360-degree view of the car in full screen. Appliances, Apple iPods, arts and crafts, furniture, and virtually anything that requires a high-quality photographic image to sell the product can benefit from QuickTime VR 3D object movies.

Universal 3D: The Next Generation of 3D and PDF

You can also view a 3D image inside a PDF file using a new file format called U3D. In this case, instead of displaying a row of photographic images, the computer's processor renders a 3D model of the data in real time. You have unlimited views of the object from all sides, and you have the additional capability of exploding the model to see how the parts fit together.

The world of CAD 3D file formats is just like digital video codecs: You have many to choose from, and they are mostly incompatible. The U3D format allows 3D CAD applications to export the onscreen interactive experience for viewing inside Reader 7 or newer. In other words, you do not need to own the application that created the product. This allows the complex product designs used to manufacture the product to be reused inside documents used by sales, marketing, customer support, online promotions, maintenance, training, and many other PDF publications.

U3D has amazing potential inside PDF, but it has been a long, hard road getting it to where it is today. Let's look at the history of the development of this format.

Photo courtesy of Cousins-Currie

The 3D Industry Forum

In 2003, Intel researchers gathered a group of leading 3D graphics hardware and software developers to discuss establishing a common standard for sharing 3D content over the Web. They wanted a specification not just for representing 3D objects but also for efficiently transferring them and making them usable by a wide variety of applications and nontechnical people. The proposed standard, U3D, is intended to be "the JPEG of 3D data."

Additional discussions with corporate users of 3D graphics revealed a desire to repurpose the 3D computer models developed for product design for use in interactive training, documentation, marketing, and sales materials. With more than 30 members, the group decided to create the 3D Industry Forum (www.3dif.org) to help promote the creation of a common standard for sharing interactive 3D content.

The 3D Industry Forum wanted to ensure that this format would be recognized as a standard, so it chose Ecma International—a non-profit industry association of technology developers, vendors, and users—to compile the submissions for approval as ISO, ISO/IEC, and ETSI standards. You can find more information at www.ecma-international.org.

Adobe's Support for U3D

In November 2004, Adobe announced it would also support the playback of the U3D format in Adobe Acrobat 7.0 software and in PDF. With this commitment from Adobe, other key 3D application developers such as Bentley Systems, Right Hemisphere, and QuadriSpace began producing software that could create and convert other 3D file formats to U3D.

One of the first companies to embrace the format was Right Hemisphere, a leading provider of enterprise software for intelligent 3D publishing. Adobe licensed portions of its Deep View technology, which supports and translates more than 120 data types to a number of formats, including U3D.

Initially, the new format didn't catch on. Although the Right Hemisphere tools were robust, the cost of the software was out of reach for most early adopters. The marketing of the U3D standard was poor (and still is) because no one company wanted to spend money marketing an open source product.

It's not that there isn't a market for 3D applications—billions are spent on video games, CG movies, and other rich 3D media. And it has been predicted that by 2008, governments and corporations will spend more than $6 billion annually for computer-based training and simulation media. But the U3D file format has not been popular enough for the major 3D software manufacturers to commit the dollars needed to include the U3D export option.

Software Solutions Focused on U3D Publishing

There are several ways to create PDF files that contain U3D models. Acrobat 3D is the most popular software that allows you to create a U3D file and insert it into a PDF. But there are other tools on the market that create the U3D file and the page containing the model.

With Adobe's release of Reader 7, QuadriSpace developed the first set of inexpensive, easy to use, and simple 3D tools, called Document3D. This software allows anyone from highly trained CAD professionals to casual computer users to leverage the power of 3D and create informative and compelling documents. Unlike 3D CAD software, Document3D focuses on producing documentation and operates like a simplified version of Adobe InDesign and Acrobat 3D in one package. The Document3D suite of 3D publishing software includes Pages3D for creating 3D PDF files, and Notes3D for translating 3D CAD files to U3D.

3D and Page Design Using Document3D

Document3D provides a complete set of page design and layout tools that let you insert pages, create and place shapes on a page, add text to a page, import and place images and photographs, add headers and footers, set up page sections, create a master page, import 3D models, and position the views of the 3D model on the page.

What makes this application so special is that it also includes all the 3D tools you need to create animations from 3D models. You can animate the movement of individual parts or the movement of the camera position, and you can create buttons that activate an animation or tables that list each procedure as step-by-step instructions. These interactive elements are published as interactive buttons in the resulting PDF file.

Dynamic text fields allow you to create areas of text that update as the 3D view changes. You can use text like this to describe a selected part of the 3D model, offer detailed procedures, or switch captions as views are selected. See our CD-ROM for more examples of U3D models courtesy of QuadriSpace.

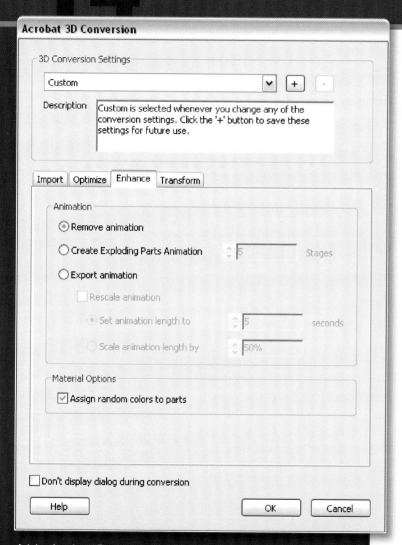

Adobe Acrobat 3D can translate CAD files into the U3D format.

Acrobat 3D

Initially, the biggest problem that the 3D community faced was converting 3D CAD designs to the U3D format for inclusion in Acrobat Professional. With the release of Acrobat 3D in 2006, it became a simple procedure to convert the many different CAD file formats to U3D and embed them in the PDF page. Acrobat 3D has all the functions of the professional version of Acrobat but also includes the 3D translators and the tools to make the 3D model interactive.

With U3D and Acrobat, you can distribute the fully animated and interactive 3D images from the original manufacturing data to a client or employee who requires it. You can import these 3D CAD file formats into a document with a simple format translation process while protecting the integrity of the design.

Acrobat 3D also allows you to control the model via Adobe JavaScript. You place form fields and buttons on the page and then program these buttons to control the converted U3D model for animation, shading and highlighting portions of the model. This document can then be sent to someone who has the free version of Adobe Reader 7 or newer to allow the viewer to make comments inside the document using Acrobat's commenting tools. Essentially, companies can develop up-to-date, accurate documentation that is easy to distribute back and forth via email.

Adobe Acrobat 3D and Adobe Acrobat 8 Professional allow you to embed U3D files into PDF documents.

Best Practices for U3D

U3D is a real breakthrough file format for industries that need to provide a virtual experience of their product, but unfortunately few people know it exists. Let's look at the average workflow for producing and marketing products and at the various ways you can utilize U3D.

Product Maintenance Manuals

In most companies, the engineering department creates a design and then releases it for product manufacture. The companies that utilize 3D CAD systems to accomplish this task typically use the models only for the design, prototyping, and analysis phases, usually within engineering departments.

The official release of the product for manufacturing, market release, and customer service functions are based on detailed 2D drawings. Therefore, all the downstream functions for representing the product definition in technical publications, product catalogs, manuals, and field service instructions are based on a limited 2D representation of the product.

The emergence of the U3D standard and its adoption in rich-media PDF publications can dramatically change this. Consider an automobile mechanic faced with the complexity of modern

cars and trucks, the sheer number of models, and then the changes from year to year. Today's mechanics already use computers to diagnose problems; these same computers could deliver 3D animations of repair procedures for particular parts so mechanics could learn new procedures as needed, right on the job. The service technician could break apart the 3D model of the engine to virtually experience the best procedure for accessing the part needing repair. Portions of the engine would become highlighted to provide part numbers for ordering replacement parts.

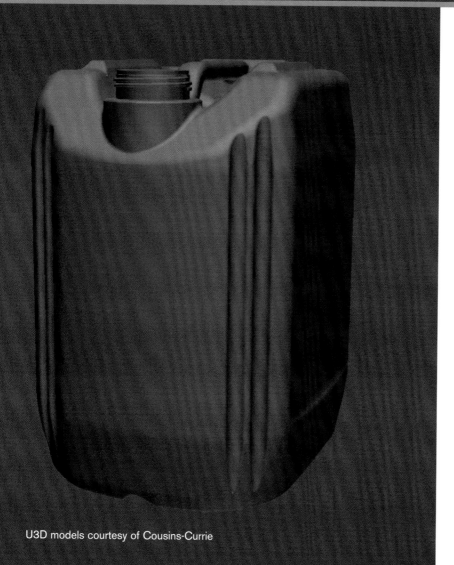

U3D models courtesy of Cousins-Currie

Animations for the appropriate removal of the engine and related components could guide the service technician through the corrective actions in the form of a 3D visual animation sequence.

With rich-media PDFs instead of printed manuals, field service engineers could carry portable computers to rapidly diagnose the situation, search and retrieve the appropriate product information, review field service instructions, and then take the necessary steps to correct the problem. Compared to the current use of 2D formats and documents, a U3D-enabled service manual would be much more efficient and precise in solving the problem.

The highest impact for leveraging 3D-based product maintenance and field service methods will be felt in industries that involve products where engineering complexity and rapidly changing technologies are most prevalent. Aerospace, defense, telecommunications, industrial machinery, energy exploration, shipbuilding, aircraft maintenance, and automotive are just a small sampling of industries that can best benefit from this technology.

Educational Manuals

The Internet has brought the classroom to your home, allowing you to take university courses online. However, it is sometimes difficult to convey a practice or procedure without actually holding the subject in your hand. For example, a human heart is a complex organ consisting of many parts that are hard to see unless the heart is dissected. Using U3D models, it is possible to remove or hide the layers making up the human heart and zoom in to explore it from the inside. Students could view the whole human body in this manner with a 360-degree view. Such virtual, on-the-spot training decreases training costs and improves training effectiveness, making it easier to reach larger audiences around the world.

How-To Manuals

3D documents can also come in handy for products that require assembly, such as large furniture products. It can be a daunting task to get all the pieces to fit together at home. Product manufacturers could provide technical support in the form of a downloadable U3D PDF that demonstrates assembly procedures via animation. Using the PDF materials in conjunction with a call center, the service technician could guide the customer through a step-by-step assembly or repair procedure via a telephone conversation.

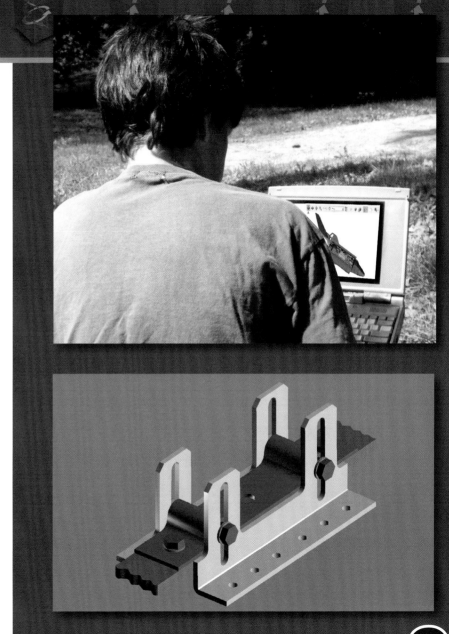

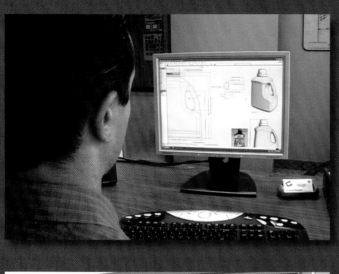

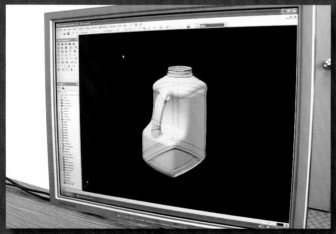

Photos courtesy of Cousins-Currie

Selling Complex Products

Using still photography to sell products and prototypes in direct-marketing print materials is common. Many manufacturers will make their promotional brochures available as PDFs on their Web sites to download and view on a computer monitor. U3D literally adds a whole new dimension, allowing 3D CAD/CAM (computer-assisted manufacturing) computer models to be leveraged to inexpensively create accurate 3D representations of the product. Simple-to-explain but difficult-to-visualize products would help people "picture it" online, in kiosks in showrooms and at exhibitions, and in CD electronic sales and marketing collateral.

In the real estate and construction industries, architectural CAD drawings for homes and condos could be ported to the U3D format and embedded inside an electronic PDF brochure to allow the user to "walk through" and experience their future home before it is built. Using U3D model "show-rooms" during the sales cycle would help the contractor convey ideas and alterations to customize the home to fully meet the customers' needs. Manufacturing companies that create molded products could send the "virtual product" to clients for approvals and feedback about the design.

Conclusions: The Future Impact of Virtual Reality Objects

Of the two formats described in this chapter, QuickTime VR object movies provide the best viewing experience if you are looking for realism, but the trade-off is the large file size resulting from the many views of images required for smooth movement. The look of U3D is not as high quality as the photographic capabilities of QuickTime VR, but U3D provides a good view of the product from all angles at small file sizes.

U3D will eventually become a standard format as widely adopted as PDF, MP3, and JPEG are today. For instance, as electronic media replaces paper-based media as a primary source of marketing information, all sales literature for both simple and complex products will include U3D or QuickTime VR representations. To be sure, kids who grow up playing 3D video games will expect the same experience with sales and marketing materials.

In fact, stock image libraries for still images and video are now quite common, so it's only a matter of time before shareware libraries of U3D or QuickTime VR products show up on the market so designers can inexpensively insert 3D models into their corporate presentations. In addition, products that require consumer assembly or configuration will gradually transition to 3D electronic-format assembly instructions.

Within the engineering and manufacturing industries, 3D will still be primarily used, shared, and viewed within proprietary CAD/CAM applications, but once the product has been manufactured, engineers will take advantage of the simple procedure to convert and reuse the computer models inside free U3D-compatible software such as Reader PDF.

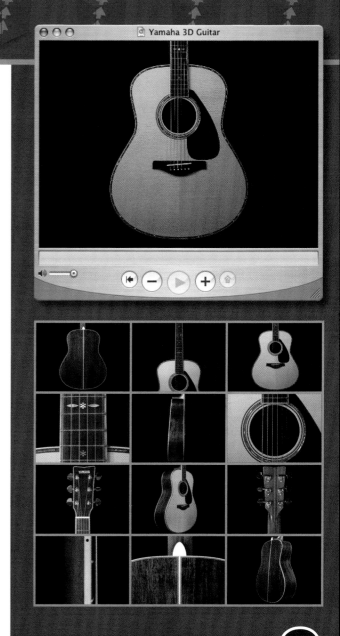

Virtual Reality Panoramic Photography

The term virtual reality is often used to describe an environment where you can experience a remote location via computer. The most common setting is in video games where you can navigate through a 360-degree scene. You can pan your field of view from left to right and from up to down to simulate standing inside the game. It's a virtual world. In the case of computer games, the computer generates the background, and when you pan the scene, the computer renders the corresponding field of view "on the fly."

15

Apple QuickTime VR panoramic photography is commonly found on Web sites that feature tourism destinations, hotels, real estate, museums, car interiors, or any scene that is best experienced from more than one angle of view. It's called *panoramic* photography because the virtual experience is accomplished by panning a viewer over several photographic images that have been joined, or *stitched* together, into one long 360-degree, seamless panoramic picture. You navigate the image by clicking and dragging your mouse over the picture, which in turn slides the image to display the desired field of view.

Photo courtesy of Jook Leung Photography

Navigation via QuickTime VR Nodes

Several scenes or locations can be combined so you can jump to another room, or node, within the QuickTime VR panoramic movie. As your mouse moves over the image, if there is a "hot spot" such as a doorway that links you to the next room, your mouse will turn into a pointer to signify that you can jump to the next location. Clicking the door will load the corresponding QuickTime VR photograph into the player.

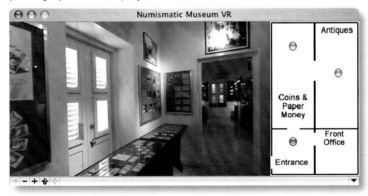

The Numismatic Museum in Aruba uses QuickTime VR Nodes to provide a virtual tour of the different rooms.

Since 99 percent of these VR tours appear on Web pages, the sizes of the images are small to allow for loading via dial-up Internet connections. This virtual experience is underwhelming compared to the large-screen video games we have grown accustomed to playing. But, when these same VR photographs appear inside a rich-media PDF file that launches full screen, the effect is quite the opposite, especially if the VR is a cubic movie.

QuickTime VR Cubic Movies

Wide-angle panoramic photographs have been around for many years, but recently, a new type of VR has gained wide acceptance; you can now look straight up and down as if you were floating in space. This view presents an entirely new perspective and is perfect for confined spaces such as the interior of a car. For example, you can look down at the armrest and straight up at the sunroof. The panoramic side-to-side view is not the priority in this case; more important is the whole 360-degree view. It's like you are floating inside a six-sided cube; hence the name cubic VR.

A full-screen cubic VR movie is a crowd pleaser when it's inside a full-screen, rich-media PDF file. Because you no longer have the limitations of a Web browser, you can author your movie to launch full screen, and your only limitation is the size of the user's computer monitor. Since the VR is embedded inside the PDF, users don't have to wait for the images to download, and they can "jump" from one location to the other almost instantaneously since all the nodes (linked scenes) have been preloaded. The large, full-screen images and the quick loading of sequential locations provide a compelling tour of a destination such as a hotel property. Still images of the hotel room leap out of the page to allow potential customers to look at everything from the carpet on the floor to the ceiling fan above the bed.

Photo courtesy of Jook Leung Photography

FIGURE 15-1 The Totally Hip LiveStage Pro user interface allows you to add wired sprites consisting of JPEG images to control QuickTime VRs.

Considerations for QuickTime VR and PDF

QuickTime VR operates differently inside a PDF file than inside a Web page because Adobe Reader overrides the QuickTime keyboard commands. The familiar QuickTime keyboard Zoom tools are not available unless you use a QuickTime-authoring application to embed zoom controls in the movie. So this is where QuickTime wired sprites can come in handy, since all navigation for QuickTime VR movies must be accomplished using a mouse. Adobe Reader 8 for the Mac was released with a bug that froze the screen if you tried to interact with the movie that was placed on the page, in full-screen mode. Wired Sprite navigation controllers allow you to get around that bug. Totally Hip LiveStage Pro allows you to add wired sprites that control the panning of a QuickTime VR (**FIGURE 15-1**).

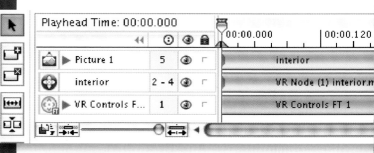

Creating a Panoramic Movie

Although the scope of this book is mainly intended to introduce you to the types of rich media you can utilize inside a PDF, I'll take some time to talk about QuickTime VR panoramic movies, which are quite simple to make if you are shooting outdoors and have the right tools. A digital camera, tripod, VR mounting plate, and the appropriate stitching software are all you require. The process is often automatic once you have all the lens settings and camera mount positions marked. Gone are the days when you had to shoot and process many rolls of film to get a good "take" for a VR movie.

Digital Cameras for Panoramic Movies

You can use several types of cameras to shoot panoramic images: one-shot cameras, two-shot cameras, four or more–shot cameras, and even digital video cameras.

One-Shot Panoramic Cameras

One-shot cameras use a mirror to capture the 360-degree image in a single frame. You then use software to "flatten" the captured donut-shaped image into the familiar wide-format panorama. You don't get the full up and down motion, but the process is foolproof because you capture the image in one shot so you don't need to stitch the pictures together. The software that comes with the camera lens mirror will dewarp the image and turn it into the final VR photograph.

Clockwise from top left:

360 One VR lens

SurroundPhoto mounting bracket with overhead mirror

Be Here 360° lens with Nikon camera mounted underneath

FIGURE 15-2 Nikon 990 camera

Dgital SLR camera with Kaidan tripod

Two-Shot Cameras

The IPIX Corporation introduced a patented process in which you join two fish-eye images to make a single cubic VR movie. To create the images, you take two back-to-back photographs using an 8 mm Nikon lens and a special IPIX tripod mount called an IPIX *rotator*. You then use IPIX software to stitch the two images into a seamless 360-degree sphere.

This process was the *de facto* VR standard for many years because of the simplicity of the software and the cubic 360-degree field of view. The quality of the image was perfect for the Internet because it did not require a high-resolution file, and the Nikon 990 camera became the VR camera of choice because it could utilize the 8 mm lens (**FIGURE 15-2**).

Four or More–Shot Cameras

When high-end digital SLR cameras hit the market at a reasonable cost, full-screen VR photographs started to appear on CDs and Web sites devoted to high-speed, broadband connections. They require shooting many images with a fish-eye lens or a wide-angle rectilinear lens, which makes straight lines in the scene appear as straight lines in the final photo. Rectilinear lenses cost more money, but the image looks less warped. You also have to shoot enough pictures to provide a 25 percent overlap in the image to allow the stitching software to be able to join the pictures into one seamless picture.

The stitching software does a marvelous job of combining the pictures, but it often requires a huge amount of post-production work with Adobe Photoshop to remove unwanted blurring in the image.

When shooting an outdoor location with moving people or cars, the overlapping part of the image often has blurring artifacts from the moving subjects that appear in one picture but are absent in the other. They appear as ghosts in the image. If you are shooting in a controlled environment, it is a simple procedure to keep moving objects out of the image; however, if you are shooting four or more pictures in outdoor traffic, it is a challenge that you can remedy only with extensive use of digital masking correction via tools such as Photoshop.

The resulting high-resolution images from these digital SLR cameras and wide-angle lenses are the mainstay of the VR industry today. They produce a cubic image that will show the top and bottom of the scene, and they are very clear inside a PDF file in full-screen mode. But you can get a high-quality VR movie in many less-expensive ways if you are willing to go with the standard panoramic VR image that does not allow for the top and bottom views.

Consumer Digital Cameras

To capture a panoramic image, you can use any digital camera, even a video camera with still-shot capabilities. But since you will not be using a wide-angle or fish-eye lens, you will need to shoot 8 to 15 images to get a 360-degree panorama. The camera must be as level as possible as you rotate it in a circle so the photographs will line up when you stitch them together later. Kaidan makes VR tripod heads with custom mounting brackets for a wide variety of consumer digital cameras.

When you take a series of images with standard lenses, you must be sure the images cover the entire 360 degrees and overlap by 50 percent. Kaidan tripod heads come with degree marks that guide you through taking shots at appropriate points, and it has models that come with detents (locks or levers) so the camera snaps into place at the exact position.

Brooklyn Art Museum, Eygpt Reborn Exhibit
Photo courtesy of Jook Leung Photography

Consumer Nikon camera with Kaidan tripod

FIGURE 15-3 Raw single-shot "donut" image from VR lens.

FIGURE 15-4 VR Worx QTVR stitching application.

Exposure Issues

One of the most frustrating moments of outdoor digital VR photography is when the sun goes behind the clouds halfway through your shooting process. If you are shooting manually, some pictures will become darker than others, and you will begin to see banding in the image where the pictures overlap. This is where the single- or two-shot process comes in handy because you can take one or two pictures quickly before the sun goes down (**FIGURE 15-3**). So, keep in mind that you need to pick the right time of day to shoot your images. If the sun is out, shoot at mid-day to keep the lighting even.

Stitching Together the Pictures

VR Toolbox (www.vrtoolbox.com) provides the latest QuickTime tools (**FIGURE 15-4**) that you'll need to stitch together panoramic movies and object movies (discussed in the previous chapter). The patents that IPIX owns covering the two-shot software seem to have become diluted by all the third-party freeware tools now available on the Web (which break the IPIX patents).

Once you have stitched together your images, you will need to convert them into Quicktime Cubic VR movies. We use a marvellous product from Click Here Design called CubicConverter (www.ClickHereDesign.com). If you want to link multiple VRs together, you can use another Click Here Design product called CubicConnector.

QuickTime VR and Rich-Media PDF Possibilities

If you look at the long history of virtual reality, you will see that it was an invention from Apple Computer via QuickTime. Before the birth of the Internet, when multimedia was distributed on CD, QuickTime was the hands-down winner for VR playback. As the Internet replaced CDs as the main source for digital media, QuickTime Player as a VR media player lost favor among photographers because it looked like Apple and QuickTime were losing the media battle to Microsoft's Windows Media Video and a new form of VR called Java, which did not require any plug-ins to play in a Web browser. When IPIX released a Java VR player, many Web developers abandoned QuickTime altogether.

But Apple kept plugging along and kept redefining the specifications to bring cubic movies to QuickTime, which resulted in the emergence of full-screen VR on Web sites targeted to users with broadband connections. One spectacular site to visit is called Fullscreen QTVR (www.fullscreenqtvr.com), which is hands down one of the best VR sites in the world.

It seems that the adoption of the QuickTime-powered iTunes/iPod has now removed the stigma that QuickTime once suffered on the Web by not being widely available, and the world is once again starting to embrace QuickTime VR photography.

Photo courtesy of Jook Leung Photography

Hotel Bedroom

The National Archives, Washington, DC

Library of Congress - Great Hall, Washington, DC
Photos courtesy of Jook Leung Photography

PDF eBrochures and Embedded VR

PDF eBrochures that promote travel destinations are becoming quite popular, and marketing managers are sending them as attachments inside email to clients who prefer an electronic copy of their printed brochure. A full-screen QuickTime VR tour of a cruise ship or hotel property is the next-best thing to actually being there.

In addition, most automobile manufacturers have decided to make their printed brochures available online via their Web sites as a PDF, and this is the perfect media in which to embed a full-screen VR movie of the interior of their automobiles. Many car companies already include a VR tour of their cars on their Web sites, so they can now re-export the panorama for full-screen playback inside the PDF.

VR in rich-media PDFs isn't limited to commercial areas; education can benefit from the technology as well. Electronic geography textbooks in rich-media PDF can provide students with a 360-degree view of the interior of The National Arhives and the Library of Congress in the United States, a dark rainforest, a breathtaking vista atop Mount Everest, or on other planets. Textbooks no longer need to be flat, two-dimensional, and boring. Thousands of QuickTime VR photographers have huge libraries of material ready for inclusion inside PDFs. Print publishers only need to look beyond traditional printed photographs and realize that an exciting world of virtual rich media is now possible inside their textbooks.

Conclusions

A good place to start your VR journey, and a great source of information for all things virtual, is at the International VR Photography Association's (IVRPA) Web site (www.ivrpa.org). The IVRPA (formerly the IQTVRA–International QuickTime VR Association) is an international association of professionals who create and produce interactive, immersive images that tell a story in a dynamic way. Their members include professional photographers, multimedia and Web developers, artists, enthusiasts, students, and companies that support VR technology with software and hardware.

The most common use of virtual tours is in the tourism industry, but they have many uses in educational markets as well. For example, those who are interested in the exploration of other planets can remotely visit Mars! Check out www.panoramas.dk/mars.html or our eBook where you can view an almost full-screen photograph that makes the virtual reality experience meaningful. Inside a rich-media PDF, the potential for directly marketing a destination or product via a virtual tour becomes compelling indeed.

Mars rover with cameras for stereo-VR photography   Photos courtesy of NASA/JPL-Caltech

VR photo of Mars

PDF Photography Portfolios

16

Models and photographers are constantly updating their portfolios with their newest look and style and will often carry a large print portfolio of their best photography with them to show clients. They will then leave behind a "comp card" or a few 8 x 10 pictures, which unfortunately often get tossed in with the mounds of print materials that inundate agencies and casting directors.

Most advertising agencies now prefer to use model and photographer Web sites to check out a sampling of the latest faces and images; if they see something that fits their needs, they make contact to request additional information or pictures. Maintaining a good Web site to demonstrate your talents to future clients can be a daunting experience for those who might be technically challenged, so some artists have found a middle ground. They utilize the direct-marketing approach using a PDF artist portfolio and the immediacy provided via the Internet.

Photo of Julia Eldridge by Paul Buceta

213

Case Study

Julia Eldridge pdfPicture Portfolio

Julia Eldridge is a former Miss Universe contestant, an artist and professional model who understands it is important to provide video and photography of herself in rich-media PDF so she can stand out from all the other models competing for the covers of magazines such as *Sports Illustrated*. She can email a rich-media PDF portfolio to art directors, publishers, photographers, sponsors, modeling agencies, art galleries, and anyone else who might be in a position to help her. "It's all in the presentation," she believes. I have included her art PDF portfolio on the book's CD-ROM as an example of how rich-media PDF can be used to present art, photography, and digital video to obtain employment. It's also good "raw content," perfect for the next generation of digital magazines.

Photo of Julia Eldridge by Glen E. Grant

Julia Eldridge Artwork Portfolio

Samples of Julia's PDF art portfolio can be seen here in these images and on the CD-ROM included with this book. Her portfolio includes a short video of her participating in the Miss Universe Pageant and some behind-the-scene footage that demonstrates how she creates her paintings of trees, fairies and dragons.

Photo of Julia Eldridge by Glen E. Grant

Tranquilisea · 40' x 48' · Pencil Crayon and Ink

4   Julia Eldridge - pdfPicture Portfolio   ◄   Index View Print Exit   ►

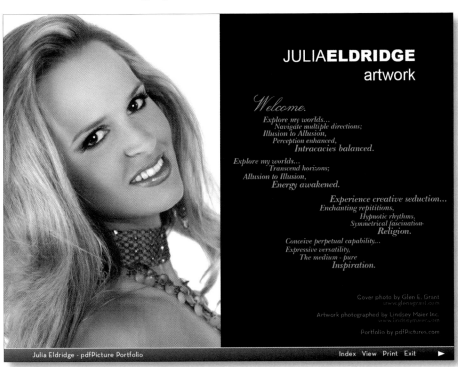

JULIA**ELDRIDGE**
artwork

Welcome.

Explore my worlds...
Navigate multiple directions;
Illusion to Allusion,
Perception enhanced,
Intracacies balanced.

Explore my worlds...
Transcend horizons;
Allusion to Illusion,
Energy awakened.

Experience creative seduction...
Enchanting repititions,
Hypnotic rhythms,
Symmetrical fascination-
Religion.

Conceive perpetual capability...
Expressive versatility,
The medium - pure
Inspiration.

Cover photo by Glen E. Grant
www.glengrant.com

Artwork photographed by Lindsey Maier Inc.
www.lindseymaier.com

Portfolio by pdfPictures.com

Julia Eldridge - pdfPicture Portfolio   Index View Print Exit   ►

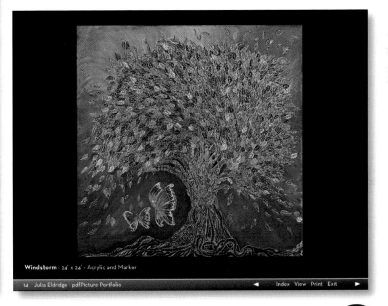

Windstorm · 24' x 24' · Acrylic and Marker

14   Julia Eldridge - pdfPicture Portfolio   ◄   Index View Print Exit   ►

Case Study

Virtual Reality PDF Portfolios

Jook Leung

Specialty: Virtual reality photography

Company: 360vr.com

Imagine yourself in Times Square on New Year's Eve at the stroke of midnight. You're dazzled by the sound of the crowds, the sight of confetti, and the warm kiss of your companion while you celebrate the coming year. It's a place many people see on TV from the comfort of their living rooms, but for award-winning photographer Jook Leung, it's an event to document for computer users around the world. Jook's specialty is capturing a virtual moment in time in 360 degrees.

The picture on the next page shows Times Square in New York on New Year's Eve, with more than 700,000 people gathered in the streets to count down the seconds while the ball drops to ring in the New Year. This photograph features Mariah Carey performing live on ABC's Dick Clark's *New Year's Rockin' Eve*.

Photo courtesy of Joek Leung Photography

Jook Leung with fisheye lens.

Live Action is Jook's Specialty

Since the process of capturing a 360-degree scene often requires shooting a series of overlapping photographs, any moving object in the scene can cause ghosting, doubling, and blurring when the overlapping pictures are eventually joined, or *stitched*, together. Jook's virtual reality photographs win awards because he has eliminated these unwanted artifacts from his images, and he actually thrives in scenes full of live action. Even in low-light situations that require a long photographic exposure, his images are frozen in sharp detail in all directions—straight up, straight down, and all sides.

He accomplishes high-quality photography by using a combination of his handheld, "human tripod" style and his Adobe Photoshop wizardry to provide a final stitched picture known as an *equirectangular image*.

This type of photograph is used to produce an interactive 360-degree Apple QuickTime VR cubic movie. QuickTime Player opens the equirectangular image and wraps it onto the inner surface of a cube so users can navigate the scene as if they were actually floating in the center of the cube.

Jook's work is best viewed in full screen because of the high-quality images he gets from his digital camera techniques. To present his work to clients, we produced a PDF portfolio with embedded QuickTime VRs of his best work so he could distribute it on a CD. Once out of the confines of a Web browser and a dial-up Internet connection, the visual impact of full-screen VR photography is truly astounding. Interactive rich-media PDF is perfect for CD because the disc can include the media players such as QuickTime Player and Adobe Reader needed to view the interactive PDF portfolio.

Jook usually deploys his QuickTime VR photography on travel-oriented Web sites, and because of bandwidth restraints, he keeps the dimensions of his VR photographs small for quick loading. To allow his work to be seen by as many people as possible, he also creates other formats of virtual reality such as iPix and Java that don't require the QuickTime browser plug-ins.

One of Jook's goals is to shoot travel destinations in virtual reality, and this is one industry where we have a lot of experience with our interactive PDF eBrochures. Our job would be to create a pdfPicture Portfolio, our brand of interactive PDF for models and photographers. By producing downloadable, interactive, rich-media eBrochures of hotel properties—the hotel rooms, pools, restaurants, and beaches—he can provide a better virtual tour for consumers who want to explore destinations using full-screen QuickTime VR.

This chapter presents a selection of his best equirectangular photography, but to get a virtual reality, 360-degree, rich-media view of these images, check out the companion interactive eBook included on this book's CD-ROM. I have also included Jook's entire 15-page PDF portfolio.

Jook Leung photographing "Tribute in Light" memorial in NYC

219

Getting the Shots

It's not a simple task to take a picture outdoors in the middle of winter with 700,000 people lining the streets. The evening in Times Square started with rain and snow, but the weather was fine in the final hours of 2005.

"I lucked out at the last moment and was the only photographer on the sound stage at midnight. The stage manager is a fan of my work, and when I asked him if I could get closer, he took me in tow and put me up there in the corner and said to me, 'I trust you'll know what to do.'"

Jook planned to use a stationary tripod but at the last minute decided to change his position to get closer to Mariah Carey. Because of this last-minute change to a handheld camera, he knew he had a good deal of stitching errors to fix later. He turned his camera in quick, rough, 90-degree positions trying to capture the peak moments in all four directions.

For these shots he used a Nikon D2x, with a Nikkor 8mm/2.8 fish-eye lens, F5.6 at 1/15 seconds, ISO 400, and Raw capture. The light level on the stage was pretty high, and the pictures were a stop overexposed. He extracted the highlight and shadow exposure in Photoshop CS2's Adobe Camera Raw from each raw file and blended with his custom Photoshop action HDRforDummies, which you can find at his Web site (http://360vr.com/HDRforDummies).

He stitched together these pictures and leveled them with Kekus Digital's PTMac, a GUI (graphical user interface) program based on Helmut Dersch's Panorama Tools. Jook explains, "If it weren't for QuickTime VR and Panorama Tools, my career as a photographer would end up as a boring one."

Collecting the Content

To create the pdfPicture eBrochure of Jook's VR photography, he sent me a good sampling of the VR images in the equirectangular format to use as still images, or poster frames, and to create the VR cubic movies to embed in the PDF.

The equirectangular images are quite dramatic to look at on their own, and I planned to use them as backgrounds with a button area to launch the full-screen QuickTime VR. Also, we imported the same equirectangular images into an application called Make Cubic to create a final QuickTime VR. Our designers then placed the background pictures and the VRs into Adobe InDesign to lay out the document and to make the QuickTime VR movies interactive.

Jook also sent us some pictures of his camera equipment because he wanted his clients to get an idea of the different gear that he uses to create the many different formats of VR. Jook's work includes simple table-top VR tripods and complicated camera rigs that can produce a very high resolution image in tight spaces.

New York City at dusk

Unlike a lot of award-winning professional photographers, Jook is a very easy-going guy and is a pleasure to work for. He shares his trade secrets with everyone he meets and we felt that a video clip of him introducing the portfolio would provide a good introduction to his pleasant demeanor. On one of his jobs, he took the added time to shoot a few minutes of raw digital video that shows him explaining the VR process, which we edited to a tiny 30-second video clip that would appear on the front cover of the interactive PDF (**FIGURE 16-1**). Since the VRs would require QuickTime for playback we decided to compress the video into the QuickTime format using the Sorensen codec.

We exported the final file that included the VRs and the video from InDesign (**FIGURE 16-2**) as a PDF and then opened it in Adobe Acrobat to add the JavaScript pop-up menu for navigation and the buttons for document interactivity (**FIGURE 16-3**).

FIGURE 16-1 Leung explains the VR process in a 30-second video clip on the front cover of the interactive PDF.

FIGURE 16-2
The final file included the VRs and the video from InDesign.

FIGURE 16-3 The JavaScript pop-up menu for navigation and the buttons for document interactivity were added in Adobe Acrobat.

Conclusions

Although the interactive PDF portfolio was for distribution on CD, the final file size was only 19 MB, small enough for downloading via a Web site. As Internet service providers increase their size limitations of email attachments, soon Jook will be able to email his PDF portfolio to anyone with a high-speed Internet connection, anywhere in the world.

PDF portfolios are starting to become quite common, but few provide the features of rich media such as video. Photographers should consider adding this feature to promote their own work as well as start offering it as a service.

Instead of handing the client a contact sheet or a CD of digital images, photographers should format the pictures in an interactive PDF portfolio so the client can use it right away for promotional purposes. To view a folder of JPEG images, the user will require some sort of picture viewer. If the pictures are nicely laid out as a PDF portfolio, its simple to use the free Reader to view the images and then email the portfolio to others who may be interested in the artist's work.

Photographers should learn to repurpose their skills so they can shoot video too. They can use the same computer they use to touch up photos to edit the digital video of the photo shoot. By combining still pictures from a photo shoot and a video clip into a rich-media PDF, a photographer can now offer something far different from the competition.

When rich-media magazines are as common as printed publications, the photographers who can provide all forms of digital content in one session—still pictures, video, and virtual reality—will be the ones most in demand.

Photo of Julia Eldridge by Glen E. Grant

QuickTime for Multipurpose Multimedia Playback

17

If you love shopping for cars on the Internet, you will likely have experienced video, Flash animations, and QuickTime VR tours of the interior and exterior of the cars. You can also embed these types of VR tours inside a PDF. In this chapter, you'll see two case studies in which we did just that for the automotive industry.

Specifically, you'll examine how you can best use Apple QuickTime to provide rich-media playback. If your rich-media PDF publication features a combination of several forms of multimedia, such as virtual reality photography and video, you should consider producing all the content in the QuickTime MOV format. VR, video, slide shows, wired sprite interactivity, and more are all available via this one media player.

I'll also discuss how to embed the media or stream it into the PDF to create bandwidth-efficient cross-platform PDFs and movies for playback on Macs and PCs.

In addition, I'll show you how to create multiple ver-sions of your PDF for delivery via email or Web downloading so your users can choose the appropriate version to meet their needs. Although some PC users may not have Quick-Time installed on their com-puters, QuickTime has become quite popular.

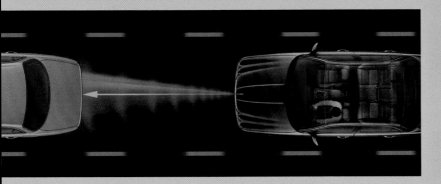

The Jaguar XJ Living Brochure

Martin Jeffery is in the direct-marketing business. His company, BrainTrain, is a full-service agency offering clients a variety of ways to communicate, including through self-mailers and brochures in print or through newsletters via email. Initially his business was creating direct-mail campaigns for his automotive clients, but Jeffery saw a future where PDF could provide a much more compelling experience using interactive rich media. He decided to name his own brand of interactive full-screen PDF the "Living Brochure," which could be emailed or downloaded via his clients' Web sites.

To take his brand to market, my company, pdfPictures, first made a PDF prototype for BrainTrain consisting of a video, a slide show, and a VR movie of a Ford automobile so Martin could present

it to a few of his direct-mail clients in the automotive industry. Jaguar and Volvo, which are owned by the Ford Motor Company, liked the prototype and agreed to become the first of many car companies to give his brand of rich-media PDF living brochures the "green light."

Luxury carmaker Jaguar had just released its new 2004 XJ model and was looking for something different to use for promotional marketing materials. Jaguar had a sizable mailing list of previous car owners and the email addresses of subscribers to its Web site. The available content we had at our disposal consisted of QuarkXPress files that were used to produce Jaguar's printed brochure and a DVD that contained four videos about the various features and capabilities of the car.

Martin and the marketing reps at Jaguar were concerned that the picture quality in the PDF wouldn't live up to the quality of the glossy 2004 XJ brochure. After seeing a few test PDF proofs that our designers produced, they were satisfied with the look of the PDF eBrochure pages. Their focus then shifted to the interactive content.

Jaguar had created a DVD to promote the Jaguar XJ, and this was mainly used at its dealerships for display on large plasma screens. The client was hoping I could maintain the high-quality video image inside the PDF. My challenge, therefore, was to keep the video's dimensions big enough to see the details of the car yet small enough in data rate and file size to allow for smooth, uninterrupted video streaming from a Web server.

The PDF also had to operate on an average home computer under the widely installed Adobe Reader 4, and the final file needed to be smaller than 2 MB–small enough to allow for download with a dial-up modem! Then, after the job was completed, everything needed to be translated into French. Not a simple job indeed.

In late 2003, at the time of this production, Adobe had just released Reader 6, but we decided too few people had upgraded to that version to allow other formats of media such as Windows Media Video to be included in the PDF. We were still living in a Reader 5 rich-media world, which would allow only QuickTime media to be streamed into the document from a Web server. The Jaguar reps were nervous that money would be wasted if only a few people could view the rich media in the eBrochure.

Versioning Is the Safest Route

After several discussions with the client about all the limitations, we decided the project would involve producing three versions of the Jaguar eBrochure. The first one was a "standard" version that had no rich media, although it would be highly interactive, with JavaScript menus. At 1.6 MB in file size, it would be small enough to email and would operate under Reader 4.

A second, "enhanced" version would also be 1.6 MB in size, but it would stream linked videos, slide shows, and VR photography from a Web server. Jaguar could email this version to customers as an attached file, but users would need Reader 5 or later to view the linked rich media.

The final, "full" version was to have all the video, slide shows, and VR tours embedded inside the PDF and would require Reader 6 or later. This version ended up being 33.6 MB in size, which was too big to email as an attached file, but Jaguar could distribute it on CD or via the Jaguar Web site.

Since the project consisted of cross-platform virtual reality and video content, users would need QuickTime 5 or newer to play the media inside the PDF. This gave my company the opportunity to create all the other rich media in the QuickTime MOV format and run everything under a single media player on both Macs and PCs, provided that a user had the required media player installed.

Previous Page   Index   Exit   Print   Display   Next Page

XJ8 with Sand interior. Shown with optional equipment.

Designing the Document

One of the nice things about converting printed automotive brochures is that many of them are already designed in landscape display. Cars are wide, and an overlapping centerfold of the portrait, two-page spread is unflattering to the curves of the car. Since the Jaguar print brochure was designed in landscape display, converting it from the print QuarkXPress file to full-screen PDF for computer display was relatively simple. Our designers imported the QuarkXPress document into Adobe InDesign and then made minor adjustments to the layout to allow the text in the document to be easily read on a computer monitor.

Designing the Interactive Navigation

There are several ways to approach the design and placement of buttons for navigation. When you send consumers an interactive PDF file that automatically opens full screen, most will find the experience a little shocking at first and ask, "What is this, a Microsoft PowerPoint presentation?" Without the Reader toolbar, the user will first try to figure out how to "turn" the page or exit the file. Everyone has become familiar with the back button in Web browsers, but interactive PDFs are something new.

I decided to take the "keep it simple" approach and instructed the design team to lay out the navigation using the words *next page* and *previous page* in the bottom corners. In that way, users would immediately recognize the book metaphor. *Index* is the table of contents, and *Print* is pretty straightforward. However, to change the view of the document from full screen to regular view, it was a toss-up between *Display* or *View*. I went with *Display*, thinking users would most likely relate to that term. (Over the years after several discussions with BrainTrain on the subject of navigation, I have settled on the word *View* to change the full-screen view and the word *Menu* to launch a JavaScript pop-up menu for the table of contents. Arrow icons now turn the pages.)

Many people think icons are part of the artwork. They just start clicking items on a page until something happens, and if the unrecognizable icon causes the page to close, they may find the experience frustrating; if so, you will lose them. In addition, if you use different types of rich media on a page, it can become confusing, with different icons for Flash animation, VR, and video.

I wanted the brochure to be easy to use, especially for people new to multimedia. Web pages have become complicated to use because designers try to provide something different to stand out from the rest. By contrast, a print brochure is easy to use; you just turn the page. So, I thought with eBrochures, simplicity in the navigation was our best bet.

We used InDesign to create the navigation text that appears at the bottom of the page, and then later I created the interactive navigation programming via Acrobat. In Acrobat, you can draw hot-spot areas over the text and then program them to perform a function using JavaScript. For example, the Index JavaScript pop-up menu allows the user to jump to any page or rich-media content in the document (**FIGURE 17-1**).

We completed the standard version with all the interactivity first and sent it to the client for approval. After a few revisions for typography issues, I got the go-ahead to add the rich-media content that was created simultaneously by our video and VR crew.

FIGURE 17-1 Pop-up menu with navigation.

Producing the Rich Media

Although Jaguar supplied the video, our company needed to create the VR photography. The car was so new it was not ready to drive to a photography studio, so we photographed the Jaguar XJ from eight viewing angles outside the Jaguar warehouse. After closely cropping around the car to remove the background, we placed the eight images of the car over a stock shot of a highway and then assembled the photos into a QuickTime VR object movie using the QuickTime VR authoring studio.

To shoot the interior pictures, the photographer used a Nikon Coolpix digital camera with a fish-eye lens. Lighting for VR photography can be difficult, as shown here by the raw shot of the interior of the car. After cropping and retouching to eliminate lights flaring in the windows, we replaced the view with a composited background of the harbor in Victoria, Canada.

Adding Interactivity to the VR

I sent the final VRs to the client for approval, and after a little bit of testing, the Jaguar marketing reps said the users might not know how to control the VR. Many people are unfamiliar with the built-in QuickTime controllers for clicking and dragging on the VR window to rotate the field of view. Using the "keep it simple" approach again, I decided to add control buttons, or *wired sprites*, to allow the user to rotate the car. I accomplished this using Totally Hip's LiveStage Pro.

Totally Hip LiveStage Pro user interface

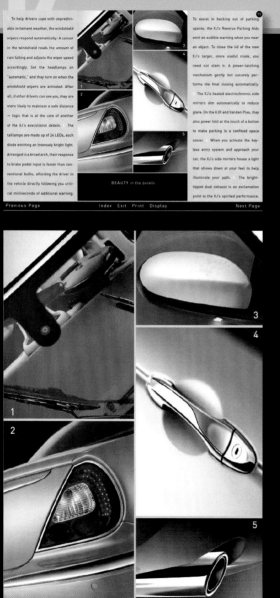

Combining Still-Image Slide Shows with Video

Although full-motion video can be compelling as a means to demonstrate the features of a car, the constraints of downloading large files from the Internet are a drawback. If the video is highly compressed, fast-moving images can cause pixelation, resulting in a blurry picture, especially if the video has large screen dimensions.

Whenever possible, I like to combine large still-image slide shows with MP3 narration in a QuickTime container. You can enlarge smaller images in the printed brochure and pan them to produce an animated slide show. Using the copy from the brochure, you can synchronize the narrated script with the pictures. You can then incorporate pictures, which in this case were not used in the final print brochure because of space limitations, into the slide shows. Just think about the hundreds of shots taken during any photo shoot that don't make the final version. Now you can use them to bring the pages of your eBrochure to life.

We used two pages of the Jaguar eBrochure to create two video slide shows. The still images came right from the QuarkXPress files used to make the printed brochure. Since the pictures were 300 dpi for print purposes, it was simple to zoom into the picture using Adobe Photoshop to create close-up still frames. You can do this, for example, by starting with a wide shot of the dashboard in one still and then dissolving to a close-up of the radio. Our programmer then used Totally Hip's Live Slide Show to create the movie, but you could use Flash. The final result looks just like video.

Combining Video and Still Images in a Single Window

The trick for succesful video integration inside a PDF is to make the video as big as possible but still allow for the small data rates required for real-time streaming via a Web site. It's simple to stream a slide show into a PDF page from a Web server, but it's a bit more difficult to stream a large video. Specifically, if the video data rate is greater than the user's Internet connection speed, the video will stutter. The solution is to make a large slide show that has a smaller video inside it.

The final Jaguar eBrochure has three videos. Each contains a smaller video placed on top of a still-image background. We captured still images from the videos using QuickTime Pro and then composited them in Photoshop to create a video background frame that was much larger than the final compressed full-motion video. We used the LiveStage Pro authoring application to join all the still-image background and the video foreground elements so they could exist inside a single QuickTime container file.

When the video streams from the Web server, the still-image background downloads first, and then the video streams into the top corner of the video window. You can also combine text to produce a QuickTime wired sprite movie. To create a French version of the eBrochure, we added a subtitle text track and synchronized it to the video to allow for language captioning. The user thinks it is just one big full-motion video when it actually consists of individual rich-media components that stream into the video window in sync. This method drastically cuts down the data rate and file size of the movie.

You can compare the result to something like the Weather Channel, where you have a small video in the top corner and the latest temperatures underneath.

Totally Hip's LiveStage
Pro authoring window

FIGURE 17-2 A Web page for downloading different versions of the Jaguar Living Brochure. Notice there are no Web browser navigation toolbars.

Resolving Web Wars

The simplest part of the whole process of delivering rich-media PDFs is Web site integration. Often a client's Webmaster will frown on outsiders encroaching upon their territory, fearing viruses, dreading password security breaches, and experiencing the general anathema of losing control. However, the simplicity of a PDF eBrochure allows you to take a "banner" approach. Just create a button or a banner, and ask the Webmaster to place it wherever it suits the look and feel of the site. Clients can then extend their marketing reach by putting the same banner on as many other Web sites as they can afford for the purpose of advertising.

In Jaguar's case, when a visitor clicks one of these banners, a new window pops up, and a Web page (called up from my company's server) opens to describe the three versions of the eBrochure. In case the user doesn't have the latest versions of Reader or QuickTime, the media player download links are there, with additional links to tech support (just in case).

For the Jaguar eBrochure, we created a Web page that would allow the user to learn about the different types of versions available (**FIGURE 17-2**).

Forcing the PDF to Download

One of the biggest problems with PDF documents on today's Web sites is that Webmasters link directly to them. This access method causes our PDF files to open in full-screen mode inside the user's browser; this means that the toolbars will not be visible in the browser window, which makes the PDF difficult to read and navigate (**FIGURE 17-3**). Make sure you put some text on the Web page to help your user to force it to download, such as a link with the words "right-click here and save target".

It is best to get your Webmaster to write a script that forces the PDF to download to the client's computer outside the browser window. This can be accomplished by a PHP script or an ASP script depending on the type of server you are using. You can also configure your Web server to force download files that have been placed in a specified folder.

When the user clicks on the link to download the PDF, the browser will display a choice to open the PDF file in Reader for viewing or to save it to the user's computer (**FIGURE 17-4**).

It's simple to create an email message with links to the download script that forces the PDF to ignore the Acrobat plug-in and prompts the Windows user to save the file to the user's hard drive. Instead of the PDF being attached to the email, one click on the email's Web link forces it to download from the Web server. Since the standard and enhanced versions of the Jaguar eBrochure were only 1.5 MB in size, the user could also email the eBrochure to others as an attachment. It's viral marketing.

FIGURE 17-3 PDF files that open in a Web browser are not full screen.

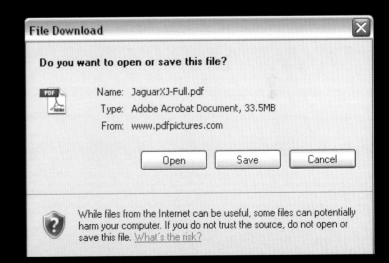

FIGURE 17-4 The File Download window allows you to choose the method of displaying the PDF file outside of the browser. If you open the document, it will not be saved on your computer.

Case Study

17

The Volvo S40/V50
Living Brochure

M artin took the Jaguar XJ living brochure to Volvo with the hope that Volvo would be interested in having its printed brochures formatted for electronic delivery as well.

The marketing reps at Volvo could see the potential and decided to convert several of Volvo's printed brochures to the living brochure brand of interactive PDF. One of the first was the Volvo Accessories brochure, which is featured in Chapter 13, "Rich-Media Slide Shows."

The Volvo reps liked the features of the Jaguar living brochure but wanted enhancements in regard to the size of the video and the virtual reality. Volvo released a new sports car called the Volvo S40, along with the companion station wagon V50, and was looking for an electronic marketing tool that would impress the younger crowd. Specifically, the Volvo reps wanted almost the entire living brochure to be interactive, and they wanted the virtual reality to be full screen.

Collecting the Content

Instead of supplying us with finished videos, Volvo sent us a Betacam SP copy of its stock footage library used to create training DVDs and other marketing materials such as TV commercials that broadcast around the world. Volvo cars are known for their safety, and the company has quite a selection of animation and video footage of Volvo cars driving on all sorts of road conditions and in crash-test situations. We planned to use this raw material to create the video elements of the living brochure. The project would entail narrating the text from the printed brochure and editing the stock footage so the still pictures would come to life as video. Users would read the text and then decide whether they wanted to view the corresponding video and animation.

The print version of the Volvo S40/V50 brochure was a QuarkXPress document in portrait format. Volvo had copies of the QuarkXPress files sent to us from Sweden so our designers could reformat them for full-screen landscape display using InDesign.

Since we had problems with floating windows on Macs using Reader 6, I decided to present the videos on the page in register with the background still images. Users would click the picture, and the video would play on top of the corresponding image or text. The embedded full versions would work on Reader 6 and newer on PCs and Macs, so I decided not to produce a linked version since the majority of users were downloading the full version in which all of the media is self-contained.

Volvo's advertising agency supplied me with the final narration on a CD in .aif files, and I edited the stock video to match the words. That part was fairly simple to do. The hard part was cropping the final video to match the corresponding size of the picture in the eBrochure. I asked the designers to keep the same look and feel as in the printed brochure; therefore, most of the final eBrochure pictures were not in the 4:3 aspect ratio used for TV playback. Using the final dimensions of the various pictures as a reference point, the designers cropped the finished videos using Autodesk's Media Cleaner Pro during compression to the final delivery codec. Once again I chose QuickTime as the file format because we were including VR photography, which would require QuickTime for playback. We used Sorenson 3 as the compression codec, which is good for cross-platform use and is excellent for video playback when using nonstandard dimensions that need to match the video frame to the picture.

 Tip: MPEG-1 video performs poorly unless it utilizes a 4:3 aspect ratio.

Capturing the VR

To create the VR photography, our photographers shot the interior and the exterior of the car using an SLR high-resolution Nikon digital camera.

To produce full-screen QuickTime VR movies of the interior of a car, you need to capture the images at the highest resolution to see the detail in the leather of the seats and the text on the dashboard. In addition, you must time the camera for a long exposure because you cannot use a flash; if you do, you will spend hours in Photoshop getting rid of the glare. You also need a fish-eye lens so you can capture the bottom of the seats and the roof in one shot.

The fish-eye photos are stitched together using PTMac (www.Kekus.com) and the final equirectangular image is converted into a QuickTime Cubic VR using CubicConverter developed by Click Here Design.

The real impact of this eBrochure is that the VR photography will replace the full-screen background images when the user clicks the picture. Especially on a widescreen cinema display, it is quite an awesome experience to navigate around the inside of the car and to look straight up and down in full-screen mode.

Lessons Learned

QuickTime gave us the capability to provide virtual reality tours of the interior of the cars, and QuickTime wired sprites allowed video, JPEG stills, text subtitles, and MP3 audio to reside in one file.

The final 22-page full Jaguar living brochure was only 34 MB in size, and the Volvo living brochure was 47 MB. The Jaguar eBrochure was smaller only because the slide shows and wired sprite videos took up less space compared to full-motion videos of the same dimensions.

If you create any rich media that uses floating windows for display, don't expect it to work properly on Macs in Reader 6 in full-screen mode. You will only hear the audio. The Mac market is not huge, but Mac users love to experiment with new media. It's best to present the video on the page instead having the video float over it if you are unsure of what version of Adobe Reader the end users have installed on their computers.

Since my company was hosting the Jaguar eBrochures on a dedicated Web server, we could track the Web page to see which versions were popular.

Downloading PDF

Download statistics and Reader requirements.

STANDARD	ENHANCED	FULL
Requires Adobe Reader 4 or later	Requires Adobe Reader 5 or later	Requires Adobe Reader 6 or later
No rich media	Linked rich media (QuickTime only)	Embedded rich media
JavaScript interactivity	JavaScript interactivity	JavaScript interactivity
No attachments	No attachments	Attachments allowed (Reader 7)
No U3D	No U3D	Supports U3D (Reader 7)

Download statistics 2003

Standard: 33%	Enhanced: 33%	Full: 33%

Download statistics 2006

Standard: 30%	Enhanced: 20%	Full: 50%

Surprisingly, in late 2003, we saw a close three-way split. One-third of the visitors downloaded the standard version (which required Adobe Reader 4 or later), one-third downloaded the enhanced version, and the other third downloaded the full 33 MB version.

Over the years, as users have upgraded to rich-media versions of Reader 6 or later, and as Internet connection speeds have increased, we are now seeing that the numbers for similar rich-media eBrochures have changed: 30 percent of users are downloading the standard version, 20 percent are downloading the enhanced version, and almost 50 percent are downloading the full version. Although the numbers for downloading the eBrochure with linked media have subsided, that version is still popular for emailing as an attached file. For almost all our new projects that feature short video clips or audio clips that do not require email capabilities, we no longer create a streaming, linked-media version. In those cases, 30 percent of users are still downloading the standard version, and 70 percent are downloading the full version that contains all of the rich media embedded in the PDF file.

Conclusions

BrainTrain's CEO Martin Jeffrey believes email capabilities have great potential for his direct-marketing initiatives. He sees a future where permission-based direct marketing via rich-media PDF will gradually supplement and directly compete with email newsletters. Broadband has arrived, and it allows the audience to download any desired document from the Web, disconnect from the Internet, and print it. Prospective customers can now take a printed eBrochure with them on the road—or if they're in the market for a new car—into the auto showroom. Print the 10-percent-off coupon from the eBrochure, and cash it in for your next tune-up!

As the publishing and advertising industries gradually transition to electronic PDFs for promotional materials, they will have to form alliances with producers who can deliver the rich-media content. Producing interactive wired sprite video and full-screen VR requires a specific set of skills and tools, which at this time are mainly used for producing content for Web pages. Flash-enabled rich-media PDF will soon become popular and provide the platform for video producers and VR photographers to expand their scope of clients and business opportunities.

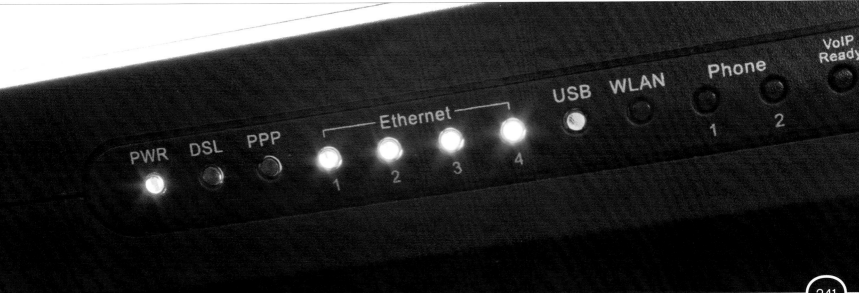

Flash SWF

18

When Adobe purchased Macromedia for more than $3 billion dollars, the industry wondered what its motivation was. The jewel of the deal was Macromedia Flash and control of the file format Macromedia had created: the SWF specification. Together they created Acrobat 8 and finally Flash worked perfectly inside a PDF file on the PC. Now, SWF is a worldwide standard for animation inside Web pages, cell phones, and even the Sony Playstation Portable device.

According to Adobe, the Flash plug-in is installed on more than 94 percent of computers in the United States, which makes it fairly safe for content creators to produce Flash-based media that can be viewed by almost everyone in the United States.

Although Adobe Photoshop is a popular moneymaker, Adobe Acrobat and the PDF server products are the breadwinners for Adobe, which means Adobe now controls the majority of software for both the print and Internet industries. Now that Adobe owns Flash and the SWF specification, both formats are working in harmony on the PC and Adobe believes the future of the Internet is Flash working beside and inside PDF.

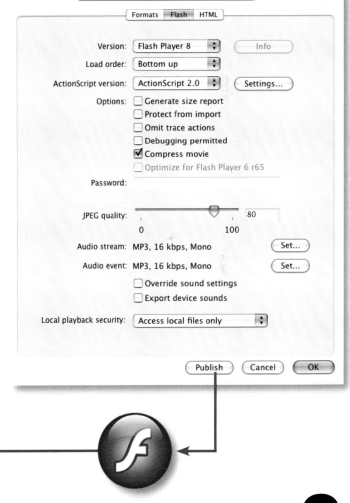

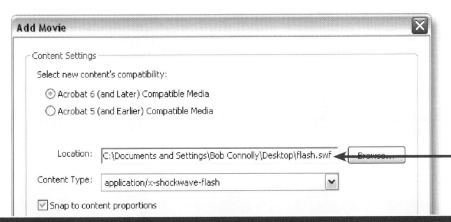

18

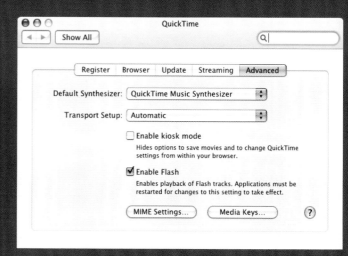

FIGURE 18-1 QuickTime preference panel for Mac showing the selection check box for enabling playback of Flash tracks.

SWF Becomes a Standard

As mentioned in Chapter 3, "Adobe's Trials and Tribulations Toward Rich-Media PDF," Flash has its roots in Macromedia Director, which was at one time the undefeated champion of applications used to produce interactive CDs. Director could animate bitmapped graphics, but unfortunately the file sizes it produced were large and unsuitable for the Internet. So, Macromedia developed a new export file format and media player called Macromedia Shockwave. Shockwave compressed and played the Director files specifically for the Internet, but the files were still too large to download via dial-up connections.

Therefore, utilizing the Director timeline approach, similar code, and a bandwidth-efficient vector-based graphic engine, Macromedia adopted a little brother for Director to produce files small enough to load quickly via a dial-up connection.

That product became Flash ("download in a flash!"), and its file format was .SWF.

SWF became popular, and even Adobe utilized it as an export format for Adobe Illustrator, for Adobe After Effects, and for its own SWF-authoring product called Adobe LiveMotion. Unfortunately, LiveMotion is now discontinued. (It was so simple to use!)

Apple Computer licensed the SWF Flash Player capabilities for its QuickTime Player but for some reason stopped upgrading SWF at Flash 5 and with its release of QuickTime 7.1.3 Apple turned off the capabilities of Flash inside QuickTime because of security issues discovered in early versions of Flash. You should consider this important limitation when creating rich-media PDFs that will include Flash.

Flash and PDF

Adobe shapes the PDF specification to suit its goals, but the Flash SWF specification caused the company major headaches. Before the purchase of Macromedia, on the PC Flash would work intermittently inside a PDF file depending on which version of Flash Player and Adobe Reader the user had. It was a real nightmare with each new version of SWF and PDF. Now that Adobe controls both the PDF and SWF specifications, they have designed the formats to work together.

When Adobe released Reader 8, the world of interactive rich media inside a PDF file took on a whole new dimension for the PC world. Not only does it work properly, but instead of PDF being a one-way street where the Flash rich-media data streams into the PDF file from a Web server, you can now submit data to a Web server via Flash without relying on QuickTime to play the Flash file. The latest versions of Flash play perfectly. Now, you can embed whole Web sites created in Flash inside a PDF. This allows Flash to live outside a Web browser and function just like a Web site in a PDF. It's now just a waiting game until the world upgrades to the latest version of Reader to experience this synergy.

Unfortunately, the Mac world cannot experience the advanced features of Flash inside a PDF because Flash playback is available only via QuickTime if the user turns on this capability manually using the preference settings inside QuickTime Player (**FIGURE 18-1**), and it is limited to Flash 5 files because Apple has not updated QuickTime to support the latest version of the SWF specifica-

tions. Adobe is currently in the process of re-writing reader so that it does not rely on QuickTime for Flash playback.

Mac users can still author their productions to include Flash for Windows. We have included many examples of Flash animations in the following chapters but have restricted most of them to only play on Windows. The restricted Flash files require either a fast processor that QuickTime is not capable of playing smoothly or they contain code that is not recognized by Adobe Reader 8 for the Mac.

In the following chapter, the cartoon characters will animate if you are using a windows computer. If you are using a Mac and attempt to play the file using QuickTime, you will be presented with a warning box notifying the user that Adobe Reader "Cannot play the media clip because there is no player available that can play the media while satisfying the author's intentions as well as your security settings" (**FIGURE 18-2**). When Adobe rewrites Reader to play SWF files on the Mac using the Flash Player, the user will be able to experience the animation in these restricted files.

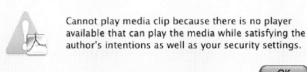

FIGURE 18-2 Adobe Reader's media clip warning.

18

Tip: If you want to create a cross-platform PDF that uses animation, it is wise to create a rendition of your Flash file using QuickTime wired sprites so that Macintosh users can experience a similar animation in a Mac-compatible format.

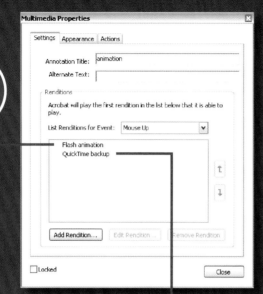

Beyond Flash 5 for a Windows-Only World

Although you may be tempted to create some really cool Flash content to dazzle your audience, don't expect everyone to have Reader 8, which can play a native SWF file on a PC. Also, remember your Mac audience. Consider using QuickTime wired sprite renditions to replace your Flash files on the Mac.

If you are not worried about producing a cross-platform PDF and think your product is so compelling that users will upgrade to the latest version of Reader 8 or newer to play your Flash files, the Windows world is your oyster.

If you are into database-driven content, keep in mind that PDFs allow for all sorts of cool applications such as Flash message boards, ecommerce, chat services, and advanced games—virtually anything a Flash-based Web site can do, you can do in a PDF. And if you are into Flash video, you can also use the latest high-quality video codecs that offer alpha channel support for keying video over backgrounds.

To play advanced Flash content, PC users must upgrade Reader to at least version 8. But users are slow to upgrade their software unless they see a reason to do so. I estimate that it will be at least three years until a good majority of the population has upgraded to a version of Reader that can play native SWF files. So, Adobe, Apple, or some other publishing company needs to create some really compelling rich-media Flash products such as rich-media PDF magazines or games to motivate users to upgrade to the latest version of Reader.

If you are in a situation where you know your audience and the technology they use—for example, they had to sign up to receive your specific product such as a rich-media PDF newsletter—then it is a perfect opportunity for you to provide them with the latest Flash-enabled PDF technology. If you adopt this business model of a subscription format that requires the latest version of the free Reader, you might find some success. You might also consider using the proprietary Zinio Reader, which is popular with magazine publishers; it just requires a special download to view its PDF files.

If you are new to Flash, be prepared for a steep learning curve if you want to create some fancy effects with it. The ActionScript programming language is well beyond the capabilities of most desktop publishers. If you just want to create a simple slide show with audio, the Flash authoring program has a template all set up for you that you might want to try. Full-screen narrated Flash slide shows in a PDF file are quite remarkable to most people who are used to viewing bloated Microsoft PowerPoint presentations.

Now that Adobe owns both PDF and SWF, expect to see some exciting new Flash applications such as Adobe Flex being utilized to add electronic commerce to rich-media PDF publications.

You can produce SWF-based applications that run inside PDF that can take advantage of advanced database-driven services for managing data interactivity.

Traditional Web browsing is constrained by page-based HTML programming where there is limited request/response-based data access. Flex applications provide a more seamless user experience by utilizing powerful data services that synchronize data and support real-time data push. This allows the PDF to "live" and allows for updating on the fly every time you open up the PDF.

Messaging capabilities enable more robust applications that continue to function after network connectivity is lost and allow multiple people in different locations to browse or chat in the same application. These features, plus the ability to seamlessly integrate audio and video, open the door to new ways of interacting with your audience.

Flash Story eBooks

19

The workflow for traditional cel animation has changed since the adoption of computers to draw the graphics. Some artists are starting to teach themselves how to use Adobe Flash and other applications that can generate SWF files, which allows them to create animation in their home studios and then email the final products to their clients.

In this chapter, you'll see how one person is using his traditional hand-drawn artistic talent in combination with his expertise in Flash to become a much-sought-after freelancer with a unique vision of the future.

Mike Hogue

Animate Your Designs
Using Flash

CALL FOR HELP

Mike Hogue
Flash Animator & Artist

CALL FOR HELP

Jinx the Black Cat

M ike Hogue is a graduate of the Classical Animation program at Sheridan College in Canada, where many of the top animators in the world learned their trade. After graduating, Mike worked at 20th Century Fox in feature animation as an "in-between artist" on the film *Anastasia* and advanced to be an assistant animator on the animated space epic *Titan A.E.*, which mixed hand-drawn animation and computer animation.

He moved from that studio to work as a cinematic computer animator at a Nintendo video game company. It was during this phase of his career that Mike decided to become a freelance animator to use his expertise in traditional hand-drawn animation with Flash to work with other animation studios. This independence provided the freedom to create his own characters and bring them to an even wider audience via the Internet.

He decided to start his own company, Sketchbook Animation (www.sketchbook-animation.com). Since then, he has worked closely with award-winning studios such as Nelvana and Studio B in Vancouver, Canada, to produce Flash animation for weekly TV shows and DVD projects. Using Flash, Mike is able to work from home and upload the tiny Flash animation files of his work to various production studios located all over the world.

His experience in Flash has also made him a well-known TV personality through his regular guest appearances on *Call for Help* on the G4Tech-TV digital channel, which is hosted by Leo Laporte. In addition to the freelance animation work and TV tutorials, he also makes time for personal projects. He has decided to create, develop, and market via the Internet, his own interactive cartoon character called Jinx the Black Cat.

jinx *theblackcat*

Collecting the Content

Mike submitted a few scenes from his Jinx the Black Cat project to allow us to experience a glimpse of the future where children's story eBooks come alive to provide hours of entertainment. Downloading, reading, interacting with, and printing them—all inside one Flash-enhanced rich-media PDF—are only a click away.

He first sketches his characters on paper to fine-tune the designs, which also helps him work out the personality of a character. Drawing these poses also allows him to see whether the design will move properly when animated.

Bringing some of these sketches into the Flash application, he then creates the cat as a vector-line design so he can later animate it. Jinx consists of 18 main parts, which are all animated on their own layers. Everything from Jinx's eyes, body, and tail is a separate piece. Mike can control the position and transition of each part from one pose to the next. Most of these parts are black, which allows Mike to perform some visual tricks to make Jinx appear three-dimensional. The combination of all these elements is what creates the illusion that Jinx is alive.

Mike brings the personality of this cat to life through realistic animation poses. Like many professional animators, he first observed the mannerisms and personality traits of animals and people in real life. Jinx is a typical cat. He sleeps a lot and likes attention when he wants attention. He's curious and cautious, which can lead to embarrassing situations…but he does his best to keep his cool.

Since Mike animates the character using two-dimensional Flash-based vector graphics, he enlarges the animation to fill the entire screen without degrading picture quality, provided the movement of the larger images remains at a minimum. Panning the scene or sliding backgrounds can cause the animation to jerk as the computer attempts to redraw the whole screen. Character animations in the foreground are usually no problem.

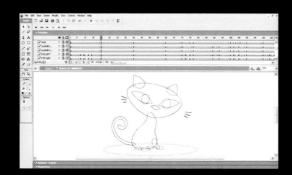

Playback Issues

Mike emailed me the individual SWF files in the Flash 5 format to include in the companion eBook and to allow for playback on Macs. Adobe Reader uses Apple QuickTime to play all rich media on the Mac. But at this time, QuickTime can play only those SWF files that are Flash 5 or older and the QuickTime Flash preferences setting must be turned on.

Another problem I had to deal with was that early versions of Reader before 8 can't play embedded Flash files on PCs. To make sure everything would work in a cross-platform situation for this book, I saved the Flash files in Flash 5 format. Therefore, Reader can read the .SWF extension and force QuickTime's built-in Flash Player to play the animations in QuickTime Player.

Minimizing Bandwidth Using Vector Graphics

The file size for each SWF scene was smaller than 500 KB but created the illusion of bandwidth-intensive, full-screen, high-definition video. Instead of exporting the scenes as video and joining them using video-editing software, as is usually done for TV production, I placed each scene's SWF file on a separate page to provide a storybook experience. The user interacts with each scene and then "turns" the page to continue the story. It's also possible to link the SWF files into one long animation to provide a traditional TV-viewing experience inside a single-page PDF, but for the companion eBook, we wanted to provide an example of what it would be like to navigate backward and forward within the story.

Dynamic Media: Music, Video, Animation, and the Web in Adobe PDF

FIGURE 19-1 Flash SWF files are placed over corresponding images on the rich-media layer.

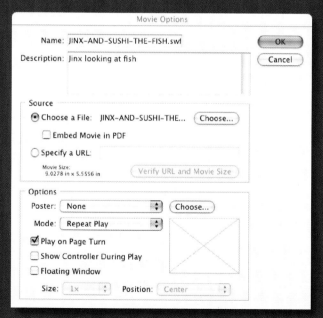

FIGURE 19-2 You can set the SWF file to launch when the user clicks the picture or set it to play on a page turn.

Creating the PDF Document

One of the drawbacks with Flash media (unless it's FlashPaper) on Web pages and in PDFs is that you cannot print it. Adobe Acrobat will generate a low-resolution "poster" preview of a Flash file inside a PDF if you set the Poster Setting to "Retrieve poster from movie," but the best way to present the page to the user is to create a high-resolution image as the background for viewing and printing. As such, Mike used Flash to export high-resolution 300 dpi JPEG images of each scene for use in the printed book and the companion eBook.

Then, using Adobe InDesign, our designer placed each image in a page just above the background layer, and then placed the corresponding Flash SWF files over the top in the rich-media layer (**FIGURE 19-1**).

You can set the SWF file to launch when the user clicks the picture or set it to play on a page turn, and depending on the speed of the user's computer, it usually takes only a few seconds to call up the QuickTime Player on the Mac or the Flash Player on the PC to play the Flash animation, which seamlessly loops until the user turns the page. If you set the movie to play automatically when the page turns (**FIGURE 19-2**), in some cases this can become annoying and will slow down the computer if the user decides instead to flip through the pages or quickly browse the eBook.

To view the animated characters on these pages, make sure you check out this book's companion eBook to experience a day in the life of Jinx the Black Cat. Jinx has a home on the Internet too. He's a virtual pet you can visit at any time at his official Flash-animated Web site at www.jinxtheblackcat.com.

The Future of Flash Comics

Jinx the Black Cat is just a small example of what you can do via Flash and PDF. It's up to you to imagine what an army of animators can come up with to produce a long-form story using traditional cartoon TV characters.

You can now repurpose PDF comics, short-story animated children's books, and traditional animated media for full-screen computer viewing. And if you spend the time to program the cartoons to be interactive via Flash, you can then provide a game-like experience.

However, some multimedia developers have complained that the Flash application has grown into a monster that is just too complicated for the average Webmaster to grasp. Each new release of Flash comes with new coding procedures (called ActionScript, which has become a sort of programming language for the professional developer). The interactive capabilities are now truly astounding, but the drawing and animation tools are lacking, which has opened the door to other software vendors, such as Toon Boom, to fill this void.

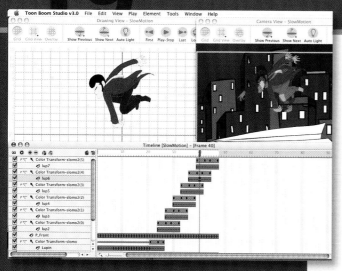

Toon Boom: Traditional Animation Using Flash Files

If you just want to create stunning Flash animations, you don't have to learn the scripting capabilities of the Flash application. The Toon Boom software development company (www.ToonBoom.com) has produced a line of computer applications that uses traditional cel animation-like tools but has interfaced them with a bare-bones SWF vector-rendering engine. The Toon Boom applications make vector drawing and animation simple yet powerful enough to provide the user with instant feedback via a Flash-like player.

There are no programming tools to add interactivity such as "Go to this page," "Launch this Web link," and so on. Toon Boom Studio software is built strictly to help you create and color vector graphics, keep the graphics grouped for simple animation, and provide camera views to allow for zooming, panning, and camera point-of-view "fly-throughs" of a scene just like 3D animation applications have.

You can open Toon Boom Studio files in Flash if you want to add interactivity. This export/import method has become popular for creating highly interactive games that feature animated characters.

Toon Boom applications even feature advanced tools for syncing up audio with characters' mouths by allowing you to automatically animate the vector graphics for the mouths using waveform information found within the corresponding digital audio file.

All these enhanced features are the reason why the Toon Boom family of software has now become the preferred animation suite for TV cartoons. Toon Boom recently won the 2005 Primetime Emmy Engineering Award for its Opus application in well-known TV series such as *Family Guy*.

Nelvana's Cartoon Series

Nelvana is a Canada-based animation house that helped develop Toon Boom's Harmony animation software. One of Nelvana's most popular Flash-based projects is an animated cartoon series called *6Teen* that airs on several TV stations in North America. I have included a video about Nelvana's workflow, and some of the raw Toon Boom SWF project files in this book's companion eBook so you can watch the video and interact with the characters of the show in native SWF.

Most of Nelvana's previous work consists of hand-drawn cel animation content. Using the Toon Boom Studio software, you could convert the cel drawings to vector art and animate them to allow for conversion to the SWF Flash format. You could adopt a revised workflow where you deliver cartoons to the public via rich-media PDF using the native SWF data files. Let's examine this workflow.

Creating Flash Cartoons for TV and Rich-Media PDF

Since Flash is based upon vector shapes, artists draw an outline or trace over an existing drawing using a pressure-sensitive tablet, and then the computer automatically fills the shape with a color. Vector designs essentially consist of connected lines and shapes filled with colors.

For example, a triangle consists of three anchor points connected by three straight lines. A circle could potentially consist of eight anchor points connected by curved lines. Altering the points that make up the object can change these shapes. It's all mathematical, so you can scale vector artwork to any size without losing quality because the software understands that the image consists of connected lines and points. Instead of manually drawing and painting a series of individual frames to create an animation, the artist can easily manipulate the Flash vector outline, and then the computer will create a series of in-between frames all nicely painted in smooth, fluid motion.

During the design process, the artists will export a preview of their work as an SWF file and view it in Flash Player to check the progress of the scene, which is often only a few seconds in length. When everything is good to go, they then export the scene as a high-resolution, uncompressed 30 frames per second video for broadcast TV. This process converts or renders the vector files to a series of video still images using a codec suitable for digital video editing.

The animator then imports these tiny video segments into a nonlinear editing program such as Avid Media Composer or Apple Final Cut Pro to join the scenes into one long animated scene. Finally, the animator can add narration, music, and sound effects to the video in an audio recording studio and save it to digital videotape in one of the various formats required by TV broadcasters.

261

The many million frames of video rendered to produce an animation at 30 frames per second for high-definition digital videotape will result in several hundred gigabytes of data. This is a dramatic difference from the original SWF Flash files used to create and then preview the animation. But the high-definition video and the SWF files look almost identical on a computer monitor. In fact, the SWF files are better looking and extremely small, in some cases smaller than 1 MB per minute of animation depending on how the animation is created. If the animation uses bitmapped graphics for backgrounds and the background moves, you will then notice that the computer cannot redraw the frames fast enough, and the motion will be jerky. On a computer, Flash files are at their best when they are generated, displayed, and moved based on data as vector shapes; video for TV, on the other hand, is displayed using individual frames of full-screen rendered images—usually 30 images per second.

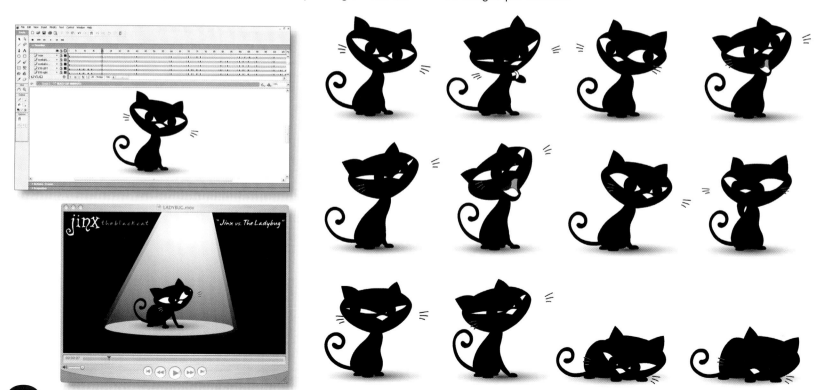

Conclusions

With the release of Acrobat 8, the capability of linking and embedding Flash SWF files inside a PDF became a reality, so the potential to deliver TV-style cartoon eBooks via PDF is enormous. If you carefully consider the delivery of a Flash-based rich-media PDF while developing a cartoon, it's possible to put a whole animated TV show inside one PDF file that is smaller than 30 MB.

This opens a whole new revenue and distribution model where users can download cartoons and animated TV shows and then view them on a computer monitor. If the Flash content is entirely vector based, it can be enlarged to full screen without degradation in picture quality. The producers need only to learn to work within the constraints of SWF files and the speed of the home user's computer processor. Cartoons such as *The Simpsons* and *Family Guy* are perfect for this type of rich-media PDF because they use simple SWF vector shapes.

And without digital recorders like TiVo, which allows you to skip over TV commercials, imagine the sponsorship possibilities where you can embed cartoons inside a PDF—when the user turns the page, a traditional Web-like rich-media banner advertisement appears with links to the sponsor's Web site for more information. Users can't zap the Flash commercials because they are embedded inside the PDF pages between the episodes or scenes. The user then turns the page, and the next rich-media episode begins.... Interact with the character, ask them a question.

Digital Magazines and Rich Media

Many attempts have been made to produce electronic versions of the print magazines found at the corner newsstand. Most of them are straight conversions to PDF using the same layout and style, which unfortunately makes them difficult to read. Instead of reformatting the layout for computer display, the publishers print or "distill" the QuarkXPress or Adobe InDesign document to PDF.

In this chapter, you'll explore some of the ways you can include rich media in a PDF magazine so it is easy to read, fun to interact with, provides a source of revenue, and stands out from all other current offerings.

265

20

Current Digital Magazines

For a good selection of digital magazines, visit Qmags (www.qmags.com) or Zinio (www.zinio.com). Qmags uses Adobe Reader for displaying the document and JavaScript for navigation. Nothing is stopping users from sharing the documents, though, which are not locked to the computer. The documents consist mostly of technical publications, and some also feature rich media.

Zinio, on the other hand, has licensed the PDF libraries from Adobe and has added a few features that mimic the "page turns" often found in Adobe Flash–formatted magazines. Publishers can add Flash, video, and audio to documents for a rich-media experience; since the Zinio staff takes care of the conversion process and the distribution, it's fairly simple and convenient for publishers to try this digital format.

The drawback to the Zinio platform is that you are locked into Zinio's proprietary file format, and therefore users must download yet another media player. It's not an open system like Reader PDF.

A number of U.S. magazine publishers have bought into the Zinio system because it has a fairly secure digital rights management and distribution process; in other words, users can't share the electronic documents. But since most magazines make their revenue from advertising instead of subscriptions, publishers should not worry about their magazines being shared. In fact, they should be trying to get the magazine seen by as many people as possible so they can report the higher readership to their advertisers. After all, their sponsors focus on the number of Web site visits when buying banner ads, so what's the difference between a digital magazine and a Web site to an advertiser? The free content found on Web sites is one of the main reasons why print magazines are losing subscribers and more advertising revenue is moving to the Web.

To me, it seems at this time, the publishers are testing the market and cannot justify the costs of designing two versions of the magazine, one for print and one for computer screen display. So, for the time being, we are forced to live with an unpleasant navigation experience that requires zooming into the text to read the document.

I feel the brand of digital magazine that will win in the end will be the one that is specifically created for full-screen display using the magazine's own look and feel. It should be free, financed by advertising just like Web sites, and made widely available using the open standard, Adobe Reader PDF electronic format.

Most digital magazines are difficult to read!

Samples of digital magazine Web sites

www.newsstand.com

www.qmags.com

www.texterity.com

www.zinio.com

Dynamic Media: Music, Video, Animation, and the Web in Adobe PDF

Rich-Media Reader PDFs Provide an Alternative

It's strange that publishers of electronic magazines spend enormous amounts of money on their Web sites and nothing on the electronic versions of their print publications. They format their Web sites for computer display and offer great video, Flash advertising from sponsors, message boards, games, recipes, newsletters, and so on, but they don't seem to care about the viewing experience of the electronic versions of their magazines.

This creates an ideal opportunity for smaller niche market publishers that want to take advantage of convergence. By reusing portions of their Web site inside reformatted, electronic versions of their print magazines that display properly on a computer screen, publishers can now offer their advertisers and their subscribers a much more compelling experience. Instead of the magazine being converted straight to PDF, publishers can reformat the Web site materials as a rich-media PDF to produce the electronic magazine, allowing users to download it in one click as a magazine.

It offers a lot to think about: print interviews featuring video and audio clips of famous people, advertising in Flash animations, interactive crossword puzzles, contests that readers could win on the spot using gaming software, animated political comics from the print magazine, and more.

Let's examine a scenario in the next few pages where rich-media can be utilized in a magazine format designed for display on a computer monitor.

IN THIS ISSUE OF

RMM

Rich Media Magazine

VOLUME XXV VERSION 2.1

Free!

FLASH GAMES
Interactive Bowling
Virtual Slot Machines

TV SERIES PROMOS
Timeless Places: Mysteries of the World

iPod AUDIO BOOKS
Take them on the road!

eBOOKS
Beyond the Handheld

Feature Article
Larry Feign
Creating Cross-Media Animation
for Web Broadcast and Print

269

Digital Magazines of the Future

To convey the look and feel of traditional printed magazines you may want to consider using three columns of text like we have here in this section of our book. Narrow columns are very easy to read and can contain many graphic elements within the body copy. A digital magazine should provide more than the printed product. The writer should try to present the reader with an interesting story that will retain the reader's attention past the first paragraph. The editor will usu-

The "pull quote" appears as a video, and the advertising is highly interactive

ally pull interesting quotes from the article and put them in bold type so that readers who are merely browsing the magazine will take notice and stop to read them. The sales department will then try to place an advertisement that is complementary beside that article. It has been that way since the birth of the printed magazine format, and little has changed in the electronic age.

But a digital rich-media magazine could create a whole new world of possibilities where the article provides the story, the "pull quote" appears as a video, and the advertising is highly interactive.

Interactive Advertising

If you pick up a fashion magazine, you'll notice that more than half the pages are ads. What would TV be like if we were bombarded by that percentage of ads? Everyone would own a digital recorder like TiVo. But in the unregulated world of advertising in print magazines, to the publisher the bottom line is advertising, and the editorial takes a backseat. Hence, readers are migrating to the Internet to get information for subjects about health, wealth, and travel.

In fashion magazines, if the advertising would allow you to spin the fashion model around to look at the clothing from the front, back, and sides, well, that would be fun.

Women's Clothing 50% OFF
This week only at
Bea's Fashions

Interactive Gaming for Sport and Pleasure

Another example is a sports magazine. A sport is something you play; reading about it does not have the same effect. But create advertising that operates like a sport, and, well, now you are in the competition. Instead of passing over the advertisement, users are drawn into it. In the digital world, an advertisement that says, "Are you a player? Prove it to me!" will probably get a response.

Electronic magazines can include games such as tennis, golf, pool, and bowling. Loads of people like to bowl professionally and for entertainment. Bowling tournaments take place all over the world, and an interactive advertisement that promotes these events while allowing users to bowl a few games should get the bowlers' attention. In addition, providing a link somewhere in the game that takes users right to the sponsors' Web sites is a great way to increase "click-through" rates. You can even include a purchase order form for eCommerce right inside the PDF file to purchase the product online.

Interactive Contests

The world of Internet gambling is ever expanding. Even Grandma likes to go online to play "party poker" with her friends. Thousands of sites operate 24 hours a day, and all you need is a credit card to play digital versions of black jack, roulette, and slot machines. Many Web sites are driven by Flash engines using random generators to provide an honest possibility of actually beating the computer. It's possible to program Flash to weight the odds so you can provide the user with a fair chance of winning. So, why not try a Flash game in a PDF magazine?

Every print magazine that hits the newsstands has at least one contest that offers a prize in exchange for the reader's mailing address. Contests are also a good way to judge the effectiveness of the advertising because the entry form has the magazine's ID number.

Now imagine a game that does the same thing inside a rich-media magazine. All users need to do is provide their name, address, and email (no credit card needed)

to get the chance to play the game, win, and claim their prize. This is an ideal way to get readers to part with their personal information so the sponsors can judge the effectiveness of their advertising campaigns–get the readers hooked on playing games where they can win the sponsors' products.

The Rich-Media Slot Machine?

Creating a rich-media PDF is just like gambling. When I take on a new interactive PDF project that is a bit complex, I carefully consider all the possibilities and uncertainties I have to address. Does this project deserve video, or will a slide show work? If I decide to use video, what media player will I use–QuickTime or Windows Media? Or perhaps I will include both formats using renditions to play it safe. But the file size will be too large to download, so I had better stream the video from a Web server. Will my client need to take it on the road to make presentations? What happens if an Internet connection is not present? What happens when a new version of the media player is released that causes the production to be rebuilt to accommodate the alterations? It's really just a gamble in many situations. Sometimes I go with a gut feeling, sometimes I toss a coin, and sometimes I just click a button!

Visualize and Puzzle Your Mind in New Ways

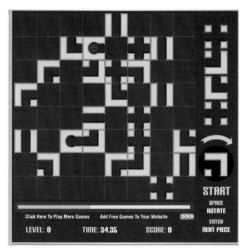

surely multiply because the puzzle is inter-active. Playing against the computer as your opponent is a way to sharpen your senses and provides an alternative to the reams of text and pictures that make up the articles in a PDF magazine.

Video Interviews

Current photojournalists need to start think-ing about taking pictures that will support their story, and it's time to think motion pic-tures. For rich-media PDF, a simple home video camera will work perfectly. The new-est cameras on the market are inexpensive and easy to use because they are fully automatic; in addition, because people are used to watching reality TV shows, the broadcast quality is acceptable. For Mac users, the software to edit the video comes with the computer. All you have to do is just plug the camera into your computer, launch Apple iMovie, and edit the footage at your leisure.

Many magazines provide crossword puz-zles. Rarely will you find a tabloid in the doctor's office that does not have the crossword puzzle filled out. People are fascinated by a challenge. The success of the prime-time show Jeopardy proves you can't ignore the addictive qualities of a good brainteaser.

Now, put the same experience inside a PDF magazine. The addictive power will

Now, when you write your story, you can supply your publisher, subscribers, or users

with a much more in-depth video interview. You can add a button to the story in PDF that displays "Click here for the extended version" of this story in video. Pictures and advertising in the magazine can now come to life with behind-the-scenes foot-age of how they were created. Readers can hear the emotion of the words, listen to the sound effects, and see the location of the shoot. In their eyes, you will be an exceptional photojournalist who has shot additional footage to support your story so that the video is not just a "talking head."

Television and Movie Trailers

Everyone likes to get a backstage pass to a concert or a movie set to see places usually reserved for the cast and crew. Digital magazines with rich-media interviews can present the same experience. It's something special–something that the printed page could never convey.

Movie studios spend millions of dollars creating promotional "behind-the-scenes" videos of upcoming feature films and TV shows. They send them to TV entertainment programs such as *Entertainment Tonight* hoping the station will edit a small clip from the promotional "b-roll" and air it to get free publicity for the film. They also send these promotional reels to newspapers and entertainment magazine editors, but in this case, it is for informational purposes only because the editor has no idea what to do with it after it has been viewed.

In other words, the rich-media content is out there. For example, you could digitize the behind-the-scenes promo reels for the internet. The most obvious use of rich media would be to include the advertisng for a TV program or movie inside a digital magazine, then embed or link the promotional video to it. It could stream right into the movie poster from a Web server.

I have included an example of the process using a promotional video from one of our travel TV series that that aired on a speciality channel called Travel + Escape.

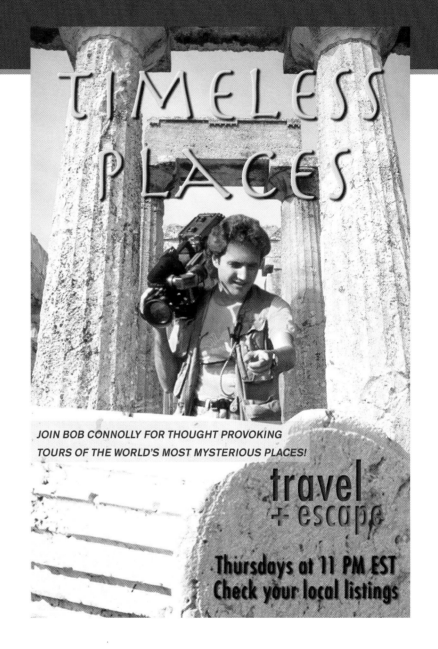

JOIN BOB CONNOLLY FOR THOUGHT PROVOKING
TOURS OF THE WORLD'S MOST MYSTERIOUS PLACES!

travel
+ escape

Thursdays at 11 PM EST
Check your local listings

Photography by Annika Feign

Feature Article

Larry Feign
Cartoonist animator

American-born Larry Feign is a household name in Hong Kong where he made his mark as a political cartoonist during the volatile era before the colony's handover to China. His work has appeared in hundreds of publications worldwide such as *Time* magazine and *The Economist*, and he has published 14 books of cartoons and humor. His home and studio are located in a tiny Chinese village on an outlying island an hour's ferry ride from the city of Hong Kong and are surrounded by wild egrets, white sand beaches, water buffalo, and a few snakes that inspire his work.

At age 7 he began publishing cartoons regularly in his school magazine, and at 10 he made his first "claymation" and stop-motion films with his father's 8mm movie camera. His adult career has been varied and wide ranging, both artistically and geographically, taking him from drawing caricatures on Waikiki Beach in Hawaii to working on the *Heathcliff the Cat* animated cartoons in Los Angeles and finally to working in Asia.

In spite of his success as a print cartoonist, animation remained his first love. In 2001 he founded a small animation studio called STVDIO Media in Hong Kong. Larry identifies closely with Walt Disney because he shares a birthday and has developed programs for Walt Disney Television International. He designs and creates animated television programs for the Asian market using expensive, high-end animation software and the more affordable application software that produces the Flash file format.

Photography by Annika Feign

275

Cross-Media Flip Book

One of STVDIO Media's in-house productions is called *Snake Soup*, which was conceived as a true cross-media animation for Web broadcast and for print. Larry decided to produce a *real* "digital" animation in the true sense of the word. According to *Webster's Dictionary*, the primary meaning of *digital* is "of and having to do with the fingers." So, he decided to create a promotional flip book, one you hold in your hands and use your fingers to play the animation. It's also perfect for a political cartoon inside a rich-media PDF.

Larry came up with the concept of a cartoon that features a person with the personality of a snake that gets eaten by a real snake.

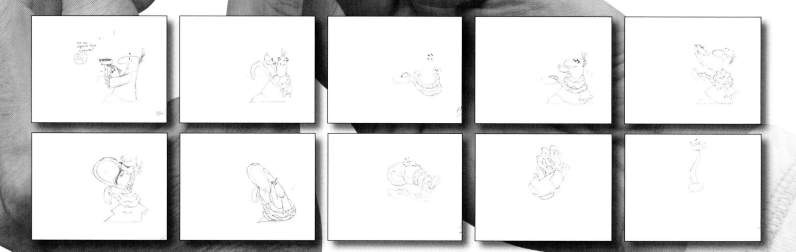

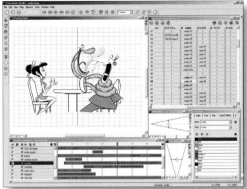

FIGURE 20-1 Larry imported individual pages into Toon Boom Studio for tracing.

The Road Ahead for STVDIO Media

With his background as a cartoonist for magazines and books and his experience in animation, Larry is excited about the convergence of stationary and moving media in the form of PDF-formatted downloadable eZines and eBooks. His company is prepared for the day when publishers will commission cartoons that can be printed in a glossy magazine, viewed as an animation inside a Web page, and viewed in a downloadable rich-media PDF magazine.

You can get your own copy of the *Snake Soup* flip book by visiting STVDIO Media's Web site at www.stvdio.com.

He provided a rough animation to allow his team to produce the intermediate elements—an 80-frame pencil drawing created on paper by animator Royce Ramos. To produce the final product, he then scanned the individual pages and imported them into Toon Boom Studio for tracing using its superb digital ink and paint capabilities (**FIGURE 20-1**).

He rendered an image sequence as single frames and sent them to the printer to produce the flipbook. To create an interactive Web version of the animation, he imported the Toon Boom project into Flash to provide interactivity.

Just attach an iPod-friendly audio file such as the industry-standard MP3 or Apple's preferred AAC (Advanced Audio Codec) file to a PDF magazine, and users can transfer audio files to their iPod to take the complete audio interview with them.

Journalists can re-use audio material that they have archived or capture new audio with a simple handheld video camera. Instead of writing important points of the conversation on paper, the digital video camera can capture the whole interview so the journalist can review it later—no more missed quotes. The journalist doesn't need to worry about lighting the scene, focusing the camera, and making everyone uncomfortable; he can just capture the audio with a lapel microphone. The journalist can use the audio as a guide to write the article, but he can also edit the raw audio into a finished product for a podcast.

Attach Your Audio Book to the PDF for iPods

Audio books that were once available only on cassette tape or CD are now downloadable via Apple's iTunes store. You can listen to a book, often read by the author, while you jog, relax, meditate, or drive to work. Podcasting is also an exploding phenomenon where you can visit a Web site and download all sorts of spoken material—including university lectures, comedy, self-help speeches, religious sermons, and more—right into your iPod for audio narratives on the go. Electronic magazines can provide a similar experience using attached MP3 audio files.

Audio Interviews and the iPod

With the release of the free Reader 8, it is possible to extract file attachments that have been included inside a PDF. In previous versions you needed Adobe Acrobat to remove the attached file, but Adobe has now provided this capability for free. This allows writers and journalists to insert digital audio in an electronic magazine.

Conclusions

Rich media can make an electronic magazine very cool. The rich media content providers, up until this point, have locked up their audio and video archives, waiting for the day to arrive when they can sell their media in a digital format suited for downloading. But advertising drives the publishers, and many advertising agencies are unaware of the power of rich media in PDF magazines.

Steve Greenberger, senior vice president and director of print services for media-buying company Zenith Media, said, "[Advertising reps are] interested, but I don't think they've been educated well enough. The greatest impact is being able to click on the ad and see video, hear music, and hyperlink to a related Web site."

It's just a matter of time until the rich-media PDF magazine format becomes popular with the average consumer, possibly by Zinio

subscribers who will provide the initial momentum. Eventually the print publisher will understand the market and advertising revenue stream for the special brand of a rich-media PDF magazine developed in-house by their print designers and downloadable from the magazine's Web site.

When *Playboy* magazine featured Marilyn Monroe as its first centerfold, it got a lot of attention for being different. At one time *Life* magazine was one of the most popular publications because it took you behind the scenes using a photojournalism approach. Its interviews were memorable. The same can happen with rich-media magazines. The industry needs a publisher with a vision to step out from the rest and try something new in easy-to-read, full-screen interactive rich-media PDF.

Server-Side PDF Custom Publications

Although the majority of the PDF documents you'll encounter are created using desktop publishing tools such as QuarkXPress, Adobe InDesign, and Adobe Acrobat, other tools known as *server-side* PDF applications create PDF files on a server located in-house or on the Internet. This method is currently most often employed by organizations that need to provide their clients and employees with customized forms or even books.

Server-side PDF documents have many advantages for governments and financial institutions because each document can be customized for a particular person and include information such as employee name and ID numbers, up-to-the-minute pricing of products and services, the time of document creation, and much more.

This chapter will explore the various ways you can use server-side PDF tools to produce searchable PDF documents that contain rich media. You will also learn how to combine several PDF files "on-the-fly" using PDF search engine results.

Create your final PDF

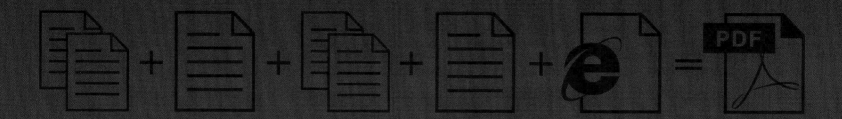

Server-Side PDFs
Using Database Content

Most of the PDF files you encounter on the Internet are "prebuilt" using software such as Acrobat to convert or "print" a Microsoft Word or QuarkXPress file to a PDF document. You can also install software on a Web server that allows you to generate a PDF file from HTML text.

Usually, this involves a "shopping cart" tool that captures the HTML or XML (Extensible Markup Language) data from several Web pages on a site and then merges the information into a single downloadable PDF file. The PDF is generated on the Web server's side using PDF libraries and source code licensed from Adobe or other vendors.

For the most part, you'll utilize these server-side PDF files when you want to provide information that the user can customize and present in a manner that is much more appealing than a Web page when printed.

Text, logos, and pictures look much better when printed using a PDF file because they are PostScript formatted, and multipage PDF documents are easier to print than low-resolution Web pages because the user just clicks one button to print all the pages at once. In database-driven server-side PDF files, all the content such as text, pictures, logos, and rich media reside inside a dynamic database where information that often changes, such as product pricing, can update "on the fly" via a Web browser connected to the content database.

Server-Side Technologies

Adobe also has a wide selection of server products that can produce custom documents.

Adobe Output Designer software is an easy-to-use design tool that lets you create electronic document templates for use with Adobe solutions for document generation. Using Adobe Output Designer, you can create electronic documents that exactly replicate existing paper documents.

Adobe Central Pro Output Server software enables businesses to generate professional-looking documents from core applications such as CRM, ERP, and legacy systems for improved customer communications. Documents such as purchase orders, invoices, and checks are dynamically generated for delivery via Adobe PDF, the Web, email, fax, or print.

Adobe Document Server software enables businesses to dynamically generate customized Adobe PDF documents for more targeted and effective customer communications. XML-based data from enterprise applications is flowed into Adobe PDF templates to create, assemble, and manipulate complex, content-rich documents on a server.

Adobe LiveCycle Policy Server allows you to apply persistent and dynamic security policies to documents that enable you to specify who has access, what they can do, when, and for how long. And best of all, authors can update security policies at any time, even after distribution, so organizations can manage and track access no matter where a document resides.

Third-Party Vendors

Since PDF is an open format, there are a wide variety of vendors that create applications to convert HTML or XML data on the fly. A good starting point is PDFlib, a company that licenses PDF libraries to accomplish that task. PDFlib (www.pdflib.com) is the leading developer toolbox for dynamic PDF creation on a Web server.

PDFlib is a widely used programming library that allows the programmer to generate and manipulate files in Adobe's well known Portable Document Format (PDF) and integrate this ability into any application or server environment. This is where many programmers go to get the code to create custom PDF applications. PDFlib also makes a server product called PDFlib Personalization Server. Block processing is the main feature of the PDFlib Personalization Server.

PDFlib introduces a new concept to PDF: Blocks are customized fields on top of PDF files that can be filled automatically with variable data. Blocks are created and designed interactively using the new PDFlib Block plug-in for Adobe Acrobat and can be filled with text, images, or PDF pages using PDFlib's new block filling functions. It's cool stuff if you are a seasoned computer programmer.

For a good starting point to find vendors that specialize in creating server-side PDF applications visit www.PlanetPDF.com or www.PDFzone.com.

The Server-Side Evolution

This server-side, made-to-order application of PDF presents a load of opportunites for custom publishing where you can customize books, catalogs, and magazines for individuals. Several automotive companies deploy this technology on their Web sites to allow users to create their own brochures for a car they are interested in purchasing. The user can choose the color of the interior and exterior, add accessories, and get updated pricing information within the PDF. Users can then download the eBrochure, view it, and print it on their home computer, or they can send the PDF via the Internet to a commercial printing house that has a high-quality digital printer.

Xerox, which is known for its photocopy technology, is now one of the leaders in this one-off "print-on-demand" technology.

Unfortunately, this system has some drawbacks, and it usually involves the layout of the final document. In the case of a dynamically generated PDF that uses HTML or XML information, even though the text and pictures are high quality, the page layout usually is "boxy." The text and pictures often are all neatly spaced in symmetrical placeholders. You might find large gaping holes appear where the dynamic text does not fill areas of the page. Text cannot wrap around the curves of an image, and you will often see a *widow*, a short line at the top of the page, or an *orphan*, a single word of text at the bottom of a paragraph of text. Basically, the server–side dynamic software does not have the same typography skills as a seasoned layout type designer. So if you want to retain a high-quality, designed-by-hand look to your documents and retain the capability to customize it, you can use a combination of dynamic content and prebuilt PDF pages.

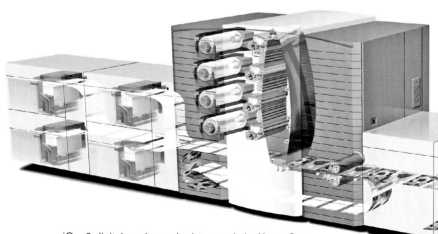

iGen3 digital on-demand printer made by Xerox Corp.

Server-Side PDF Using PDF Pages

PDF technology has been well accepted in the business world because the security of the file format is rock solid. That being the case, it is rare to find an IT department that will not allow a PDF file to pass through the corporate firewall (a safety mechanism to stop computer viruses). In fact, the U.S. government is now enforcing rules and regulations that require its agencies to submit PDF electronic documents for contracts, import/export forms, and reports. Not only can the document be password protected, but the creator can also set an expiration date. Using Adobe Policy Server technology, you can even track the document to see just who is reading it. These security issues—in addition to the elimination of paper—have worked so well that a major effort is currently underway to modernize every area of the government where archiving and disseminating information is vital.

For example, agencies such as NASA are currently in the process of scanning and converting thousands of printed pages in its archives, which were created on outdated word processors that are no longer supported, into the "U.S. government–sanctioned" PDF.

Text-to-Speech Documents

The U.S. government has created regulations to make the same documents that are available to the general tax-paying public available to individuals who are reading impaired. It is now a simple procedure to have the converted text read aloud to you using the "text-to-speech" capabilities built into every PDF document and free Adobe Reader application.

285

FIGURE 21-1 A Google search results page shows listings of links to PDF files and Web pages.

Server-Side PDF Workflow

Like many government agencies, the dilemma NASA faces is organizing the many millions of PDF pages in a way that will make it easy for its staff and partners such as research universities to search and retrieve information. A search engine is the key to the success of this initiative, and desktop publishers are now learning some techniques used by Web site developers to make their PDF pages search-engine friendly so their contents can be called up and displayed on a page. Once that is accomplished, users will be able to combine the PDF pages into a single PDF file.

PDF Search Methods

Google, the world's premier search engine, is continually altering the way it provides results for keyword searches. You may have noticed that quite a few PDF files show up in Google search results (**FIGURE 21-1**). Google formulates its search results page of Web site links by using keywords typed into its search box field. This marvelous process is based on Google's robots, which constantly visit and revisit every Web site on the Internet to "capture" the visible text and invisible metadata stored inside Web pages.

This metadata includes the title of the Web page, search keywords, and a short subject description of the Web page. This metadata is stored on the servers at Google, and when your requested search words match the metadata at Google, you are presented with a search result page consisting of the links to the Web pages and short descriptions of each page. Sometimes descriptions are based on similar keywords found in the body text of the corresponding Web page, and sometimes it comes from the description metadata information.

PDF Metadata

Just like Web pages, PDF documents can also have titles, keywords, and description metadata, but virtually no one utilizes this capability, which is one of the reasons why you don't see even more PDF files in the search results from Google. Most desktop publishers and Webmasters don't know this capability exists, which is unfortunate, because Google's search robots are programmed to go to great lengths to capture the metadata contents in PDF files on the Internet.

Web sites that have their own search engines often employ the same techniques used by Google except they limit the search to the contents of their own site. In cases like this, it is possible to filter the results page to display only PDF files. The results Web page text (**FIGURE 21-2**) comes from the information found in the "title" and "author" and "subject" tags in the PDF Document Properties window containing the keywords for which the user searched. In this situation, it is possible to create a dynamic Web page that uses only the metadata text information found inside a PDF. To update the Web page or the Web site, you just add or remove PDF pages from the Web site.

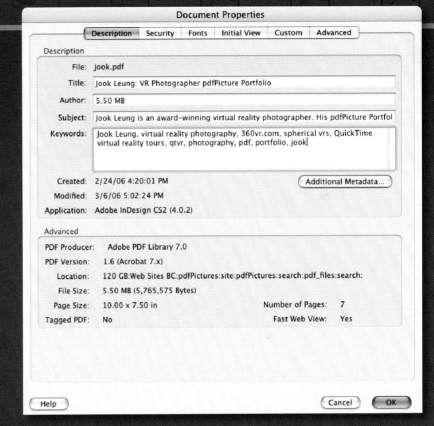

FIGURE 21-2 A search results Web page (below) is generated from data that resides within the Subject metadata seen in the Document Properties (above).

Your search returned 1 result

☐ **Jook Leung** | File size: **5.50 MB**

Jook Leung is an award-winning virtual reality photographer. His pdfPicture Portfolio features full screen virtual tours of cruise ships, hotels, restaurants, monuments, museums, and more.

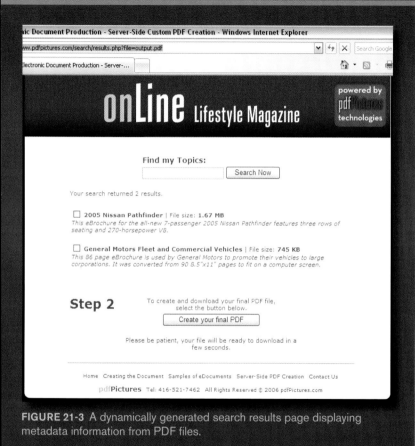

FIGURE 21-3 A dynamically generated search results page displaying metadata information from PDF files.

For a sample of a Web page that uses a PDF search engine, visit www.DynamicMediaBook.com/search.

PDF Search

For example, let's say you searched for *car*, and you had two PDF files containing the *car* keyword available for download from the results Web page. Each time the Web page was displayed, your custom application would retrieve the information that was stored in the four "description" tags in the PDFs and display it as HTML text on the page. Your Web page will consist only of the text found in the PDF descriptive metadata. If you took one PDF away from the server, the page would display information only from one PDF file (**FIGURE 21-3**).

To update the text on the Web page, you would just change the text in the PDF and upload it via FTP to the folder that holds the PDF files.

If your site contains thousands of PDF documents, this is an ideal way to facilitate the quick and easy retrieval of information in the HTML format. Your results page is actually a fully functioning Web page providing a good amount of information on its own. The "description" tag can supply paragraphs of information—not just one line of text like Google. Now, once users have read a brief synopsis of what is contained in each PDF, they can select one or more PDFs for printing or, if there is rich media involved, for viewing.

Where server-side PDF comes in handy is when you want to combine or merge the search results from several listings into one self-contained, downloadable PDF. Search for the documents you want, select the ones you want, append the documents together, and then download them as a single self-contained PDF.

Appending Server-Side PDFs

In a process called *appending*, you can combine individual PDF pages into a single document and stamp or merge additional text or pictures into "fields" of the page. The source PDF files can be single or multipage documents created using traditional desktop publishing tools, and they can contain rich media. You then upload the finished pages to the Web server where they reside inside a folder.

When a visitor searches for a particular topic, a Web page presents a listing of PDF files, with check boxes allowing the user to select the PDF files they want to append into a single document. Fields on the Web page allow users to fill in their names or other information such as credit card data to be included in the final PDF. The user can also create a password to protect against others opening the document once they have downloaded it to the computer.

During the combining process, the server-side application appends the requested PDF pages, and the Web server "stamps" each page with a sequential page number. The user's name can be inserted into the cover page or every page inside the document.

Once the user downloads the document, each PDF file selected by the user can appear as an interactive link in a "Table of Contents" (**FIGURE 21-4**) page to allow the user to quickly jump to chapters consisting of the individual PDF files. Any interactive JavaScript navigation programmed into the individual, original PDF—such as turning the pages, printing, quitting, and

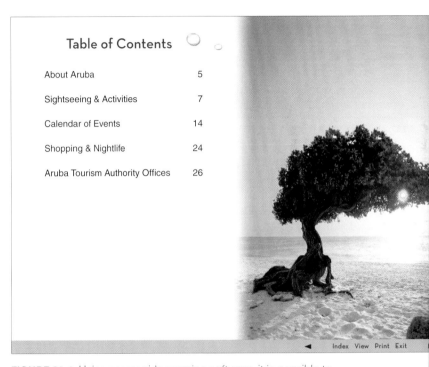

FIGURE 21-4 Using server-side merging software, it is possible to generate a Table of Contents page that contains interactive links to chapters within the eBrochure.

so on—is carried through from one document to the next. Finally, and most important for your purposes, each page can contain embedded rich media such as video, audio, and animation. Visit www.DynamicMediaBook.com for more information.

289

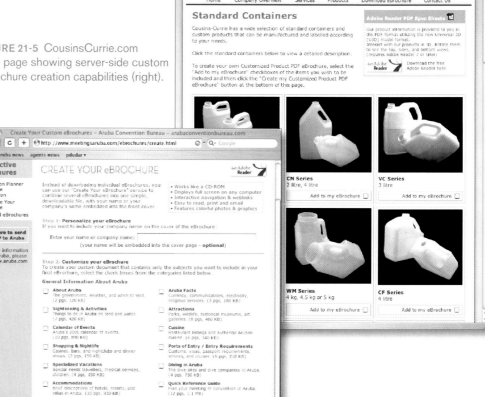

Server-Side PDF Samples

Our company has produced several Web sites for the manufacturing and tourism industries that feature the use of server-side PDF. Cousins-Currie (**FIGURE 21-5**) is one of the largest manufacturers of blow-molded products, and they utilize server-side PDF to create custom brochures of their products. To sample this feature, visit www.cousinscurrie.com.

The island of Aruba (www.aruba.com) has downloadable tourism rich-media eBrochures of the hotels, destination management companies, tour operators, and islands.

In addition to offering downloadable individual eBrochures, these Web sites contain a "Create Your eBrochure" Web page consisting of the individual eBrochures, short descriptions of their contents, the number of pages, and the file size of the individual PDFs. Users can check a box to select the eBrochures they want to add to the final PDF document, and they can use a single form field to add their name to the front cover of the final PDF.

Visit www.MeetingsAruba.com for a sample of this process (**FIGURE 21-6**).

FIGURE 21-5 CousinsCurrie.com Web page showing server-side custom eBrochure creation capabilities (right).

FIGURE 21-6 Create a customized eBrochure from MeetingsAruba.com.

Server-Side Possibilities: Search, Merge, and Converge

With all this technology at your command, it is now possible to create electronic documents that can become another viable solution for video on demand (VOD). Consider all the specialty TV channels that have huge libraries of video sitting unused on production company shelves. A 13-part one-hour TV series contains about 130 five-minute video clips, and if the series runs for several years, potentially more than 500 video clips for content are at your disposal.

For example, travel shows could take advantage of server-side rich-media PDFs for their online visitors, and sponsors could become involved with this service by purchasing advertising inside the PDF. Let's say you want to learn about traveling Europe. You visit a travel Web site owned by a TV channel that specializes in travel, and you search for *Europe*. This returns a list of PDF segments for TV episodes that include document keywords and descriptions so that only the PDFs containing the word *Europe* appear in your search results.

The metadata inside the PDF page generates the search results, and each page consists of one video segment about Europe from the travel TV series.

The Rich-Media Video Server-Side Workflow

Most TV programs contain a hidden closed-captioning track for the hearing impaired. When you turn it on, it appears on the TV screen on top of the picture and runs in sync with the narration. These closed-captioning tracks originate as just plain text, so you could easily import them into Adobe InDesign and design them as PDF pages. In fact, you could digitize, compress, and insert the video segment from the TV show into a PDF page along with corresponding text from the closed-captioning track. You could either link or embed the video clip beside the corresponding text, which would allow you to read the text and watch the video at the same time. Or you could launch the video full screen like traditional TV shows.

For sponsorship opportunities, you could also add advertising from print materials to the PDF. You could embed Flash advertising from the travel Web site or even TV commercials into the final PDF file too.

To create the final custom TV show, the user would check several PDFs related to different TV segments that demonstrate various travel destinations and then click the Build My TV Show button. This would tell the server-side PDF application software to collect the selected PDF files and append them into one document. Then, the PDF would download to the user's computer to allow for full-screen playback.

Essentially, visitors to the Web site could create their own, customized rich-media TV show using PDF server-side search and merge technology as the delivery method. It's VOD inside a custom publication that uses only the content from a TV show. Imagine the possibilities with the amount of programming that exists at TV production companies. You could package shows about fishing, home improvement, fitness, health, sports, hobbies, and so on, for rich-media delivery inside PDF TV programs.

Conclusions about Server-Side PDF

Server-side PDF is a perfect way to allow users to customize, combine, and download more than one PDF at one time. Instead of downloading a large PDF document, users can select only the chapters or individual pages in which they are interested. For example, magazine publishers could put articles from previous issues online as individual PDF pages so subscribers could create their own version of the magazine with only the content that interests them.

In addition, the customization capabilities that allow users to add their own names and passwords are great ways to personalize the publication. And for content security, the publisher could embed the purchaser's credit card information in the document, which would stop users from sharing the file. After all, who would want to give away their credit card number and password?

By attaching, embedding, or streaming rich-media video to the document, you can have a viable Video on Demand (VOD) capability that is perfect for the next generation of Internet TV-viewing possibilities presented via computers using Intel Viiv or Apple Front Row technology.

The customization process described in this chapter is not something far off in the future. These capabilities are currently being widely used by the banking and financial industries to customize digital documents according to credit history, currency fluctuations, mortgage rates, and so on. It will just take a little bit of teamwork and a lot of cooperation from the various production departments that make video media—such as that used in training, for example—to be included in each relevant PDF.

For more information about Server-Side PDF tools and news, check out this book's companion website DynamicMediaBook.com.

HTML SWF PDF

Closing Remarks

I am hoping that this book has helped you to better understand the history, complexities, and the possibilities that exist within the PDF format. It's important to understand that with each new release of Adobe Reader come a whole new realm of multimedia wonders. QuickTime video and VR have been available on the Mac and Windows platform since Reader 5, and as you now know, there are plenty of iTunes users out there ready to experience rich-media PDF without upgrading anything on their system. iTunes runs via QuickTime.

For the most part, video inside PDF is what most users will want to see, so your safest bet is to make renditions of the video—Windows Media video for the PC and QuickTime for the Mac. The ability to embed and play Windows Media video became available in Reader 6. Acrobat 8 and Reader 8 is the turning point for rich-media PDF because the popular Flash SWF format finally works perfectly inside PDF on the PC.

Since the desktop publishing community is well versed with PDF creation, these artists are the ones most likely to benefit from this new digital delivery medium. There is no need for them to learn HTML, QuickTime VR, digital video, or Flash. They only need to hire the freelance digital video and Flash content-creators that supply similar services for Web site producers. They can also just repurpose the video and Flash content already available on most Web sites. It's fairly simple to integrate the rich media in their InDesign page layout and then make the document interactive via Acrobat. The successful interactive media producers of the future will be the the ones who are able to bring together a team of talented people that all share the rich-media PDF vision.

The world has gone broadband. Rich-media PDF is truly a new medium and with it comes the resistance from industries that have the most to lose. Printed products and Web sites will never vanish, but PDF will soon converge traditional print, radio, television, and Flash media outside of the cumbersome Web browser. The splash Web page of the future might present the user with the following choices:

Click Here for HTML - Click Here for Flash
Click Here to build and download your PDF.

Index

E

F